I SPEAK OF FREEDOM

I SPEAK OF FREEDOM

Kwame Nkrumah

PANAF
London

I SPEAK OF FREEDOM

First Published 1961
Panaf Edition 1973

ISBN   0 90 1787 14 0

Panaf Books
75 Weston Street
London SE1 3RS

Dedicated to Patrice Lumumba,
late Prime Minister of the Republic
of the Congo, and to all those
who are engaged in the struggle
for the political unification of Africa.

By the same Author

Africa Must Unite
Axioms of Kwame Nkrumah
Class Struggle in Africa
Consciencism
Dark Days in Ghana
Ghana (Autobiography)
Handbook of Revolutionary Warfare
I Speak of Freedom
Neo-Colonialism
*Revolutionary Path**
*Rhodesia File**
*The Struggle Continues**
Voice from Conakry
What I Mean by Positive Action

Pamphlets

The Big Lie
Ghana; The Way Out
The Spectre of Black Power
Two Myths: The Myth of the "Third World"
               "African Socialism" Revisited
What I Mean by Positive Action

* Published Posthumously

CONTENTS

PREFACE

The movement for independence in Africa which gained momentum after the Second World War has spread like a prairie fire throughout the length and breadth of Africa. The clear, ringing call for freedom which the eight independent states of Africa sounded in Accra in April 1958, followed by the All-African Peoples' Conference in December of that year, stirred up the demand for independence from Conakry to Mogadishu, from Fort Lamy to Leopoldville. The 'wind of change' has become a raging hurricane, sweeping away the old colonialist Africa. The year 1960 was Africa's year. In that year alone, seventeen African States emerged as proud and independent sovereign nations. Now the ultimate freedom of the whole of Africa can no more be in doubt.

For centuries, Europeans dominated the African continent. The white man arrogated to himself the right to rule and to be obeyed by the non-white; his mission, he claimed was to 'civilise' Africa. Under this cloak, the Europeans robbed the continent of vast riches and inflicted unimaginable suffering on the African people.

All this makes a sad story, but now we must be prepared to bury the past with its unpleasant memories and look to the future. All we ask of the former colonial powers is their goodwill and co-operation to remedy past mistakes and injustices and to grant independence to the colonies in Africa.

The new African nations from the very nature of things cannot but be economically weak at the early stages of their nationhood as compared with the older and long established nations of the world. The long dependence on European and American financial and technical enterprise has prevented the growth of local capital and the requisite technical knowledge to develop their resources. They need economic help, but in seeking outside aid they lay themselves open to a grave new danger which not merely threatens but could even destroy their hard-won freedom.

It is unreasonable to suppose that any foreign power, affluent enough to give aid to an African state, would not expect some

measure of consideration or favour from the state receiving the
aid. History has shown how one colonial empire in liquidation
can easily be replaced by another, more insidious, because it
is a disguised form of colonialism. The fate of those territories
in Europe and North Africa which once formed the Turkish
Empire is a warning to Africa today. It would be a tragedy if the
initial weakness of the emergent African nations should lead to
a new foreign domination of Africa brought about by economic
forces.

It may be argued that the existence of the United Nations
Organisation offers a guarantee for the independence and the
territorial integrity of all states, whether big or small. In actual
fact, however, the U.N. is just as reliable an instrument for
world order and peace as the Great Powers are prepared to
allow it to be. The present division of the world into rival blocs,
and the dictates of power politics, offer little hope that this
international body will ever become an effective instrument for
world peace. Recent events in the Congo have not helped to
foster confidence in the U.N. in the face of Great Power interests.
Patrice Lumumba, democratically elected Prime Minister of
the Congo Republic, who himself invited the U.N. to the Congo,
was murdered along with two of his Ministers because the U.N.
failed in its mission to maintain law and order.

It is clear that we must find an African solution to our problems, and that this can only be found in African unity. Divided
we are weak; united, Africa could become one of the greatest
forces for good in the world.

Although most Africans are poor, our continent is potentially
extremely rich. Our mineral resources, which are being exploited
with foreign capital only to enrich foreign investors, range from
gold and diamonds to uranium and petroleum. Our forests
contain some of the finest woods to be grown anywhere. Our
cash crops include cocoa, coffee, rubber, tobacco and cotton. As
for power, which is an important factor in any economic
development, Africa contains over 40% of the total potential
water power of the world, as compared with about 10% in
Europe and 13% in North America. Yet so far, less than 1%
has been developed. This is one of the reasons why we have in
Africa the paradox of poverty in the midst of plenty, and
scarcity in the midst of abundance.

Never before have a people had within their grasp so great

an opportunity for developing a continent endowed with so much wealth. Individually, the independent states of Africa, some of them potentially rich, others poor, can do little for their people. Together, by mutual help, they can achieve much. But the economic development of the continent must be planned and pursued as a whole. A loose confederation designed only for economic co-operation would not provide the necessary unity of purpose. Only a strong political union can bring about full and effective development of our natural resources for the benefit of our people.

The political situation in Africa today is heartening and at the same time disturbing. It is heartening to see so many new flags hoisted in place of the old; it is disturbing to see so many countries of varying sizes and at different levels of development, weak and, in some cases, almost helpless. If this terrible state of fragmentation is allowed to continue it may well be disastrous for us all.

There are at present some 28 states in Africa, excluding the Union of South Africa, and those countries not yet free. No less than nine of these states have a population of less than three million. Can we seriously believe that the colonial powers meant these countries to be independent, viable states? The example of South America, which has as much wealth, if not more than North America, and yet remains weak and dependent on outside interests, is one which every African would do well to study.

Critics of African unity often refer to the wide differences in culture, language and ideas in various parts of Africa. This is true, but the essential fact remains that we are all Africans, and have a common interest in the independence of Africa. The difficulties presented by questions of language, culture and different political systems are not insuperable. If the need for political union is agreed by us all, then the will to create it is born; and where there's a will there's a way.

The present leaders of Africa have already shown a remarkable willingness to consult and seek advice among themselves. Africans have, indeed, begun to think continentally. They realise that they have much in common, both in their past history, in their present problems and in their future hopes. To suggest that the time is not yet ripe for considering a political union of Africa is to evade the facts and ignore realities in Africa today.

The greatest contribution that Africa can make to the peace
of the world is to avoid all the dangers inherent in disunity,
by creating a political union which will also by its success, stand
as an example to a divided world. A union of African states will
project more effectively the African personality. It will command
respect from a world that has regard only for size and influence.
The scant attention paid to African opposition to the French
atomic tests in the Sahara, and the ignominious spectacle of the
U.N. in the Congo quibbling about constitutional niceties
while the Republic was tottering into anarchy, are evidence of
the callous disregard of African Independence by the Great
Powers.

We have to prove that greatness is not to be measured in stock
piles of atom bombs. I believe strongly and sincerely that with
the deep-rooted wisdom and dignity, the innate respect for
human lives, the intense humanity that is our heritage, the
African race, united under one federal government, will emerge
not as just another world bloc to flaunt its wealth and strength,
but as a Great Power whose greatness is indestructible because it
is built not on fear, envy and suspicion, nor won at the expense of
others, but founded on hope, trust, friendship and directed to the
good of all mankind.

The emergence of such a mighty stabilising force in this strife-
worn world should be regarded not as the shadowy dream of a
visionary, but as a practical proposition, which the peoples of
Africa can, and should, translate into reality. There is a tide in
the affairs of every people when the moment strikes for political
action. Such was the moment in the history of the United States
of America when the Founding Fathers saw beyond the petty
wranglings of the separate states and created a Union. This is
our chance. We must act now. Tomorrow may be too late and
the opportunity will have passed, and with it the hope of free
Africa's survival.

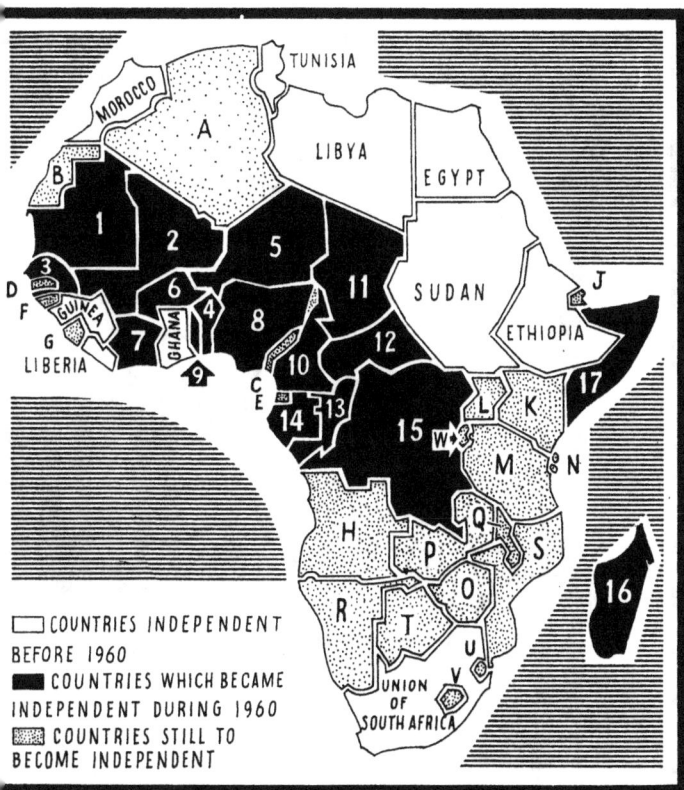

1—Mauritania. 2—Mali. 3—Senegal. 4—Dahomey. 5—Niger.
6—Upper Volta. 7—Ivory Coast. 8—Nigeria. 9—Togo. 10—Cameroun.
11—Chad. 12—Central African Republic. 13—Congo (formerly French).
14—Gabon. 15—Congo (formerly Belgian). 16—Madagascar. 17—
Somalia.

A—Algeria. B—Rio de Oro. C—British Cameroons. D—Gambia. E—
Rio Muni. F—Portuguese Guinea. G—Sierra Leone. H—Angola. J—
French Somaliland. K—Kenya. L—Uganda. M—Tanganyika. N—
Zanzibar. O—Southern Rhodesia. P—Northern Rhodesia. Q—Nyasa-
land. R—South West Africa. S—Mozambique. T—Bechuanaland. U—
Swaziland. V—Basutoland. W—Ruanda-Urundi.

GHANA

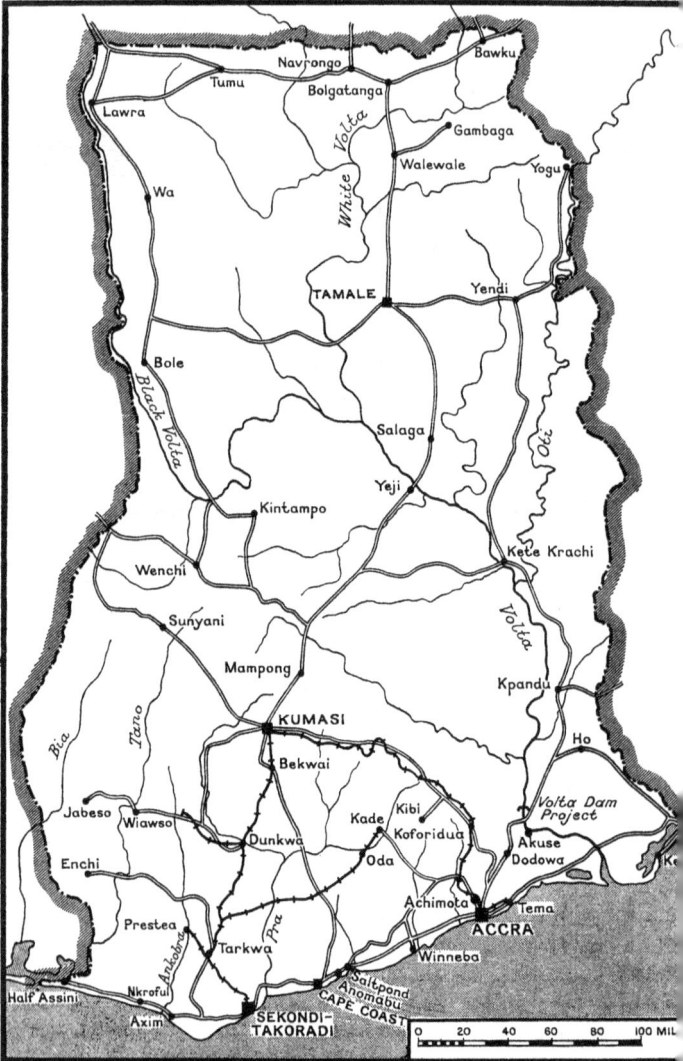

Navrongo • Bawku

Tumu Bolgatanga

Lawra

Gambaga

Walewale

Wa White Volta Yogu

TAMALE Yendi

Bole

Black Volta

Salaga

Yeji Oti

Kintampo

Kete Krachi

Wenchi

Sunyani

Volta

Mampong

Kpandu

KUMASI

Ho

Bekwai

Jabeso Kibi Volta Dam Project

Wiawso Kade Koforidua Akuse

Enchi Dunkwa Oda Dodowa K

Achimota Tema

Prestea Pra ACCRA

Tarkwa Winneba

Nkroful Saltpond
Half Assini Anomabu
Axim CAPE COAST

SEKONDI-
TAKORADI

0 20 40 60 80 100 MIL

Bia Tano Ankobra

CHAPTER ONE

RETURN

In December 1947 I returned to my country after twelve years in America and the United Kingdom. I had been asked to become general secretary of the United Gold Coast Convention, a political organisation set up to secure independence 'in the shortest possible time'. The U.G.C.C. was slow to make much impression on the country as a whole, probably because it was composed mainly of business and professional men, especially lawyers. My task as general secretary was to widen the membership and to turn the U.G.C.C. into an active, popular movement.

I must confess that on my return there was little outward sign of the great changes that the next few years would bring. Ghana was then the Gold Coast, a so-called 'model' colony under British rule. A new Governor, Sir Gerald Creasy, had come to the ancient castle at Christiansborg. The government, consisting at that time of an executive council of European civil servants, was satisfied with normal security measures. My return was carefully noted but not apparently viewed with any great concern. This rather surprised me. My work in London for the West African National Secretariat and my membership of the revolutionary group known as 'The Circle' were well known. For years I had worked for West African unity and the destruction of colonialism, and my views had been summarised in a short book *Towards Colonial Freedom*, published in 1946. So I half expected to be questioned when the ship docked at Takoradi and the immigration officer read the name on my passport. But the immigration officer was African; he was delighted to see me and said so.

For a fortnight I stayed in Tarkwa resting and taking stock of the political situation. There had been a considerable political awakening in the Gold Coast between 1919 and 1947. The gap was widening between the new African intelligentsia and the colonial government. But I could see that the rate of development was not fast enough. Some people thought that a big step towards self-government had been taken in October 1944, when

Sir Alan Burns told the Legislative Council that the Colonial
Office had approved a new constitution by which Africans were
to be appointed to the Executive Council. But the more
politically educated among us scorned the half-hearted gesture.

In those months following my return I eagerly read the local
newspapers, *The Spectator Daily*, *The West African Monitor* and
others. I wanted to take the pulse of the country. In January,
there was the royal funeral of Nii Tackie Tawiah II, Ga Mantse
and President of the Ga State Council. The great state umbrella
which accompanied him everywhere no longer shaded his
palanquin but hung sadly over his coffin. Mourning ceremonies
followed him; the sacrifice of animals, the ritual sprinkling of
blood, and, as a final parting gesture, the firing of guns. The old
stateliness of chieftaincy still counted for something, both socially
and politically.

But change was in the air. The longing for self-government
showed itself from time to time. In a New Year message at the
beginning of 1948, journalist F. Therson Cofie wrote:

> Once more the wheel of time is rolling out of existence the old
> year with all its attendant fortunes and misfortunes and is
> ushering in the New Year with all it has in store. Year in and
> year out we make resolutions, most of which are never carried
> out; we formulate lofty plans which seldom materialise . . .
> in the face of this unsteadiness how on earth do we expect to
> march as one man toward the goal of our aspiration, namely
> the much talked of self-government?[1]

At this time the world news showed that the big nations were
only just recovering from the Second World War and there was
unrest everywhere. A crisis between East and West, the first of
many, occurred in 1948. The North Atlantic Pact was signed.
This was closely followed by the Berlin blockade, when Russia
would not allow any communication between the West and
Berlin. For a time it looked as if war might ensue, but the crisis
passed.

In India, Gandhi was assassinated by a member of the
Orthodox Hindu Organisation. Hindu women were restrained
from destroying themselves on his funeral pyre, and all India
observed thirteen days of mourning. We too mourned his death,
for he had inspired us deeply with his political thought, notably

[1] *The Spectator Daily*, 2 January 1948.

with his adherence to non-violent resistance. In Cape Coast *The West African Monitor* paid its respect in true Akan fashion by printing the message of the talking drums, *Dammarifa due; dammarifa due, due.* All over the world the news was of trouble. In Shanghai, Chinese Communist forces estimated at 50,000 had launched a drive on the strategic Manchurian railway town of Sinming thirty miles north-west of Mukden. From Switzerland it was reported that King Leopold of the Belgians, in exile, had sent a message to the Belgian Government insisting that the question of his return be put to popular vote.

But in the Gold Coast the unrest was of a particular kind; it was a movement rejecting imperialism and foreign rule. It was an urgent feeling which soon spread into the hearts of all. At a meeting held by the Nzima community of Aboso in February, I told the two thousand people who had gathered to welcome me that success could only be achieved through the united support of the people:

> Without organisational strength we are weak; unity is the dynamic force behind any great venture. In whatever sphere of labour you are placed we want you to work so well that when the time comes for you to serve your country you will be the right man at the right place.

I ended by explaining the aims and aspirations of the U.G.C.C., and expressed the hope that a new branch of the Convention might be formed. There followed a most moving incident. A fisherman, Brepon Yaw, rose to his feet, and said:

> I am an honest fisherman. This talk of self-government has so captured my imagination that I gave two shillings during the silver collection. I now hand over my last four shillings to help in speeding the work of the Convention. Believe me, if I had more I would give it. That is all I have to tell you.[1]

As the fisherman finished speaking, thunderous applause broke out. His spontaneous, touching gesture had moved that vast crowd deeply. In my travels up and down the country I was to have many other moving experiences. The Convention was indeed becoming a popular movement with the growing support of all sections of the community.

At that time the Gold Coast was poor. It is well known that

[1] *African Morning Post*, 16 February 1948.

economic distress often precedes political change and some
would go so far as to say that it is the main cause of it. Certainly,
rising prices and the threat of inflation in 1948 would have
aroused even the most apathetic. On Thursday, 5 February
more than six hundred demonstrators marched through the
streets of Accra carrying slogans: WE WILL NOT BUY; WAIT
UNTIL PRICES ARE REDUCED; TIME AND TIDE WAIT FOR
NO MAN. In Kumasi the anti-inflation campaign under Krobo
Edusei caused petty traders in the Central Market to close their
stalls. Nii Kwabena Bonne II, Mantse of Osu Alata, organised
a boycott of textiles throughout the country. 'Believing,' he
declared, 'that the work which I am doing is one which will help
my country, I am prepared to die if only it will make the Gold
Coast a better place.' [1]

The editorial in *The African Morning Post* of 7 February was no
less determined:

One fact on which the exploiters and oppressors of the African
generally bank is that the black man is incapable of collective
action. On the contrary, events have time and again falsified
this view. The wonder is that the foreign elements in this
country have continued to hold this exploded opinion. . . .
The African may appear to be sleeping over his own interests,
but once he is aroused from his slumber he takes up the fight
with might and main. . . . The Gold Coast African is today
awake; yes, wide awake; and there is reason to believe that
he will sleep no more. For years on end he has been im-
poverished and economically crippled by those who have
come into this country for the purpose of trade – heartless,
soulless, unsympathetic creatures who take delight in sucking
the lifeblood of the aborigines. Africans all over the world are
awaking from their age long slumber . . . Gold Coast, now is
your chance.

When I spoke to a rally of thousands of young people in Accra
at the end of January, I linked the economic crisis with the
political situation. 'Let the government of the Gold Coast pass
as quickly as possible into the hands of the Gold Coast people
themselves,' I told them, and continued:

A fierce fight against the economic system is raging. It does
not matter whether those who have promoted that economic

[1] *Ashanti Times*, 5 February 1948.

system are black or white. The Convention is against anybody who identifies himself, be he black or white, with that economic system. The present struggle is a historical one, for down the ages this fight has been raging with unabated intensity and has pointed all along to one goal – complete independence for West Africa.[1]

The young people clapped and cheered and it was some time before I could continue. When my voice could be heard again I told the audience that the people were not organised and therefore they had no strength. The chiefs found strength in the Government and so they naturally leaned towards it. But as soon as the people were organised and strong the chiefs would probably return to them. If they did not, they could pack up and follow the Europeans out of the Gold Coast.

My speeches were usually reported in the papers, and so my words reached people all over the country, and sometimes abroad. I spoke without notes, sometimes for hours. Some journalists were flattering. They spoke of personal charm, a lively manner and an infectious enthusiasm. What I think more important is the ability to communicate with the people. Not just with any particular class; not only with professional men but with everyone, and at any time. If I have any special gifts in speaking I count that the greatest.

Perhaps my success as a speaker may also be put down to the fact that my mind is clear and my policy decided. People listening to my speeches throughout the years could not have failed to notice two recurrent themes. The first is freedom of the individual. The second is political independence, not just for Ghana or for West Africa, but for all Africa. I do not know how anyone can refuse to acknowledge the right of men to be free.

[1] *The African Morning Post*, 21 January 1948.

CHAPTER TWO

THE CAMPAIGN BEGINS

The work of the U.G.C.C., combined with the growing economic tension in February 1948 led to a state of affairs which was highly inflammable. Sure enough, at the end of the month an event occurred which proved to be a decisive step in the struggle for independence.

Saturday, 28 February 1948 is still clear in my mind. I was addressing a meeting in Saltpond when news reached me of rioting in Accra. Police had opened fire on a body of ex-servicemen as they demonstrated at Christiansborg Castle crossroads, about 300 yards from the Castle itself, where the Governor lived. They were unarmed and two were shot down. Pandemonium followed. Angry crowds rushed through the streets of Accra looting and destroying as they went, smashing cars and setting shops alight. For a time the police were powerless.

The looting and the rioting continued all Sunday with Indian, Lebanese and Syrian as well as European shops being attacked. The large stores of the United Africa Company and the Union Trading Company were burning. By Sunday evening extra troops had moved in and the situation was gradually brought under control. But as a result of these disorders, 29 people died and 237 were injured. The trouble had not been confined to Accra. In Kumasi there was systematic looting also and a riot broke out in Nsawam where three looters were shot.

I arrived in Accra while the rioting was at its height and saw for myself the complete breakdown of law and order. At a hurried meeting of the Executive Committee, we decided to send two telegrams to the Secretary of State for the Colonies, Mr Arthur Creech Jones. We asked for a special commissioner to be sent immediately to hand over the administration to an interim government of the chiefs and people, and to see to the calling of a constituent assembly.

Meanwhile, Accra was slow to settle down to normal life again. The police were jittery; it was a time of repression and arrest. On Tuesday, 9 March *The West African Monitor* came out with great gaps in its columns and a heavy black headline reading THE MONITOR RAIDED BY POLICE. Many other newspapers shared the same fate. Rumours that the police were looking for the leaders of the U.G.C.C. reached me. I laid low for a while in the house of two women supporters and spent the time planning the development of the Convention People's Party.

It was not long, however, before the police caught me. I was arrested during the night at Cape Coast. The police also arrested the other leaders, Danquah, Ofori Atta, Akuffo Addo, Ako Adjei, and Obetsebi Lamptey. We were known as the Big Six and we were taken off to be detained in various parts of the country. I was taken to Kumasi and then to a lonely part of the Northern Territories.

But our telegrams to the Secretary of State had not been in vain. A commission of enquiry was sent out under the chairmanship of Aiken Watson, and we were duly released to give evidence before it. I must confess I was glad to have the chance to give my views in public again. It seemed the Commissioners were worried about my influence with the people. They wanted above all to classify me, politically. Was there a label to fit? Was I a Communist? Was I just anti-White?

I was questioned again and again about my speeches and newspaper articles. A copy of *The Spectator Daily* was laid before the Commission. In it there was an article signed 'British Democrat' containing an assurance that the people would achieve independence 'sooner than most of you dare hope'. The article then continued:

> I would like to offer some advice to you, my friends; that is, join the Gold Coast Convention as soon as possible; not only the menfolk but also the women. To the men I say assist the women to take an active part in the political life of the country, for remember, no country can be truly democratic in which women do not have equality with men. In the case of literacy which is the strongest weapon of the Imperialists in holding your people down, I would suggest that every literate person in Africa teach at least one person who is at present illiterate to become literate; you owe it to your country and your children.[1]

The ideas expressed in the article were certainly in keeping with my own views, and could have been written by me.

[1] *The Spectator Daily*, 23 February 1948.

'Have you any connection with that article?' asked Colonel Buckmaster.

I cannot recall my answer. The questioning continued:

'In Sierra Leone you made a speech?'

'Yes, I have been making several speeches.'

'Did you make a speech at Saltpond on 29 September?'

'No.'

'I am sorry, the 4 December, at Sekondi?'

'Yes.'

'And do you remember saying that this was the last Governor?'

'Yes. I said so.'[1]

I told the Commissioners that I had never advocated violence. I wanted to see the Gold Coast people organised in their demand for self-government. When the organising period was over, the strength of the organisation would have to be tested by means of peaceful demonstrations. If these failed to produce the required results, then boycotts and strikes were the only weapons left.

The Commissioners were interested in discovering how far my views were shared by other leaders of the Convention. To judge from some of the questions asked, they expected to find disunity amongst us. Much importance was attached to the fact that an unsigned Communist Party card was found in my possession at the time of my arrest. I made it quite clear that although I associated with Communists, as well as with members of other political parties when I was in London, I was not a member of the Communist Party. It was true that one day I hoped to see a united West Africa. 'It is a private dream of my own,' I told them.

'Is it a dream that you wish would come true?'

'Yes.'

Later in the same interrogation I was asked:

'Would you describe yourself as a person trained to engage in political revolution?'

'No.'[2]

The commission soon completed its enquiries and issued its report in June. Briefly, it advocated a greater share of self-determination for the country and recommended that a committee should be set up to consider the drafting of a new constitution. For a time there was comparative quiet, but the cam-

[1] *The Spectator Daily*, 20 April 1948.
[2] *The Spectator Daily*, 20 April 1948.

paign for independence continued. *The West African Monitor* now heavily underlined its motto: ON THE PEDESTAL OF TRUTH, KNOWLEDGE AND FRATERNITY WE WAVE THE TORCH OF AFRICA'S EMANCIPATION.[1]

I had by this time begun to address meetings again. At the end of May I went to Kumasi, where I was given a tremendous welcome. A crowd gathered at the station to meet my train and as I stepped from the compartment a burst of cheering greeted me. I was swept off my feet and carried shoulder high to the waiting taxi. About forty other taxis lined up in procession and we drove through all the principal streets in town, including Bantama. I stood up in the car so that all could see me; the cheers of the crowds made me very happy.

Significantly enough, Empire Day was celebrated with little enthusiasm that year. In some places, the day passed without any notice at all being taken. The Omanhene of Essikado, who owned the recreation ground at Sekondi where Empire Day was usually celebrated announced that the ground was not available. He could see no point, he said, in going to salute a flag under which the people were nothing 'but poor slaves'.[2] He had a gong beaten throughout the town forbidding school children as well as adults to go to the park. His orders were obeyed and the twenty-fourth of May came and went, uncelebrated. Very wisely, the white administrative officers made no attempt to interfere with the Chief's directions.

As the summer went on, dissatisfaction grew. The Watson Commission had brought no immediate relief, though a constitutional committee was to be set up later on. The ordinary people in the country were getting restive. It was at this time that serious differences arose between myself and the Working Committee of the U.G.C.C.

While I was away on a Party rally, Obetsebi Lamptey and William Ofori Atta raided my office in Saltpond. They searched for and confiscated any letters in which I had used the word Comrade; this, they thought, was clear proof that I was a Communist. At length I appeared before the Working Committee to answer various charges. To my amazement, they accused me of acting outside my authority in founding the Ghana National College for students who had been expelled for striking in sup-

[1] *The West African Monitor*, 28 May 1948.
[2] *The West African Monitor*, 8 June 1948.

port of us at the time of our imprisonment. To make a long story short, I was relieved of my post as general secretary, and became treasurer instead. It was known that already I had a strong personal following, and it was feared that the movement might fail if I left it entirely.

On the very day on which I ceased to be general secretary the first issue of my paper, *The Accra Evening News*, appeared with its famous fighting motto: WE PREFER SELF GOVERNMENT WITH DANGER TO SERVITUDE IN TRANQUILLITY. Through the columns of this paper I was able to reach a wide circle of readers. Day after day, in various ways, I hammered home the message of full self-government, not in the shortest possible time, but now, NOW.

The early success of the *Evening News* (as it was popularly called) fully justified the time and expense involved in getting the paper established. At first we could print only a single sheet. But in the columns of that single sheet we daily reminded the people of their struggle for freedom. A mysterious columnist, 'Rambler', examined the worst abuses of the administration. Any injustice, however small, which came to the notice of the paper was publicly condemned and this quite often landed us in trouble. One day I received a letter from the Solicitor General threatening a libel action on behalf of a member of the Education Department, who, it was alleged, had been slandered in my paper; £500 was claimed unless I published an unqualified apology. For answer, I published the Solicitor General's note and re-published the offending article.

The case was brought and I lost. With the help of friends I paid the damages. This was just the sort of thing I envisaged when founding the paper. It was to be a place where grievances could be aired, where abuse of power and injustice in any form could be made known.

Demand for the *Evening News* rose by leaps and bounds. I now had another means of reaching the people. My pen, as well as my voice, had entered the campaign. At this time the phrase SELF GOVERNMENT NOW began to appear on walls and buildings up and down the country. Stirring headlines kept the issue in readers' minds. The theme of self-government was never allowed to grow cold. *The West African Monitor*, using another

motto SERVICE NOT SERVITUDE, published many inspiring
articles in the last months of 1948. A correspondent wrote:

We are at the brink of our national existence. We must either
move forward towards political autonomy or retreat and fall
into the pit of national servitude. We cannot, we must not
retreat. We must move forward towards political autonomy
even if that means detention, imprisonment, exile or even
death for some of our number. . . . Have faith that God is on
our side.[1]

The Daily Echo used economic arguments:

West African cocoa earns five times as many dollars in a year
as Britain receives from sales to America of motor-cars, ships
and locomotives. Last year the total dollar earnings from cocoa
sales in the United States amounted to 140,000,000 dollars.
But the goose that lays the golden eggs is being strangled.[2]

The writer of the editorial in the Cape Coast paper agreed
about economic exploitation:

We can, at best, chuckle at the fatuous notion shamelessly
expressed by some of the foreign merchant houses out here
that they are here to serve the country. The godly truth for
them to confess is that they are here to encompass the undoing
of the poor, ignorant and defenceless African.[3]

About this time the Extra-Mural Department of the University
College held a meeting in Accra at which Major Lillie Costello
of the Public Relations Office spoke on 'The Press and Government'. He was at pains to point out that the press had a very
important part to play in the life of the country:

'The Press in this country, as in any other country, can be a
tremendous carrier of goodwill if it so wishes, or, it can just as
easily follow a policy of racial division and all that policy
entails . . . the Press in this country, as in other countries, is
one of the main channels of information to the public. Now,
my aim and desire with the voluntary co-operation of the
Press is to swim in that channel.'[4]

[1] *The West African Monitor*, 3 September 1948.
[2] *The Daily Echo*, 16 September 1948.
[3] *The West African Monitor*, 21 September 1948.
[4] *The Spectator Daily*, 23 September 1948.

He denied that he wished to see a government Press. All he wanted for the government was a fair hearing. *The Spectator Daily* reported his speech in full with no comment.

Although the *Evening News* took up much of my time, I continued to address large meetings in many parts of the country. About this time there was a particularly successful gathering at Sekondi. The subject of my talk was 'The True National'. I described such a man as morally strong, skilled in action, honest, free from bribery and corruption. He should have compassion and a firm determination. It was customary at these meetings to take a silver collection in aid of the U.G.C.C. On that occasion, in Sekondi, £10.8.1. was collected. Soon afterwards, I spoke to a large audience in the Town Hall, Accra on 'The Liberty of the Subject'. I told them there was a big difference between the meaning given to liberty in England compared with the liberty practised in colonial territories. 'Only by attaining self-government,' I said, 'can the people of this country think freely, talk freely and say whatever they want to say. There is nothing to fear but fear itself.'

At the end of my talk I launched a 1,000,000 shillings appeal fund in aid of the Ghana College. The fund was started at once, with two guineas contributed by the only European in the audience, David Kimble of the University Extra-Mural Department.

It is true that at this time I was very largely concerned with the political goal of self-government. Some argued that this made me blind to any good in the administration and to faults in my own people. This was not so. There is, for example, very strong condemnation in the *Evening News* of disorders in Odumase in the issue of 14 November 1948. One of Rambler's ubiquitous scouts reported a 'strong and hideous' mob, 'their faces besmeared with white powder and charcoal, holding knives, cutlasses and cudgels and other mankilling implements' which had run through the streets of the town looking for Ako Adjei, a Convention speaker who was to have lectured in the Presbyterian Secondary School. Rambler's scout discovered that certain leaders of the district were behind the frenzied crowd that day. 'Is this form of totalitarianism not worse than Communism?' he asked:

Is it not Hitlerism? Has that state not gone to the abyss of the inglorious old days? All sorts of interpretations are being put

on this display . . . and unless an official statement by that
state claiming or disclaiming responsibility is issued, Manya
Krobo and the people of that state have their good name to
lose. My scouts are alert.[1]

In December, the Coussey constitutional committee which
had been set up as a result of the findings of the Watson Commission, began its work. The campaign for self-government went
on with, if anything, increased vigour. More 'SELF GOVERN-
MENT NOW' slogans were pasted up on walls and buildings.
People seemed to talk of little else. Komfo Atta, writing in the
Evening News, warned the Coussey committee against drawing
up a constitution unacceptable to the people of the Gold Coast,
'We as a people in our own God-given land must be given a clear
chance to act freely, and live freely,' he said.[2]
    One of my most successful speeches was made at this time.
The occasion was a meeting of the Youth Study Group in Accra.
Over three thousand people attended and I spoke to them for
well over an hour. I briefly traced the history of the Gold Coast
since Europeans first came to the country. Then I went on to the
question of a new constitution. It must, I said, provide for
universal adult suffrage, a national assembly and a board of
ministers collectively responsible to the national assembly.
About education I had this to say:

    Imperialism thrives only where the people are divided and are
    ignorant of their rights. That is why the educational system
    is so bad. In fact there is no system at all. It is one big muddle.[3]

Under the headline KWAME NKRUMAH STORMS ACCRA the
editor of one newspaper wrote:

    Three thousand people make quite a crowd in a city the size
    of Accra . . . and Kwame Nkrumah delivered to this crowd
    what may without exaggeration be classed as the best political
    harangue that has ever been heard in this country. . . . The
    25,000 words which he must have uttered in these 90 minutes
    were each a nail in the coffin of colonialism and imperialism
    in Ghana.[4]

1 *The Accra Evening News*, 22 November 1948.
2 *The Accra Evening News*, 11 December 1948.
3 *The Accra Evening News*, 23 December 1948.
4 *The Accra Evening News*, 23 December 1948. Note that already the name
'Ghana' is current.

Certainly the eager response and enthusiasm of that youthful audience filled me with confidence for the future. At Christmas, through the columns of the *Evening News*, we appealed to the youth of the world. We called especially upon the youth of Britain:

We trust that you, the youth of Britain, will co-operate with us in our struggle for freedom and self-government, so that we can both freely work together to build the Brave New World which is the dream of our Youth.[1]

The New Year message to readers of the *Evening News* was clear. It fixed a date for independence:

Let all the sons and daughters of Ghana, on the eve of the era of freedom stand resolute, determined that they will get their self-government in 1949.[2]

And so the New Year dawned. The battle for self-government went on, not with weapons and bloodshed, but with words. The wonder is that new words could be found for the ceaseless reiteration of the call for freedom. I once told a gathering of dancers that they were dancing their way to self-government. They might have replied that I was talking my way to freedom!

[1] *The Accra Evening News*, 30 December 1948.
[2] *The Accra Evening News*, 31 December 1948.

CHAPTER THREE

ORGANISATION FOR FREEDOM

Early in 1949 the Governor left suddenly for London. There
were rumours that he had gone because of trouble over the
banning of a Ghana Youth Conference in Kumasi. The secrecy
which surrounded the Governor's departure only heightened
tension in the country. More British troops arrived. Planes landed
at Accra airport day and night. Many people believed that arms
were being distributed to the Europeans. The African reaction
was well summed up in the editorial column of the *Evening News*:

> Bullets or no bullets, British troops or no British troops, there
> is nothing that can deter us from our determined march
> towards the goal of complete Self Government and Inde-
> pendence.[1]

But the people were still not organised enough. 'Organise!
Organise!! Organise!!!' we urged:

> Let individuals, men and women, join any of the political
> organisations, farmers' unions, trade unions, co-operative
> societies, youth movements. No section of the people of this
> country should be left unorganised. No individual person
> should be without membership in some organisation. . . . The
> strength of the organised masses is invincible. . . . We must
> organise as never before, for organisation decides everything.[2]

The youth of the country were already organised. The Youth
Study Group which I founded had grown into a nationalist
youth movement known as the C.Y.O. (Committee on Youth
Organisation). All youth organisations, clubs and societies were
invited to affiliate with the C.Y.O. Applications poured in, and
soon members of the Working Committee of the U.G.C.C. began
to object. They feared the growing strength of the youth movement with its programme of 'Self Government Now'. They saw
in it a threat to their own power, particularly as most of the
members of the C.Y.O. came from the less privileged section of

[1] *The Accra Evening News*, 13 January 1949.
[2] *The Accra Evening News*, 14 January 1949.

the people. On 20 January 1949, we published a copy of the Constitution drawn up by the C.Y.O. at the end of 1948. The main proposals were universal adult suffrage without property qualifications; a Board of Ministers (from the Assembly) with collective responsibility, and itself responsible to the Assembly; a fully elected Gold Coast Assembly; a House of Chiefs, and Self-Government 'this year' (1949).

Many individuals and organisations sent telegrams and letters to the Governor and to Justice Coussey supporting the constitutional proposals. We appealed to others to follow suit:

> This country has too much at stake in the deliberations of the Coussey Committee, and we must let this Committee know what we feel and want. Every Ghanaian is expected to do his duty.[1]

Throughout February and March I travelled up and down the country addressing meetings. I spoke to a Keta audience on 'The Political Significance of Unification'. Six days later, I addressed a large crowd in Kumasi. From there I went to Tamale, and chose for my subject 'Poverty versus Plenty'. The Northern Territories people were particularly receptive to economic arguments. They looked forward to a higher standard of living once independence had been achieved. Economic freedom, I told them, would follow political freedom. While I was carrying on the struggle with speeches, my paper, the *Evening News*, kept up a ceaseless flow of encouragement:

> We believe in constitutional methods, but at the same time we do know that never in history has self-government been handed to a colonial and oppressed people on a silver platter ... the dynamic must come from us. So to the people of Ghana, we say be calm, but nevertheless firm in your demand for self-government; if you don't demand it now, who else will do it for you?[2]

At this time Rambler reported that Europeans were taking bets on my future. One officer was said to have wagered that I would be assassinated within three months. He seemed sure of it. Certainly I must have been very unpopular with some people. I was held personally responsible for all that the *Evening News* contained. Occasionally, people called at the *News* Office and

[1] *The Accra Evening News*, 1 February 1949.
[2] *The Accra Evening News*, 9 February 1949.

demanded to see me. I remember an incident early in February 1949 when an angry white soldier called to complain about certain articles concerning the West African Command. The staff managed to calm him down, and he left with a free copy of the *Evening News* in his hand!

About then, there was considerable interest being shown in the Accra election to fill a vacant seat in the Legislative Council. I regarded the increase in the voter's list from 20,000 names to 36,000 as most encouraging. It meant that a further 16,000 people intended to avail themselves of the opportunity offered to elect their own man to represent them. Formerly, even some registered voters did not bother to vote, because they knew the 'Legco'[1] was all a farce, and there was no point in troubling to go to the polls. At last, the people were waking up to the fact that political freedom was the key to national existence, peace and prosperity. The Convention candidate, Obetsebi Lamptey, was opposed by Kofi Adumoa Bossman, a known supporter of imperialism. Bossman lacked any real political backing and withdrew his candidature about a week before the election. Lamptey was elected unopposed. Bossman's withdrawal was a straw in the wind pointing clearly to the growing political consciousness of the people.

Throughout the early months of 1949, I continued to address meetings. I spoke on a variety of topics, but they were all variations on a single theme, Independence. The welcome I received in some places alarmed the authorities. Some of my supporters were arrested. Rambler reported the arrests, and added, 'We march on to victory, and those arrested because of their hero will return in triumph.'[2]

A fund, called the Kwame Nkrumah Defence Fund, was started to raise money to help pay for my defence in legal actions brought against me. As publisher of the *Evening News* I came in for many libel actions. But the fund was generously supported and I survived, although by July damages claimed from me totalled some £4,750.

In March, a new phase of the political struggle began, the period of preparation for Positive Action. It had become evident that unless we organised our potential strength more vigorously, the granting of Independence might be delayed indefinitely.

[1] Legislative Council.
[2] *The Accra Evening News*, 18 February 1949.

The Coussey Committee was taking a long time to do its work. It was therefore necessary to adopt a definite programme of political action. I explained what I meant by Positive Action. It was, I said, the application of constitutional and legitimate means to cripple the imperialist forces in the country. The weapons would be strikes, boycotts and non-co-operation, based upon the principle of non-violence. Again and again we urged the people not to relax:

> The history of colonial liberation movements shows that the first essential thing is ORGANISATION. Some may say 'unity', but unity presupposes organisation. At least, there must be organisation to unify the country; one person cannot do it; a few leaders cannot do it, but when the masses and the leaders share common ideals and purposes they can come together in an organisation, regardless of tribal and other differences, to fight for a cause.
>
> Leaders may come and go; they may rise and fall; but the people live on forever, and they can only be joined together by an organisation that is active and virile and doing the things for which it was established. The role of an organisation, especially in the colonial struggle, is of paramount importance; for victimisation, bribery and corruption, defaulting of leaders, these test the preparedness of the people for emancipation from age-long imperialist bondage, and both leaders and followers are to be wary of the imperialists even when they offer gifts. One thing we must bear in mind is that imperialism never gives way until it cannot help it.[1]

On 12 June came the split with the U.G.C.C. and the founding of my own party, the Convention People's Party. The editorial in *The Morning Telegraph* summed up the reaction of a large section of the people:

> With the formation of a new People's Party the upsurge of political activity in the country has gathered fresh momentum. There are no more cross roads, no more hallucinations, and there is no more aimlessness in outlook. The new Convention People's Party founded by Kwame Nkrumah has come to serve as a vanguard and an incentive towards volume constitutional agitation for a Greater Tomorrow.

All over the country, people hurried to join my Party. The whole Convention group in the Wassaw district threatened to

[1] *The Accra Evening News*, 18 May 1949.

join the C.P.P. if the U.G.C.C. failed to comply with certain demands. This group was one of many. I was referred to as the 'Apostle of Freedom'[1] and the 'Ghandi of Ghana'.[2]

Branches of the C.P.P. were opened in more and more places. Women as well as men flocked to our meetings. I travelled vast distances to explain our policy and to introduce the new Party. I received a great welcome in Kumasi on 24 June when 5,000 people gathered in the Prempeh Memorial Hall to hear me speak about the C.P.P. On that occasion £190 was donated to Party funds. But it was not all plain sailing. A section of the Press deplored my break away from the U.G.C.C. Osei Kodwo, writing in *The Spectator Daily* spoke of the need for unity, and urged his readers to follow the Convention leaders 'as a body, instead of following Nkrumah or Danquah or Ofori Atta as individuals'.[3]

There was bound to be a certain amount of confusion until it became increasingly clear that the U.G.C.C. no longer represented the wishes of the majority of the people. My call was for 'Self-Government Now', as opposed to the U.G.C.C.'s 'Self-Government in the shortest possible time'. Again, the C.P.P. did not intend to accept the Report of the Coussey Committee.

On 1 August I formally resigned from the U.G.C.C. In my letter of resignation I said:

> I am fully aware of the dangers to which I am thus exposed, but firm in the conviction that my country's cause comes first. I take the step and chance the consequences. I am prepared if need be to shed my blood and die if need be, that Ghana might have self-government now.

Many local branches of the U.G.C.C. met and passed resolutions dissolving their membership, and joining the C.P.P. Telegrams of support poured into the *Evening News* office. I carried out a nine-day tour of Ashanti and Nzima and visited the newly formed C.P.P. branches.

In the midst of all this, Sir Charles Arden-Clarke arrived to take up his position as Governor and Commander-in-Chief. I published a letter of welcome in the *Evening News* on 11 August. After explaining the political mood of the country and expressing the hope that he would see our demand for self-government was granted, I ended:

[1] *The Spectator Daily*, 23 June 1949.
[2] *The Morning Telegraph*, 27 June 1949
[3] *The Spectator Daily*, 9 July 1949.

Friendship and Empire are ill bedfellows. . . . We will not
tolerate any ideology of friendship within the Empire until we
have been liberated from the paralysing grip of imperialism,
when friendship can then be on equal terms.

Your Excellency, much lies ahead of you. Your stay with us
will be good or bad as you wish it. Those who think that they
can still govern us from Downing Street against our will are
tragically mistaken, and it is up to you to inform and advise
them as 'the man on the spot', that Britain can only henceforth rely on the friendship and co-operation of the Gold Coast,
our beloved Ghana, by first granting her her freedom now.
Your Excellency, Welcome to Ghana.

When the Coussey Report was made public, late in 1949, it
became clear that we were going to be offered a so-called 'improved Constitution', a very poor substitute for self-government.
I called a Gold Coast People's Representative Assembly to discuss the Coussey Proposals, and said:

The destiny of the Gold Coast is at stake, and we are to consider whether this country is only worthy of an improved
colonial status or is entitled to a free political existence.
Imperialism knows no law beyond its own interest and it is
natural that despite the pretensions of its agents to justice and
fair play, they always seek their interests first.

We shall not tolerate any half-baked constitution nor allow
any bogus one which deprives us of the right to govern ourselves to be forced down our throats. . . .

Let every citizen who loves his country come together for
this august and momentous assembly. . . . Let us show our
detractors that we mean to manage our own affairs. Ghana
shall be free.[1]

The Assembly was a great success. Thousands of people
attended, many of them delegates representing clubs and
organisations all over the country. I outlined the object of the
Assembly and drew attention to the inconsistencies and anomalies
of the Report. Several delegates spoke and in the end we passed
a resolution rejecting the Report and demanding immediate
independence within the British Commonwealth. A copy of the
resolution was sent to the Secretary of State.

And so 1949 drew to a close. It had been a most eventful year.
It began with the appointment of the Coussey Constitutional

[1] *The Accra Evening News*, 14 November 1949.

Committee, whose Report was rejected by the people in favour of a full 'Dominion-status' constitution. The political struggle had been carried a stage further with the foundation of the Convention People's Party, and the country was ready for Positive Action. In my Christmas message I spoke of the future:

There is now a new awakening which is irresistible and will surely re-assert our inherent and inalienable right to govern ourselves at no distant date. But that is only possible if we press forward our legitimate demands with dogged tenacity. . . . We are already in the thick of the fight; let us finish it nobly; let us struggle hard and victory shall be ours very soon.

CHAPTER FOUR

CONSTITUTION MAKING

The political and social revolution in Ghana may be said to have started at midnight on 8 January 1950, when Positive Action began. It was clear by then that the government had no intention of calling a constituent assembly to let the people decide for themselves whether they would adopt the Coussey Report or not. The economic life of the country was paralysed and trouble was unavoidable. The story of my subsequent arrest and imprisonment has been told in my Autobiography. It is sufficient here to say that during the fourteen months I spent in James Fort prison, the campaign for Independence never stopped. My supporters outside, led by Komla Gbedemah, kept in touch with me and I was able to get messages smuggled out to them.

In the General Election of February 1951 the C.P.P. won the majority of seats in the Assembly. I was elected for Accra Central with the largest poll ever recorded. The Governor ordered my release, and I left James Fort as the elected leader of the first African-dominated government of the Gold Coast. Thousands of people crowded round the car, singing the C.P.P. song, waving and cheering. As our slow procession wound its way into Horse Road, men, women and children stood on roof-tops and leaned from windows. Every inch of the way, the crowds seemed to grow larger. Finally, about 30,000 people assembled at the West End Arena to hear me speak. Gbedemah told of how he had completed the task entrusted to him as deputy leader while I was in prison. He called for three cheers in honour of the released men; for with me had also been freed Kofi Baako, Nana Kobina Nketsia, Awoonor Renner, Blankson Lartey, Jerron Quarshie and H.S.T. Provencal. Then he asked me to speak.

It was not the moment for a long political speech, nor yet for talk of revenge against the administration. I spoke for only three minutes. I thanked the people for all they had done towards our release and for the wonderful welcome they had given us. 'I find that within your hearts,' I concluded, 'you have some place for us. It is for us now to show that within our hearts we also have some place for you. The struggle continues.' My final words could hardly be heard, so loud was the cheering.

The following day I gave a Press conference at which I said that the constitution under which I was to act as Leader of Government Business was 'bogus and fraudulent' but would serve as a stepping stone to self-government. It was bogus because the ministers were without power. Yet the C.P.P. elected members would accept ministerial posts if they were offered them. While co-operating with the administration, we would not alter our demand for full self-government within the Commonwealth. I also said that we should turn first to an extensive programme of education and prepare a five-year plan for development. In a message which I issued a week later to Party members, I referred once more to the Constitution:

There is a great risk in accepting office under this new Constitution which still makes us half slaves and half free. It is all too easy to identify oneself with such a Constitution and thereby be swayed by considerations of temporary personal advantage, instead of seeking the interest of the people. Hence we call for vigilance and moral courage to withstand the evil manœuvres of imperialism.

Bribery and corruption, both moral and factual, have eaten into the whole fabric of our society and these must be stamped out if we are to achieve any progress. Our election to the Assembly shows that the public has confidence in the integrity of the Party, and that we will not stoop low to contaminate ourselves with bribery and corruption at the expense of the people.

The trust which the people have placed in the Convention People's Party is the most precious thing we possess; and as long as that trust and confidence is maintained, there is victory for us. . . . What the people of this country want is real political power to manage their own affairs without leaving power in the hands of a single person appointed by an alien power, however paternalistic or kind.

In due course the new Legislative Assembly met, with myself as chief minister, called Leader of Government Business, and with seven members of the C.P.P. as ministers. Ultimate self-government had become a certainty.

The following month I was elected life chairman of the C.P.P. at a conference in Saltpond. Earlier I had addressed a mass rally in an open space just outside the town. On that occasion, the theme of my address was solidarity, and the continuing need for organisation. I made it clear that opportunists had no place in our Party. 'I am finding ways and means to check opportunism in the Party and have asked the National Executive to expel at once any opportunist in the Party,' I said. I expressed the same determination to rid our organisation of bribery and corruption:

> I have maintained and I shall continue to maintain that I will fight against bribery and corruption whenever I find it. Wherever I find it, I will expose it, even if it is within the Assembly.

About this time I addressed Party members and supporters almost every week at rallies throughout the country, or in Accra. In all, I must have spoken before hundreds of thousands of people, and dealt with almost all the questions connected with our policy. At Suhum, the problem of chieftaincy came up. I assured my audience of some 20,000 people:

> I am not in the Gold Coast to abolish chieftaincy. All that the people expect our natural rulers to do is to respect the wishes of their people. I plead for mutual respect between chiefs and people. Let me make it plain to all that even when the C.P.P. has been able to achieve self-government for Ghana, there will still be chieftaincy in the Gold Coast.

At Winneba, two months later, addressing a most friendly durbar and rally, I recalled that political power was not yet absolutely in our hands, and that we must advance to it step by step. There were still many problems:

> My chief problems are the workers, the farmers and the ex-service men. I am determined to have them well placed. This is the time to match reason with reason; this is the time to apply wisdom to wisdom, and this is the time to stop, look and give sound judgement.

At Anomabu, birthplace of Kwegyir Aggrey, I reasserted some of the principles by which our Party stood:

> My hatred against imperialists can never dwindle, but what I want everyone in this country to remember is that we are fighting against a system and not against any individual, race or colour.

Shortly afterwards I left with Kojo Botsio, then Minister of Education, for a visit to the United States, in the course of which I received the honorary degree of Doctor of Laws from my old University of Lincoln. I was deeply touched by the spontaneous welcome we received everywhere we went. My speeches in America were mostly of thanks, but at the same time I did try to explain the political situation in the Gold Coast, and the need for support. On our way back through London, I met Seretse Khama. We were attending meetings in adjacent committee rooms of the House of Commons. Botsio and I then listened to part of an all-night Commons debate from the Distinguished Strangers' Gallery. Earlier in the day I had given a Press conference in the Government's hospitality centre off Park Lane. Questions were asked about swollen shoot, the cocoa disease, and about our plans for education and industry. Some of the questioners obviously knew very little about the Gold Coast; others showed real knowledge and interest.

Enthusiastic crowds greeted our arrival back in Accra towards the end of June. It was nice to be home again. But there was no time to relax. On 29 June I announced a 'new deal' for cocoa. For each fully grown tree removed by the authorities because of disease, compensation would be paid at the rate of two shillings a tree each year for five years. Hitherto, only two shillings a tree had been paid. Payment would only be paid when a diseased tree was removed and burnt and a new tree properly planted in its place. I said:

> The Government appreciates the loss of livelihood felt by the farmer while his replanted trees are growing; this is its method of safe-guarding his interest when he himself is taking steps to safe-guard the country's interest by co-operating in the reconstruction plan for cocoa which I am launching.

I explained that a new variety of cocoa which was quicker growing and started bearing in two years would be introduced into the country. The Government was investigating the marketable properties of this type of cocoa and hoped it might be attractive to dealers and manufacturers. The new deal for cocoa was only part of our programme for development. In a broadcast on 25 July I announced other changes. A medical school would be built and maternity facilities extended. Housing schemes were being planned for various parts of the country.

There was a plan to develop teacher training centres and secondary and technical education. A Professor of Agriculture would be added to the staff of the University College. To deal with the question of unemployment, a Labour Advisory Committee was to be set up. On the question of the high cost of living I said:

> We want to control more effectively the prices of essential commodities such as maize, sardines, corned beef, sugar, flour, kerosene, cement and wax, and fancy cotton prints, and to check the prevailing black market in these articles. We also hope, with the co-operation of consumers, to see that laws regarding conditional sales are rigidly enforced.
> We are at present examining the report of the Rental Enquiry Committee and we intend to bring under control the present soaring rents.

When the Legislative Assembly met on 15 August I moved that the aims and objects of the Development Plan be approved. The total estimated cost at that time was £74,000,000 and the Volta River project a further £65,000,000. I said that one of the fundamental objectives of the plan was to exploit the natural resources of the Gold Coast to the maximum. Unless we demonstrated the stability of the Government to the outside world we would not get foreign financial assistance. After some discussion, the Plan was approved.

While we were planning the economic development of the country, we did not lose sight of constitutional issues. Until full self-government was achieved, we could only scratch at the surface of the problems which confronted the country. I have always maintained that political freedom must precede economic emancipation.

My position as Leader of Government Business was clearly unsatisfactory and further constitutional reforms were necessary. For some time, Party members and others had been insisting that I, as leader of the predominant party in the Legislature, should become Prime Minister. As a result of talks between the Governor and the Secretary of State, constitutional reforms were agreed upon and on 5 March 1952, Sir Charles Arden-Clarke announced them to the Assembly. I became the first African Prime Minister in history.

When opening the debate in the Assembly on the proposed

constitutional changes, I said I would like to make it clear that
the achievement of the Gold Coast people was not the result of
the efforts of any one party, organisation or individual. I told the
House that the words and actions of the Members would be
examined from many angles and in many parts of the world.
'The future of Africa and peoples of African descent,' I said,
'depends on the success of the people of the Gold Coast in their
struggle for self-government.' I paid tribute to the political
leaders of the past, and said they should never be forgotten. I
spoke of the actual changes in the constitution:

> The change which has been made is no mere window dressing,
> no matter what our critics and detractors may say. The office
> of Prime Minister is the highest office in mature, self-govern-
> ing democratic countries. By getting it into our constitution
> now, we have made a big step forward. . . .
>   We are making sure that there are no more Civil 'Masters'
> in this country as under the old Colonial regime, but Civil
> 'Servants', as in other countries, dictating no policy but faith-
> fully carrying out the policy decided by the Cabinet. I must
> say that the great majority of expatriates in the Civil Service
> have adjusted themselves well to the new constitution and
> many are working really hard and loyally for the good of the
> country, in support of the policies of our government. . . .
>   Let us live by deeds, not words, and stick to our policies
> like firm rocks and not shift like quicksands. We shall prove
> ourselves by our fidelity to our purpose, by our faithfulness to
> our cause, our upholding the confidence of the people and,
> above all, by our assiduously maintaining the solidarity of our
> Party in the Assembly.

As Prime Minister, my responsibilities increased. I knew that
the eyes of the world were on me, as the first African Prime
Minister, and that the political future of the rest of Africa might
well depend on my success or failure. In a broadcast to the
American people, I said that Africans were ready to live on
terms of friendship and equality with other races in Africa, but
they were determined to be free and equal:

> The success of our efforts in the Gold Coast is a source of
> inspiration to all Africans and people of African descent every-
> where. We can see our role in its historical setting: to bring
> democracy and human brotherhood and peace to Africa and
> the world. The new African does not fight against race, or

colour, or creed, but against any system which exploits and degrades. We believe that true internationalism is rooted in national independence of all countries.

I called for understanding and co-operation among the great nations, and appealed to the world audience of the United Nations to make the world safe for progress. Freedom brings responsibility. We had still not attained political independence, but we knew our mission. It was evident that self-government would be achieved through the C.P.P., for membership of the Party had now passed the million mark. On my forty-third birthday, I spoke to a large crowd at the Arena:

In our country today, this is not the time for looking back, for being sentimental. This is the time for looking forward, with faith and high hope, and this is the time for action. For we must act to show all the world that we have the faith and the will to complete what we have begun.

Another year in my life has served to remind me of the grim tasks that lie ahead and to fill me with determination to attack them with more vigour. I am encouraged and sustained by the good wishes that have showered on me today, and by the prayers that have been offered for the welfare of our people and our country. . . . The history of our struggle is familiar to you all. You know why we staged Positive Action, and why we chose to participate in this struggle for liberation. . . .

It is our ambition to improve the standard of living of the people of Ghana, by making great achievements such as the gigantic agricultural scheme, leading to the abolition of unemployment and idleness; the introduction of progressive socialist schemes like housing, sanatoria, the establishment of workers' compulsory education for children of all classes, maternity and child welfare clinics, and other intricate and progressive social and economic schemes that will surely transform Ghana into a modern country.

Our support has come from the masses, and in the masses we place our greatest belief and faith. And we shall not be let down. Now while Ghana needs us, for in our country we have no place for shirkers, we have place for workers, thinkers and doers. . . . And so before long this country of ours will be the land of self-help, efficiency and enterprise. It will begin to reap the reward of its courage and suffering. It will be the land of opportunity and of active minds.

In October I asked Chiefs, Councils, traditional authorities, political parties and groups throughout the Gold Coast to submit their views on further constitutional changes. I said in my statement in the Assembly, that the proposals should indicate clearly what further functions and responsibilities we ought to assume. When we had definite proposals to make, we would discuss them with the United Kingdom Government. Statesmanship of a high order was called for, because every ill-considered word, written or spoken, might damage the cause we all had at heart. I went on to suggest possible questions for discussion. Clearly the position of the ex-officio ministers would have to be considered. Did the country want a single House system? Or ought a Second Chamber to be established? Representational and electoral reform was needed. 'The world which is both critical and sympathetic,' I added, 'will watch with the closest attention how we deal with this problem. All I ask of the Chiefs and people is that they should place at the disposal of the Government the best advice they can give.' This statement was greeted with loud cheering.

Well over a hundred organisations submitted their views. The discussions and consultations formed the basis of the government's White Paper on Constitutional Reform, which in its turn led to the so-called Nkrumah constitution which came into force in 1954.

Although affairs in my own country occupied most of my time, I always kept an eye on the larger issue of African freedom and unity. In January 1953, I paid a state visit to Liberia and had some very interesting talks with President Tubman. Accompanied by Kojo Botsio and E. O. Asafu-Adjaye, I went to the Liberian Legislature and made a speech in which I spoke of African unity:

The ideal nearest my heart is the union of all peoples of West Africa. To this end I am dedicated. It is the policy of the Gold Coast government that both countries should work in closer harmony, for both are in the vanguard of African advancement, and share the same aims and ideals.

While we in the Gold Coast still cherish our bonds with the British Crown we are united in the desire to control our affairs. Our goal is almost in sight; within a very short time we expect the full burden of responsibility will fall squarely on our shoulders. It is for this reason that I and my colleagues value

so highly this opportunity to meet Liberians who have carried
this responsibility for so long.

I gave an exhaustive survey of the Gold Coast's economic
position, quoting figures to show revenue and expenditure.
Revenue amounted to about ten times the 1938–39 figure. This
was mainly due, I said, to the increased world demand for
primary products.

I have the happiest memories of my stay in Liberia. I shall
never forget the wild enthusiasm of the crowds at the mass meeting held at the Centennial Pavilion in Monrovia, when I
delivered an impromptu speech. As often in the past, the enthusiastic crowd acted as an inspiration, and the words flowed
out of me. That speech, entirely without notes or preparation,
was probably the most successful made in Liberia.

My final speech to the people of Liberia was made at the
garden party given by President and Mrs Tubman. I described
my impressions of Liberia, and added:

> I do not believe in racialism and tribalism. The concept
> 'Africa for the Africans' does not mean that other races are
> excluded from it. No! It only means that Africans shall and
> must govern themselves in their own countries without
> imperialist and foreign impositions; but that people of other
> races can remain on African soil, carry on their legitimate
> avocations and live on terms of peace, friendship and equality
> with Africans on their own soil.

The months following my return to the Gold Coast were
mainly taken up with preparing the new constitutional proposals
to be laid before the United Kingdom Government. On 10 July
1953 I placed before the Assembly the historic 'Motion of
Destiny', which called on the British Government to give the
Gold Coast its independence as soon as the necessary arrangements could be made. The Motion has been quoted in full in my
Autobiography. However, I consider it of such importance that
I make no apology for quoting parts of it again. I opened my
speech by reminding members that they were called upon to
exercise statesmanship of a high order:

> There comes a time in the history of colonial peoples when
> they must, because of their will to throw off the hampering

shackles of colonialism, boldly assert their God-given right to
be free of a foreign ruler. Today, we are here to claim this right
to our independence.

The demand for self-government, I said, was a just demand,
admitting of no compromise. The right of the people to govern
themselves was a fundamental principle, and to compromise on
it would be to betray it. The right of the people to decide their
own destiny was not to be measured by the yardstick of colour
or degree of social development:

> If there is to be a criterion of a people's preparedness for self-
> government, then I say it is their readiness to assume the
> responsibility of ruling themselves. For who but a people
> themselves can say when they are prepared?

I went on to describe the various stages in the constitutional
development of the country:

> Mr Speaker, we have travelled long distances from the days
> when our fathers came under alien subjugation to the present
> time. We stand now at the threshold of self-government and
> do not waver . . . I express the wishes and feelings of the chiefs
> and people of this country in hoping that the final transfer of
> power to your representative Ministers may be done in a
> spirit of amity and friendship, so that, having peacefully
> achieved our freedom, the peoples of both countries, Britain
> and the Gold Coast, may form a relationship based on mutual
> respect, trust and friendship. . . . Today more than ever before,
> Britain needs more 'autonomous communities freely asso-
> ciated'. For freely associated communities make better friends
> than those associated by subjugation.

After summarising the history of the Gold Coast, I stated that
in the future we would doubtless make mistakes, as all other
nations had done. But the mistakes would be our own mistakes,
and it would be our responsibility to put them right. Loud cheering followed when I said that history was being made: a colonial
people in Africa had put forward the first definite claim for
independence. I emphasised that self-government was not an
end in itself:

> It is a means to an end, to the building of the good life to the
> benefit of all, regardless of tribe, creed, colour or station in

life. Our aim is to make this country a worthy place for all its citizens, a country that will be a shining light throughout the whole continent of Africa, giving inspiration far beyond its frontiers. . . .

We must aspire to lead in the arts of peace. The foreign policy of our country must be dedicated to the service of peace and fellowship. We repudiate the evil doctrines of tribal chauvinism, racial prejudice and national hatred. We repudiate these evil ideas because in creating that brotherhood to which we aspire, we hope to make a reality, within the bounds of our small country, of all the grandiose ideologies which are supposed to form the intangible bonds holding together the British Commonwealth of Nations in which we hope to remain. . . .

Mr Speaker, we can only meet the challenge of our age as a free people. Hence the demand for our freedom, for only free men can shape the destinies of their future.

Mr Speaker, Honourable Members, we have great tasks before us. I say, with all seriousness, that it is rarely that human beings have such an opportunity for service to their fellows. Mr Speaker, for my part, I can only re-echo the words of a great man: 'Man's dearest possession is life, and since it is given to him to live but once, he must so live as not to be besmeared with the shame of a cowardly existence and trivial past, so live that dying he might say: all my life and all my strength were given to the finest cause in the world, the liberation of mankind.'

Mr Speaker, 'Now God be thanked, who has matched us with this hour.'

So great was the cheering both inside and outside, that the House had to be suspended for fifteen minutes. The Motion was debated for several days and finally carried unanimously.

CHAPTER FIVE

ALL-AFRICAN CABINET

Telegrams of congratulation on my Motion of Destiny speech poured into Accra from many parts of the world. The last phase of the struggle for independence had begun, and seemed to be off to a good start. *The Manchester Guardian* (as it then was) in a leading article commented (17 July 1953):

> Great credit is due to both Dr Kwame Nkrumah and his colleagues, and the Governor and the other members of the colonial service, for the wise and sincere way in which they have handled a situation which might have been made intolerable by rancour or ill faith or even vanity on either side.

A week afterwards, I opened the new £33,000 Nankese-Akwadum road. It was quite an occasion, because for the first time since I became Prime Minister, the Okyenhene, Nana Ofori Atta, accompanied by his elders and clan chiefs, took the chair at a public function at which I was the principal speaker. It was no secret that there had been some antagonism between the Okyenhene and myself. The crowd cheered when I spoke of our co-operation. I said that the new road which linked New Juaben with Akim Abuakwa was evidence of the government's determination to develop all parts of the country. After cutting the tape and declaring the new road open, the Omanhene and I rode to Akwadu where we were met on the new bridge over the Densu River by Nana Agyeman Akrasi II, Omanhene of New Juaben and representatives of the Koforidua Urban Council. Nana Agyeman Akrasi made a short speech of welcome, and concluded, 'We are very grateful to you as the Prime Minister of the Gold Coast for the laudable achievement you have made towards self-government within so short a time. May the Lord bless you.'

While new roads, bridges and buildings of all kinds marked the rapid development of the country, constitutional issues remained foremost in my mind. In my Christmas message I reviewed the progress made:

At home we have amicably settled the new division of constituencies; we have decided on direct elections; and we look forward to an African Cabinet of representative ministers. These are strides which we could not take but for the understanding of all true citizens, and the goodwill and support of our friends of all races both here and abroad.

Abroad, we have continued to strengthen our friendly relations with members of the Commonwealth, this year noticeably with India and Canada. Nearer home, we have re-awakened the spirit of our fathers in the idea of one West Africa which, diverse in human and material resources, shall be united in a community of noble interests.

Let us again go forward together, chiefs and people, with discipline and a high purpose. Let the message of the season remind us to recharge our spirit and our strength, making us more steadfast and firm. And let us all, in good faith and confidence of the rightness of our cause, and in the sincerity of our desire to maintain not only the right balance but the highest standards in our public life, press on to the goal before us, of political emancipation, economic reconstruction and social regeneration.

Sons and daughters of Ghana, I wish you one and all a Merry Christmas and a bright and great New Year.

Early in 1954 the political pace quickened as thoughts turned to the forthcoming general election. The C.P.P. held a big rally at New Tafo on 13 February. Fifteen miles from the outskirts of Koforidua we were escorted by two hundred cars. Thousands of people waved and cheered as we drove along. When we were five miles outside Tafo, another huge crowd met us. In my speech I said that the C.P.P. was a disciplined Party and the mistakes of individuals would not break its solidarity. The country was going through a transitional period in which obstacles were inevitable, but they would be overcome.

With the country well on the way to self-government, overseas investors were thinking hard about the wisdom of putting their money into industry in the Gold Coast. In the Legislative Assembly on 1 March I reassured foreign investors on the subject of nationalisation. If any future government decided to nationalise a particular industry, there would be fair compensation. It was to be hoped that private firms would adopt training schemes designed to provide for a steady increase in the appoint-

ment of African staff. The government, I said, was anxious to
expand the economy of the country:

> We are satisfied that there is ample scope for the establish-
> ment of many new enterprises, and as a start has already been
> made, the government proposes to take steps to build up and
> extend the industrial structure of the economy.

Another aspect of the uncertainty of this transitional period
was the question of chieftaincy. I told the Assembly that the
institution of chieftaincy was so deeply bound up with the life of
our community that its disappearance would spell disaster:

> At the same time, the government believes that chieftaincy, in
> common with other human institutions, cannot remain static,
> but that it must in large measure adapt itself to the changing
> requirement of the changing time.

I announced that a Bill would be introduced to provide that
financial contributions should be a charge on the local government revenues. Traditional authorities ought to have enough
money to enable them to play their parts 'with the dignity which
we all expect from our chiefs'.

The three-year-old Legislative Assembly set up according to
the recommendations of the Coussey Committee came to an end
in March 1954. On the last day I spoke of the corporate unity
which the House had fostered, and paid tribute to the Speaker,
Sir Emmanuel Charles Quist. I said that the Government fully
appreciated the efforts of the Opposition. Other farewell speeches
were made and the sitting ended with a short address by the
Speaker.

Then electioneering began in earnest. We adopted the slogan
'C.P.P., 104', indicating that the Party would contest the 104
seats and hoped to win them all. Anyone failing to vote for the
C.P.P., we said, would be delaying self-government. I named the
Party's candidates at a monster rally held in Accra on 2 May,
and then presented them to the people. 'It is our aim,' I declared,
'to win the 104 seats in the next Assembly, for it is that which
will demonstrate to the outside world the unity of the country
and the determination of the people to regain their independence
now.'

A number of disgruntled Party members who felt that they

ought to have been nominated for the elections, let it be known that they desired to seek election as Independent candidates. I reminded these that we were not fighting for individuals but for the Party, and what it stood for:

> The destiny of the country is at stake. The issue is too great to be trifled with, and personal desires must be sacrificed for the common good. Unity and discipline should be observed within our ranks and we must all work unreservedly for the Party's candidates to win 'Operation 104'.

The result of the general election held in June 1954 was a sweeping victory for the C.P.P. On 17 June the Governor called me to Christiansborg Castle and asked me to become Prime Minister and to form a new government. After an hour's talk, I returned to my office and held a Press conference at which I announced that the new Cabinet would include ten ministers apart from myself, all of them members of the C.P.P. Asked about the future, I said that we would intensify our negotiations with the British Government in regard to self-government. I defined the position of the Gold Coast in world politics by emphasising that it would be useless for the Gold Coast to kowtow either to the East or West. 'In my opinion,' I added, 'the Gold Coast should follow a middle course maintaining the balance between East and West. I really believe in a Third Force.' I disclosed that plans were proceeding for a united West Africa, and for annual Pan-African conferences.

On 23 June, I broadcast my first official message to the people on my return to office as Prime Minister:

> I think everyone will agree that the recent general election has been the most momentous in our history, and it has provided us with useful experience for the further steps in our hazardous journey towards independence and nationhood. I have been thinking of many things since the conclusion of this election, and so I am speaking to you, my countrymen and women, and sharing my thoughts with you, for your help is indispensable in the future, and for the achievement of the objects which are so close to our hearts. For the first time in the history of the Gold Coast we have a completely African Legislative Assembly, and an all-African Cabinet. They are charged with the responsibility of running the affairs of this country. This is a great and worthy task.

In this, my first official message since my return to office, I turn naturally to you, my people, whose confidence in myself and in my Party has been so clearly demonstrated at the polls, and on behalf of us all, and in particular, on my own behalf I say, 'Thank you'.

I congratulated the successful candidates among whom was the first woman to be elected to the Assembly:

To my countrywomen I say a special word. The election of our first woman member to the Legislative Assembly fills me with hope for your achievement. I trust that you will take an ever-increasing interest in the conduct of our affairs, and I recall with pride the words of Aggrey: 'Educate the women, and you educate the nation.'

I called on all, irrespective of party, race or creed, to work for the good of the country, saying 'We are catching up with the world, and I know that if we work together in friendly co-operation, nothing is impossible.' We were in the last phase of the fight for political freedom. The length of the phase would depend on ourselves:

Full self-government is only one step away; we must be very sure that we do not stumble at this final step in our journey to reach the end of the road. With all these thoughts in mind, we must now be deeply grateful for the blessings that we have received; for the opportunity to work towards the attainment of our ideals; for the freedom which permits us to abide by our principles, so that we need not compromise on our principle of preferring self-government with danger to servitude in tranquillity.

We need, too, to be grateful for the goodwill and fellowship of the other peoples of the world, for we are happy because we have more friends than enemies; our friends believe in us, and are sure that we can fulfil the hopes reposed in us. We must not fail them. We must succeed.

The seventy-two members of the C.P.P. who had been elected to the Assembly met shortly afterwards in Accra to discuss Party policy and other matters of mutual concern. It was agreed that all members would contribute £120 a year from their salaries to the Party's funds. Ministerial Secretaries would pay £180 as a yearly subscription to the Party; and Ministers would pay not less than £402 as their annual subscription. All the subscriptions would be collected at the C.P.P. central headquarters in Accra, and fifty per cent of each member's subscription would be sent to his constituency for incidental expenses.

During the next few months, I travelled to various parts of the country, and in February 1955 visited the Northern Territories. I paid a courtesy call on the Yabum-Wura, Paramount Chief of the Gonja, and then spoke to the Gonja Volta District Council. After mentioning the numerous developments which had taken place in the district, I referred to the extent to which Northern Territories opinion was represented in the Government at the level of Ministers and Ministerial Secretaries. During the transitional stage before independence, the Government would strengthen the machinery for consultation with the Regions. I said that the proposals of the Development Committee of the Northern Territories Council would be carefully studied to see how they could be incorporated in the Second Development Plan.

The Minister of Finance, Komla Gbedemah, in presenting his budget on 22 February 1955, proposed major tax charges to provide more revenue for our development plans. In seconding the Budget speech, I gave a summary of our achievements:

> In the field of economic and productive services, during the past four years, eighteen new agricultural stations have been set up together with eleven new cocoa stations in connection with the reconstruction of the cocoa industry. Four new agricultural training centres have been built; and soil surveys carried out over many hundreds of square miles.
>
> We have increased electricity output from 32,000 to 51,000 kilowatts, an increase of 60%
>
> As regards water development, we have constructed 940 wells and sunk 62 successful boreholes. We have installed seven new pipe supplies and four more are under construction.
>
> Turning to communications, we have during the past four years built 38 miles of new railways, re-aligned a further fifteen miles and have another fifty miles under construction. The capacity of Takoradi harbour has been greatly increased and the construction of a new harbour at Tema has been started.
>
> We have built or reconstructed 828 miles of major roads and re-surfaced with bitumen a further 730 miles. Four major bridges, including the Adomi Bridge, are under construction,

and two more have been completed. In addition, over 60 smaller bridges have been built.

We have added 270 miles of overhead telephone trunk routes and 140 miles of underground cable. We have installed 4,800 new telephones. This increases the telephone traffic capacity threefold. We have completed thirteen new post office buildings and the size of the General Post Office has been doubled. All these things, and particularly important works such as the Adomi Bridge, will bring benefits to the country which are clearly very far-reaching.

As to social services, we have doubled the primary school accommodation available, increased that for middle schools by fifty per cent, and increased the numbers attending new secondary schools by two hundred per cent. Eight new teacher training colleges have been built, not to mention what has been done in the field of technical and higher education.

Our housing programme has provided to date 15,000 room units accommodating nearly 40,000 people. As regards health, in addition to the most modern hospital in West Africa now under construction in Kumasi, we have nine new hospitals completed or under construction, and have carried out extensions to fifteen existing hospitals. Two new health centres are nearly complete.

I added that priority must be given to economic and productive services which would increase our revenue and widen the basis of our economy. Social services came next, particularly education and health. 'Social development must and will continue,' I said, 'but it must be geared to the pace we can afford.'

CHAPTER SIX

THE PARTY AND ITS PROGRESS

During the first five years after the war, an increasing number of visitors arrived in Ghana. Most of them came on business, or in connection with government development work of one kind or another. The question of accommodation became urgent. Accra needed a large modern hotel capable of catering for large numbers of visitors.

Plans were drawn up for the Ambassador Hotel, to be built near the centre of Accra. It was designed to provide not only 100 bedrooms, each with a bathroom attached, but also a restaurant, lounges, bars and a banqueting hall to seat 300 people. I laid the foundation stone on the 26 May 1955. In my speech I said that very often our lasting impressions of a country are determined by first impressions, and by the hospitality offered:

> We ourselves expect to be made to feel welcome when we arrive in a foreign country and we should in our turn put ourselves out to make strangers feel at home in our own country. But up till now we have had little to offer visitors in the way of first class hotel accommodation, and if it hadn't been for the individual efforts of the people here in receiving them into their homes, I am afraid most of them would have left us for good and would have done so with a very bad taste in their mouths and a very poor impression of us.

I went on to say that Accra, as the capital city, was the shop window of the country:

> It is here that our visitors will invariably receive their first impressions. As many of these visitors do not journey outside Accra, the impressions they receive here go for the whole country. On account of this it is most essential that we improve our capital city both in appearance and in the provision of amenities.

The Ambassador Hotel was completed in time for Independence. Government guests stayed there and enjoyed standards of comfort as good as any provided in first-class hotels throughout the world. Many other new buildings were planned in all parts of the country. They were part of our general development policy. Meanwhile, the political struggle continued. The Twelfth of June, the anniversary of the founding of the C.P.P., is the occasion each year for a notable speech to Party members in the Accra Arena. The year 1955 was no exception. We were by now confident of ultimate success, political cohesion was more than satisfactory, and we were flexing our muscles for the final attack on feudalism and imperialism. After reminding my audience of the very words used six years before, when the Party was founded, and of the principles for which it has always stood, I dealt with the question of our political opponents:

Our political opponents have been singularly confused in their aims, methods and approach and would not hesitate to make an alliance with the devil himself if by so doing they could frustrate the victorious march of the masses towards their just aspirations. Since the formation of the Convention People's Party in 1949, no less than twelve political parties have sprung up, and yet, because they failed to produce any policy acceptable to the people, none of them has succeeded. For the first and only time in the chequered history of this country, ours has been the only party to present a clear and bold political programme – for *independence, freedom, democracy* and *social justice.*

Countrymen, in our own lifetime the world has witnessed two global wars fought for the cause of freedom; other erstwhile colonial territories, such as India, Burma, Ceylon, Pakistan, Indonesia – and a host of others in Asia – have fought for, and attained their freedom. For the last few years we of this country have in our turn toiled and suffered for freedom.

And yet, when the very colonial power which has dominated us for the past hundred years now offers our freedom and independence and tells us to make arrangements for it, some of our own chiefs and disgruntled and disappointed politicians are doing their utmost to sabotage the very cause for which we have fought undaunted.

I ask you, are the suffering masses of this new Ghana of ours going to stand for that?

The reason they (the Opposition) adopt such tactics is because they fear democracy and the common man, and they try to camouflage such fears by undermining the party system and the parliamentary democracy we have been able to introduce into the country. Friends and comrades, it is only a year ago since we had our general election when the various parties put out their manifestoes and promises to the country. Our appeal to the nation was simple and direct: *Give us the mandate to obtain independence for this country and to develop our resources.* The nation heard us and responded admirably. This is the promise we are trying to fulfil.

With the end of our long struggle in sight, those against democratic government in this country are now trying to upset things. You and I know, however, that they will never succeed in sabotaging our struggle for independence. Our goal is now within reach, and it is up to each one of us to see that nothing stands in our way.

With regard to the Ashanti situation, impartial overseas observers have been able to diagnose the trouble with more frankness and candour than we ourselves have managed to do. The pity is that it should have occurred at all. As I have said time and time again, every citizen is at liberty to become a member of whatever political party he likes; he is also at liberty to form a political party of his own. After he has put forward the ideology he wants to pursue, it is up to him to persuade the people to his way of thinking. The test of whether he has succeeded in convincing them will show up at a general election. But, whatever methods he employs to impress his ideas upon the people, he should never resort to acts of violence. If he does commit acts of violence he does so at his own peril. No government will condone this and firm action will be taken to bring perpetrators of violence in this country to justice.

The C.P.P. members cheered this statement and I went on to show the essential fairness of a democratic constitution based on universal adult suffrage. Our opponents had not our political appeal, and after attacking our cocoa policy quite unjustly, and unsuccessfully, they now pinned their hopes in federation, namely a federal system of government with a number of small autonomous 'kingdoms' in Ghana. It was too ridiculous. But all this was not to deny that an Opposition Party would be welcome:

I have always expressed both in public and in private that we need a strong and well organised Opposition Party in the country and in the Assembly. My advice to opposition parties

has always been that they should organise themselves and
choose reliable and trustworthy leaders – not saboteurs and
political renegades and apostates – and that they should produce a national policy that the people can accept. They can
then contest the elections and let the people decide. That is
the democratic process through which parties come into
power. If their plans and their record are better than ours,
they will win. If ours are better, we shall remain in power.

That was the sum of the position as I saw it and my audience
was loud in approval. After recalling further disputes which we
had had on parliamentary matters I said:

What I cannot understand is why these opposition parties
don't get together and use their energy in a more constructive
and effective way by forming themselves into a nationwide
opposition party, instead of racking their brains for ways and
means of overthrowing the Party in power and believing that
the dynamiting of the houses of Party members would be as
final in its destruction as that of a child's sand castle knocked
down in a fit of rage by a fellow playmate. What they forget
is that, unlike the sand castle, the foundations of the Convention People's Party are far deeper than those of any man-
made construction.

Let them therefore come together as a Party and discuss
their grievances with us man to man. By the nature of things
the opposition parties could well be called 'Ghana Opposition
Parties Amalgamated' or G O P A. If, having formed such a
Party, they set about something constructive, the world would
think well of them. But unfortunately this seems beyond them
because they seem incapable of direction and organisation;
it appears that all they are capable of at present is abuse and
vilification, but, those who criticise us, let them look at their
own heights!

I appeal to you all, trade unionists, ex-service-men, farmers
and youth, to be active and vigilant and to keep all wolves in
sheep's clothing out of your organisations. Remember, eternal
vigilance is the price of liberty; the struggle for freedom has
depended entirely on your exertions and sacrifices, and you
must not allow your own handiwork to collapse because of the
machinations of the very reactionary forces against which you
have been fighting all these years.

I was now nearing the end of what I had to say on political
matters. At this time the Togoland issue was quiet, but our

members in Ashanti were being harassed daily by what I called
a 'feudal revolt against a democratic way of life'. I then came to
answer the charge of dictatorship, levelled by the enemies of our
Party.

I now want to answer the iniquitous and vicious allegation
made by our political opponents that the Convention People's
Party is dictatorial. If I were a dictator the Opposition Party
would have no place to stand to make the noise they are
making. But to answer this charge we have only to ask ourselves what the political record of the Convention People's
Party has been since it came into power.

In local government, the Government of the Convention
People's Party has established for the first time elected local
councils; our Government has placed the local courts, prisons,
police and administration under the elected local councils
and intends to establish a proper local justiciary in line with
the central judiciary; it has released the people of this country
from the tyranny of decadent oath-swearing, inordinate fines
and pacifications; in the sphere of central government democratic innovations by our Government include universal adult
suffrage, a fully elected legislature and a Government collectively responsible to the Legislature; coupled with this they
have been responsible for an independent judiciary under the
Judicial Service Commission and an independent public
service under the Public Service Commission.

Study for yourselves our legislative record and our Hansard
since we came into office. Is that the path of dictatorship? I
think you will agree with me that, on the contrary, the Party
has been trying to release the people from the bondage of
foreign colonialism and the tyranny of local feudalism.

I ended my review of the political situation, as I often did, on
the note of Pan-Africanism, a goal to which we in Ghana have
always turned our eyes. But although it was now far into the
afternoon my speech was not over. I had important economic
facts and plans for the future to acquaint my audience with:

It has been well pointed out that political independence is but
an empty façade if economic freedom is not possible also. I
must emphasise again, however, that economic freedom can
only be purchased by capital development, it cannot be given
from outside. Through the sound economic policy of the
Government the country is prosperous, its revenue is buoyant
and large surpluses have been accumulated both by the

Government and by the Marketing Boards. Besides this, we have financed a huge development programme all by ourselves without borrowing a penny from outside and in addition to this we have laid aside much money already for the next Development Plan.

In the space of only four years, when I and my colleagues took over the reins of government, our national income has risen from £20 million to £65 million per annum, and our expenditure from about £14 million to £52 million. We have redeemed our external debts and our total national assets from all sources amount to nearly £200 million. We can feel with confidence that our prosperity is healthy, our finances are strong and our economy is virile. But this is only the beginning! It is only when you travel round the country that you can appreciate fully the tremendous development that is going on all over the Gold Coast, and I think it would be a good thing for arrangements to be made for the various sections of the community to visit other places and see things for themselves.

How many of you, for instance, are aware of the fact that there are now thirteen hospitals in the twenty-six constituencies in the Northern Territories? I would remind you that there were exactly three before the Convention People's Party came into power four years ago. Two years ago, how many of you could travel from Accra or Cape Coast to Kumasi and back without the risk of getting bogged down and spending nights on the road?

How many of you realise the progress that has been made in education? In the four years that the Convention People's Party has been in power the number of children attending Primary schools has been doubled; those attending Middle schools have increased in number by 50%; nine additional Training Colleges have been opened under this Government and the output of students has doubled itself since 1951; eighteen new Secondary schools have been opened since 1951; and the number of pupils attending has almost trebled; the Higher School Certificate course which in 1951, was only provided for by Achimota, is now provided for by Mfantsipim, Adisadel, St Augustine's and Prempeh colleges, as well as the Kumasi College of Technology. In addition to this, those receiving technical training have increased in number from 180 in 1951 to over 1,400 at the beginning of 1954. And schools and technical institutes are still going up throughout the country. We lay stress on education because it is the antidote to feudalist despotism and ignorance and superstition.

Then there is the literacy drive and community development that is being undertaken extensively in rural areas. How many of you are acquainted with the success that has been achieved by these?

Unemployment is a problem that has been exercising the mind of the Government very acutely and we are doing everything we possibly can to solve it. It is our intention to develop economic and productive enterprises, to build more factories, industries and agricultural estates. These projects alone will provide occupation for the whole of our unemployed community for a long time to come. Have no fear, there will be a job for everybody.

As has already been stated, our second Development Plan will concentrate mainly on the development of economic and productive services and on rural development. We must set up factories, produce more electricity for expanding industrial and domestic needs, increase and improve our roads, bridges and water supply. With better sanitation, better education and ever increasing facilities for employment our people are living better, healthier, more purposeful and more prosperous lives. The Government is doing more and more to improve these facilities as a part of the general development of the country.

Countrymen, it is quite obvious that the renegades and reactionaries, incensed at the progress being made by the masses and terrified at the idea of democratic development in our country, are bent on one thing, that of causing as much confusion as possible in an endeavour to mislead the United Kingdom Government and our friends abroad into casting doubt on the African's ability to govern himself. But the United Kingdom Government and our friends know better.

On this solemn occasion, therefore, on this sixth anniversary of the Party, the people's liberation movement, I call upon you once again to solemnly re-dedicate yourselves to the struggle for independence; I call upon you, at this momentous period of our lives, to stand firm behind the Party for independence, democracy and social justice. Organise more solidly than ever before, for the struggle is fiercest near the end, in the same way as it is darkest before the dawn. Stand firm, be vigilant and organise, for remember, *organisation decides everything*.

Let us therefore, on this solemn occasion, renew our pledge to Mother Ghana by singing together the words of our Party's hymn:

'Land of our birth we pledge to thee,
Our love and toil in the years to be;
As we are grown to take our place
As men and women with our race.

Land of our birth, our faith, our pride,
For whose dear sake our fathers died;
Oh Motherland we pledge to thee,
Head, heart and hands in the years to be.'

The Gold Coast has already taken its place in the comity of nations at the Bandung Conference, and we look to the day when we shall take our place among the United Nations at Lake Success. Yes, the world is watching us. The invitation extended to the Gold Coast to participate in the recent Bandung Conference is eloquent testimony of the recognition of this country in international affairs. The Gold Coast is the symbol and the inspiration of renascent Africa; as such it is a privilege and a responsibility for us to make our experiment a success.

We are now making preparations for the celebration of the date of independence so that when the day of independence dawns, as it assuredly will, we may arise as a nation to greet it. But as freedom approaches, the responsibilities of the Party increase. Now is the time for united effort and action under the bold leadership of the C.P.P.; for this is the party which has proved itself the champion of freedom, the only party which can claim to have brought our nation to the threshold of independence. Let us therefore move forward together to build up a new Ghana – strong, clean, incorruptible, virile and cohesive, as a symbol of emulation for the rest of Africa.

I have never ceased to condemn bribery and corruption and I have warned that anybody, no matter his rank or office in the Party, who shall be found indulging in these vices shall be immediately exposed and punished. The standard of integrity in public life in any country is measured by the degree to which 'the temptations to profit' are overcome, and as a young country on the threshold of independence, it lies in our hands now to set our standard for the future. I am determined to do everything in my power to see that the standard we set is the highest possible, and I look for the support of every man of goodwill in achieving this end.

Friends and countrymen, for six years we have waged a relentless struggle for freedom and we are now at the threshold of independence. We are committed to the laying of a solid foundation for political stability, social justice and economic progress. To this end we shall exercise all the patience that is required of us. History records that it is the peaceful means that endure; the gains of violence are transient; the fruits of patience are imperishable. We shall do everything in our power to see that our country's resources are harnessed and utilised in the best interest of our people. We have got to succeed!

Africa has been left behind and suppressed for too long, but this giant continent is now awakening. We must face the future with confidence. We are grateful to all the other nations of the world that have helped us and that have spoken on our behalf, but I firmly believe that *only the African* can speak for the African and *only the African* can be the spokesman of this great continent.

Fellow countrymen, Party members, supporters and sympathisers, we look forward with confidence to the day when our dear country shall take her rightful place amongst the comity of free nations and take part fully in international deliberations for peace and progress. Stand firm! The day is not far and there is Victory for us.

With the cheers of thousands ringing across the Arena, my speech came to an end.

CHAPTER SEVEN

ACCENT ON DEVELOPMENT

By the middle of 1955, the first Development Plan was in its last
year. It was necessary to take stock of the economic position of
the country. I went to see for myself how the various development schemes were working out in the different regions. On
29 June, I visited Ho and addressed the Trans-Volta Togoland
Council.

The Trans-Volta Togoland Council was established in July
1953 to develop the territory and to advise on the spending of a
special grant of one million pounds. It recommended the building of schools, roads and bridges, a maternity centre at Peki and
many first aid stations. Under the guidance of the T.V.T.
Council, district councils formed works organisations. An extensive rural water development programme was worked out,
so that even the remotest villages might have an efficient water
supply.

I congratulated the Council on the great success of the first
Development Plan. I spoke of the new schools and hospitals, of
the towns and villages which had already benefited by the sink-
ing of boreholes all over the region.

But much still remained to be done. I told them that a second
Development Plan to increase the wealth of the country and to
develop rural areas still further, was under consideration.
Further funds would be available from the Cocoa Marketing
Board. It was essential that there should be a cohesive plan
worked out for the region as a whole. Having dealt with the
economic aspects, I then came to the political position:

I now turn to the future of trust territory. This is a matter
which is nearest to the heart of many of you here. In August,
the United Nations Visiting Mission will arrive. Its main
object will be to consult the people of trust territory on the
best way in which they can decide, in a democratic fashion,
what their future will be. The Visiting Mission will make its
recommendations to the Trusteeship Council. The Trusteeship Council will, in turn, advise the General Assembly how

the people of trust territory shall decide their future. In December, the General Assembly will give its decision, and we can expect a test of opinion early next year. The time is therefore fast approaching when the people of trust territory will have to make up their minds about their future.

I am speaking to you as your Prime Minister. It is my duty, therefore, to make the policy of my Government quite clear to you. I hope most sincerely that the people of trust territory will decide that their true interests lie in remaining with the Gold Coast. We know that the people of the northern section of trust territory have stated on numerous occasions that they want nothing more than to be united with an independent Gold Coast. My colleagues, the Minister of Finance and the Minister of Education, have just come down from a tour of the northern section, and they will confirm this. We know too that the vast majority of the people of Buem-Krachi also want nothing more than to be united with an independent Gold Coast. We hope and pray that the people of the rest of the southern section will decide the same way when the time comes.

The more I think about this problem, the more I am convinced that the union of trust territory with the Gold Coast is the only practical solution. As I have said before to this council, we cannot see the Ewes of trust territory splitting once more away from the Ewes in Anlo, Tongu and Peki. We cannot contemplate the splitting of Dagomba into two once again. We cannot conceive that the people will wish to separate themselves from the Gold Coast and lose the benefit of the central services provided by the Gold Coast Government together with all the specialist services in the fields, particularly of health and education, which they enjoy at present.

We, the people of the Gold Coast and the people of trust territory, have worked together happily for nearly forty years, to our mutual benefit. We of the Gold Coast think of you as being part of us, and I believe that the majority of the people of Trust territory, when faced with the prospect of being separated from us, will immediately realise that this would be a disaster for them. Since my Government took office in 1951, we have done more in five years for the development of trust territory than had been done in the previous twenty years. We are soon to start on our second Development Plan, and we have asked your advice as to how this should be framed in T.V.T. I can speak for my Government, and, I think, for any future government of the Gold Coast when I say that trust territory will always get a fair deal from the government of the country.

As regards the future of your T.V.T. Council after the people of trust territory have given the right answer in the test of opinion, I cannot at this stage speak so categorically. I would hope that it would continue to exist and have delegated to it such responsibilities as may be delegated to the regional councils in the Gold Coast. You may at least be assured that it or a similar body would have an important part to play in the development of the region.

The Gold Coast is shortly to obtain independence, and it will be the first country in Africa to emerge from colonial status to full sovereignty. As I said on a previous occasion, we are already in command of our own internal affairs, and you are assuming that responsibility with us. Soon, we shall be in command of all our affairs.

Since you have been with us for nearly forty years, we do not want to leave you behind in some form of trust, or in a dependent or colonial status when we ourselves will have gained our freedom and independence.

That is why the vast majority of you will want to take this final step with us, and end your trustee status. That is why I believe that few will be misled by those who advocate separation from the Gold Coast. We are confident therefore that when the time comes the vast majority will see that it is in their interest to march forward with the Gold Coast to freedom and independence.

Shortly afterwards, delegates and Party members from British Togoland and from all parts of the Gold Coast met in Kpandu for the sixth Annual Delegates Conference. During 1955, the actual organisation of the C.P.P. underwent certain changes. I explained the reason for the altered composition of the National Executive and said that in future, representation would be on a regional basis:

Each region is expected to send six regional representatives, one of whom is to be a woman. These form the National Executive and meet quarterly. Added to these are the nine members of the Central Committee which our Party's Constitution allows the Life Chairman to appoint and which meets weekly. We have also a Working Committee which meets once a month. Besides these, we have a number of committees dealing with certain specific aspects of Party organisation.

I must remind Party members that the strength of the Party's organisational machinery depends on the strength of the branches. Every branch of the Party is expected to keep an up-to-date enrolment register of members. There should be regular meetings to discuss current political, economic and social affairs. The branches, through their Branch Executives, should be in constant touch with the Constituency Headquarters, the Regional Headquarters and the National Secretariat. A new membership card is being planned for 1956. This will be renewed each year, the colour changing with each fresh issue, and they will be kept in the pocket of your membership books. By this means we shall be able to assess the strength of the Party and the contribution of Party members to the Party.

I then came to the vexed question of Ashanti, and here I spoke in general terms. I had already dealt extensively with the subject in my Arena speech on the sixth anniversary of the Party. But the resignation from the Party of certain well-known men such as Joe Appiah, Kurankyi Taylor, De Graft Johnson, R. R. Amponsah and others, made it necessary for me to say a few words on the broader question of unity of purpose within the country if independence was to be achieved in the shortest possible time.

I went on to speak of the new Ghana which would develop after Independence. There would be equality of opportunity, and the development of the natural resources of the country for the benefit of all sections of the people:

Our talents and resources must be developed to the full. Uneconomic agricultural holdings must be consolidated and the forests protected against wasteful use. To consolidate agricultural holdings effectively it will in many cases be necessary to use expensive equipment and to employ professional and highly trained personnel. To this end our technical and secondary educational programme must be fully expanded. Government and Cocoa Marketing Board scholarships are being granted to our young men and women in order to prepare them to take their place in this programme. In the case of small farmers whose holdings are consolidated and who constitute themselves into co-operative groups, they will be given agricultural loans and technical assistance. In order to protect the farmers from extortionate money-lenders and to put long and short term credits within their reach, a system of Land Banks or Co-operative Banks will be instituted.

The problem of unemployment in rural areas must be solved by creating industries in the rural areas, for example, the growing, processing and preserving of food, local handicrafts including textiles, the manufacture of sugar, salt and soap and the expressing of edible oils. All these provide the foundation of economic progress. With this in view the Government must see that the people are educated in agricultural economy and that by means of preventive medicine and improved sanitation, the villages are made healthy places in which to live. It is up to the Government to get these things done and the Convention People's Party solemnly pledges its word that they shall be done.

The concentration of labour in industrial areas and modern factories require large capital investment which the resources of most under-developed countries cannot bear. A democratic Ghana should not develop a propensity for the consumption of foreign capital, except what is absolutely necessary. It is therefore important to build up local industries in the villages and to encourage the workers to live among their own people and to develop their respective surroundings, rather than they should be forced in their search for employment to migrate to the towns and cities where the industries are centred.

The unity of the country depends upon transport facilities which alone will make possible the free movement of men and goods. Therefore, transport by rail, by road and by civil aviation will be given high priority. Power resources need to be developed. In this connection the results of the most up-to-date researches will be studied and applied so that Gold Coast industries will not start with obsolete equipment. Power resources in the form of oil and hydro-electricity will be fully exploited. Next in order of importance will be a building programme for essential administrative and social services.

Democracy, as against imperialism, despotism and autocracy in the Gold Coast, must have its roots in rural reconstruction. It is in the rural areas that the forces of feudalism are entrenched. There can be no social advancement or complete overthrow of imperialism as long as the vestiges of feudalism still remain in this country. An effective system of democratic regional, district and local councils must therefore be established in order to make the wishes of the common man decisive in the consideration of rural problems and programmes. Homes for the people, education for the masses, rural communications, health and sanitary needs, water supplies, facilities for education with special emphasis on the acquisition of modern skills, housing and social amenities will be in importance second only to that of the development of rural industries. Our development plan must be essentially a plan for rural reconstruction.

Our Party has given the country the beginnings of a national banking system, a fiscal policy which we intend to use to cover the country more effectively and to establish an equitable system of taxation. We have accumulated financial reserves which will enable us to participate in the establishment and financing of industries here. In fact we are in a position to take a comprehensive and bold view of the political and economic future of our country. Where local private investors are unable or unwilling to supply capital, public funds will be provided to finance new industries independently or in partnership with foreign private investors. The institution of public corporations is an essential feature of our planning. Thus the economy of the Gold Coast will have three sections: public, co-operative and private.

These are the points we have to consider as we move towards independence and with these plans we hope to face our independence and our future thereafter.

My final words were an appeal for unity. I invited the people of British Togoland to advance with the Gold Coast under the banner of the C.P.P. to independence, prosperity and social justice.

We were all one people, and it was the policy of my government to set up Regional Committees so that the needs of the various regions would be considered in the light of the individual wishes of the people who lived in them. Committees were first set up in the Northern Territories and in Trans-Volta Togoland. A Western Regional Committee was formed in 1955, and I spoke at the first meeting which was held in Cape Coast on 5 August. I outlined the reasons for setting up Regional Committees. They would, I hoped, provide a forum where the wishes of the people living in the region could be expressed. At the same time, they would ensure maximum co-operation and understanding between central and local government.

I explained that the Western Region Committee's first task was to consider government proposals for the second Development Plan, in so far as they affected their region. It was essential that committee members should approach the problem realistically:

> Your outlook should be regional in character and not local. We know that each of you has responsibilities to your own particular locality, but what Government seeks in this particular context is your advice as a representative body of the Western Region. In the final reckoning, therefore, the purely local interest must be subordinate to the common interest of the region as a whole, and while I am well aware that it is not always easy to accept this, I am confident that with goodwill it can be achieved. And I wish you to appreciate that, while the plans put before you may be subject to reconsideration in the light of comments you make, financial limits for the Second Plan period have already been fixed for each Ministry, and suggestions which would involve large-scale increases in these allocations cannot be entertained. The pace of development is limited by availability of finance and the physical capacity to do work, and however anxious we may be to get things done we can only do so within the limits of our capacity.

The Government had made special provision of funds in 1955 for all Regional Development Committees, and proposed to make further funds available throughout the Second Development Plan period. The funds had been allocated to regions on a population basis, and the Western Region had been granted £105,000. 'The planning of the expenditure of this sum is your responsibility,' I told them, 'and here again I should like to plead for a realistic and responsible approach.' I outlined our thinking on this:

> 1. The funds are allocated for regional development and should be spent on projects of regional significance.
> 2. The greatest care should be taken to avoid any encroachment into the sphere of district or local councils on the one hand or any risk of duplication of a planned central government project on the other.
> 3. In planning programmes, priority should be given to revenue-producing projects and projects which would strengthen the economic structure, primarily water supplies, electricity and communications.
> 4. No project should be carried out which would give rise to a recurrent commitment on the central government or to a recurrent commitment which the local authority or authorities concerned would be unable to meet.

5. Taking into account the plans of central and local governments, projects planned by Regional Development Committees should be evenly spread throughout the region with no undue concentration in any one area.

The careful observance of these principles is essential if your Regional Development Committee is to discharge its planning function effectively and without confusion.

I concluded my speech by expressing the hope that Regional Committees might one day evolve into statutory Regional Councils:

I shall watch the progress of your Committee with the greatest interest and I hope that with God's guidance you may work in that atmosphere of harmony which is so necessary to constructive and fruitful deliberation.

CHAPTER EIGHT

SHAPING THE FUTURE

I was once asked by an incredulous young man whether it was really a fact that during my student years in the United States of America I had to work as a shoeshine boy, a factory hand, and a bellhop on board ship, in order to pay my university fees. He seemed hardly able to believe me when I told him it was perfectly true, and that those struggling student days were some of the happiest days of my life.

On the whole, the youth of today seems to believe that money alone can open the gate to knowledge, to university degrees and to success in life. Every day, I receive numerous letters from young people asking for financial assistance to proceed with their education. They seem to think that without money they are doomed to a life of ignorance. I fear that if I had waited in the hope of receiving money to start even my preliminary education, I would never have ventured beyond my little village of Nkroful.

Happily, however, our young people today are in a much more fortunate position. Primary and secondary education are there for all to enjoy. Whether the pupils proceed to university or technical colleges thereafter, depends entirely upon themselves. This, of course, is how it should be.

I have always enjoyed speaking to audiences of young people, and I gladly accepted an invitation to address the boys of Adisadel College on their Speech Day on 10 November 1955.

Students from Adisadel College, the famous secondary boarding school in Cape Coast, have distinguished themselves in the commercial world, the professions, the Church, the civil service, in fact in every walk of life. When I visited the school, there were several old boys in my Cabinet. The Commissioner for the Gold Coast in London at that time was also an old boy.

I spoke of the school's contribution to the country:

The purpose of all true education is to produce good citizens. And this is a task which I consider secondary boarding schools like Adisadel College are particularly able to carry out. By studying at boarding school a student automatically learns those principles of good citizenship which will help him to take a full share of the work of the community when he leaves school. He learns to shoulder responsibilities, to share with his fellows both the good and bad things of life, to understand the importance of team spirit and to take a personal pride in the successes of the school community. And, perhaps more important still is the fact that he learns to live in tolerance and co-operation with his fellow students.

Another facet of the training in citizenship which a student can receive here is discipline. Now I know from my own school days how hated is that word. But in later life you will realise how important it is both for your own and for other people's happiness. Freedom without law is anarchy. And discipline is just as important on the playing fields as in the classrooms. You know full well that unless you are prepared to keep to the rules of the game, neither you yourself nor any of the other players are going to enjoy it. In a game of football, for instance, there is nothing more boring both to the other players and to the spectators than to watch a man dribbling a ball and refusing to pass it on. It is wrong and it is simply not playing the game. In a broader sense this applies well to life in the community. Greed and selfishness in any form are antisocial and should be strongly discouraged.

In the field of sports, it is the concern of my Government that an independent Gold Coast shall stand second to none. The National Sports Council has the full support of the Government and it is our intention to encourage national competitions which will produce sportsmen and athletes for national and international contests. These competitions must run through the entire educational system in order to provide us with continuous supplies of distinguished sportsmen. Self government for the Gold Coast means a fuller and a richer life which cannot be attained without the spirit of fair play and enterprise which sports can provide.

The Gold Coast is now passing through a very testing time, a time when we need the services in our community of all men of goodwill. But, if the Gold Coast is going to achieve all that we have set before us, it is important that students like you, who have been fortunate to receive the best possible education available in the country, should be prepared to contribute to the service of the state. At one time the emphasis was on lawyers. Today, however, if we hope to catch up with the modern world in its advance, we need more urgently, technicians, engineers, medical men, scientists, agriculturalists and geologists. There is much to be done in the country with regard to industrialisation and development. And we need our own specialists to attend to this. See to it that you are on the job when the time comes!

I was glad to think that those boys in front of me would soon be helping to shape their country's future. I told them that they had a responsibility not only to the Gold Coast, but also to the rest of Africa:

Set yourselves up as an example and prove to the world that you are both capable and ready to put your country on the map, to hoist her flag and to keep it flying.

Above all, don't become know-alls, for nothing is more objectionable and nothing makes one look more of a fool. Education makes us humble and tolerant. You can do well to remember these lines of William Cowper:

'Knowledge is proud that he has learned so much;
Wisdom is humble that he knows no more.'

It has made me very happy to be here among you this afternoon. It is not my usual custom to accept invitations to school speech days, but I wanted to take this opportunity at this momentous time in our history to address these words to you in order that through you, my words may also reach the students of all secondary schools in our country.

In conclusion, I would like to wish you all, Mr Hammond, the masters and pupils, the very best of luck for the future.

To the students I would like to say that when the time comes for you to depart from this great school, may you be well equipped to tackle successfully whatever may face you and may you ever be a credit to Adisadel College.

A few weeks later, at the end of 1955, I broadcast a New Year message. It was a good opportunity to review our position. Each year brought us closer to our final goal of independence. I spoke of the way in which the country had developed:

Most of you will have seen for yourselves the completion of hospitals and health centres in the most outlying places, and if you are living in Kumasi you will have seen the virtual completion of the great Kumasi hospital. Through your children you will be aware of the continued rapid development of educational facilities. There is a noticeable improvement in our water supplies and in feeder roads in the rural areas. You may have travelled on the new roads between Accra and Winneba or Mampong and Bolgatanga. You may know of the improved methods of boat-building being used at Takoradi, and elsewhere. Those of you who are in trade and commerce will realise the value of the double track railway line between Takoradi and Manso; you must also be aware of the tremendous significance of Tema harbour now under construction; I would mention also the now almost completed new rail link between Achiase and Kotoku.

These developments would not have taken place were it not for the harmonious co-operation between you, the people of the Gold Coast, your Government and the thousands of its employees of all ranks.

Then I turned to the future. Independence would shortly be achieved, and the country must be ready:

Racialism and tribalism and violence must cease to be political factors in our national life. Violence must be completely rejected as an instrument of policy. I make this appeal not only for the happiness and well-being of our own country. I would like every citizen in the Gold Coast – on the Coast, in Ashanti, in the Northern Territories – to remember that the hopes of millions of Africans living in our great continent are pinned upon the success of our experiment here. They want us to prove by our performance that we can, peaceably and responsibly, with give and take and fair play manage our own domestic affairs. And there are other groups here in Africa who, unhappily, hope equally vigorously that we shall fail and that they will be able to point the finger of scorn at us and say, 'See, leave them to run their own affairs and the result is violence, bloodshed and tribal strife.' Let every citizen make a vow now in his heart that we in the Gold Coast, in this last solemn year before Independence, will do everything we can, by our calmness, our co-operativeness and our good sense, to fulfil the hopes of our friends and to disappoint the men of ill-will who expect to see us fall. And in all we do, may the good God be our guide.

At the beginning of this momentous year I feel it would be helpful for each one of us to pray for guidance through the days that lie ahead. And so, finally, I would like to invite you, on behalf of the churches of the country, to observe Sunday,

the 8th of January, as a national day of prayer. And what
better words can we use on such an occasion than those of the
following prayer:

> Grant me serenity to accept things I cannot change,
> Courage to change things I can
> And Wisdom to know the difference.

Although my speeches usually have a strong political content,
there are occasions when I keep strictly away from politics and
economics. One such occasion was when I opened the African
Art Exhibition at the British Council in Accra, in March 1956.
African art, music and dancing have played a very significant
part in the artistic revolution which has taken place all over the
world in recent years. For example, some of our old tribal dances
have gone into the making of High Life, the Calypso and other
similar dances. African carvings in ebony, ivory and cast bronze
have found their way into art exhibitions in Europe and elsewhere, and have aroused considerable interest.

Although no artist myself, I was glad to accept the invitation
to open the African Art Exhibition. It was not the first Exhibition
of its kind. There had been three previous ones, in which the
work of Gold Coast artists, the Akwapim Six, had been shown.

In my speech, I referred to their work. Like the works of Pablo
Picasso, Modigliano, Matisse, Henry Moore and their contem-
poraries, African art has to be understood before it can be fully
appreciated. The fact that it is today becoming more and more
widely sought after is proof enough that not only has the world
at last begun to appreciate its value as something more than a
mere curiosity, but also, by so doing, it has demonstrated that
it has begun to understand and respect the mind of the African.
The Akwapim Six, I said, had done yeoman service in promoting
the country's art, and had set a fine example for others to follow.
I hoped there would be many more exhibitions:

> Exhibitions are of great value, not only to the artists whose
> works are being displayed, but also because they offer a tre-
> mendous incentive to the would-be artist. Without being pre-
> sumptuous, I am sure that we have all at some time during our
> lives believed sincerely that, but for the workings of fate, we
> would be ranking among the great artists, musicians or writers
> of our day. This is quite a natural feeling for, without the
> desire to create, man would soon become stagnant and un-

interesting. It is true that among such people, some do show
definite talent, but there is also a large sprinkling of those who,
like myself, discover to their dismay that they can't even draw
a straight line. But the most important thing is to give them
the chance to prove it: to encourage them to draw lines,
dabble about with paint and potter's clay, hack and chisel at
wood and stone, until they have exhausted their creative
instinct and either returned to live as a forgotten hero or com-
menced to climb the ladder of fame. In any case Mr Chairman, they should not be allowed to bury their creative urge
before they have had a chance to prove whether they have
talent or not.

Of course, I am not saying that they should give up their
jobs and rely on their embryo art for their daily bread: after
all, we don't want a country of starving art enthusiasts. My
advice to the youth of the country is to study hard in their
spare moments, to follow in the steps of the Akwapim Six and
form themselves into groups where they can pool their ideas,
suggestions and criticisms and learn by exhibiting their work
to the public whether they are any good or not.

Another non-political occasion was the opening of the Ghana
Library in Accra on 17 May 1956. A good national library and
a good national museum are the custodians of a nation's culture
and wisdom. In my speech, I spoke of the Gold Coast Library
Board, established in 1949, whose duty it was to establish, equip,
manage and maintain libraries throughout the country. The
Library Board was fortunate in its early days, in that it had
premises and a stock of books immediately available. The library
wing in the King George V Memorial Hall had been built as a
result of a donation made by Bishop Aglionby, the first person to
envisage the provision of a public library in the country. The
books were provided by the British Council, and the library
services which the British Council had started formed the
nucleus of the future work of the Library Board.

Undoubtedly the greatest achievement of the Library Board
was the building of the magnificent new Ghana Library, which
followed closely on the opening of regional libraries in Kumasi
(1954) and Sekondi (1955):

Accra now has a library fitting to its position as the capital of
Gold Coast. A public library, moreover, which I have reason
to believe is second to none in the whole of the continent of

Africa. A library of which to be proud, and which will be used to its limits I hope by the Gold Coast people. Of special value is a large reference library which will seat almost one hundred people. For the first time the scholar, the research worker and the casual enquirer after knowledge will have congenial surroundings in which to work, and a collection of books which the Library Board intends to make one of the best reference collections in Africa. Its staff will be always ready to help, and if material is not immediately available every effort will be made to obtain it.

The Library Board and its services will play its full part in the further development of the country when we achieve independence. The public library cannot be regarded primarily as a part of the formal educational machinery but must instead be developed as an independent, though complementary, organisation designed to further not education alone but any and every phase of thought and action in which books can be of value. The future Ghana will possess a library service of which it can be justly proud, a library service which can serve as a pattern for other rapidly developing countries, and which moreover compares very favourably with much longer established systems.

We have been fortunate with the help we have had in the past from bodies like the Commonwealth Education and Welfare Trust, which took especial interest in our children's libraries and also helped substantially in the building of the Ashanti Regional Library, and the British Council under whose auspices the visit of the President of the British Library Association was arranged, but much credit must be given to the Gold Coast Government who were sufficiently far-sighted to vote money for this most essential work, and who will continue to interest themselves in the expansion and development of libraries throughout the country.

CHAPTER NINE

A DATE FOR INDEPENDENCE

Throughout 1956 the pace towards independence quickened. The issues still to be settled had been progressively narrowed and clearly defined in the negotiations between the Gold Coast government and the United Kingdom government which preceded the granting of the then existing constitution; by the report of the Select Committee of the Gold Coast Assembly appointed on 5 April 1955; by the proposals of the constitutional adviser, Sir Frederick Browne; and by the searching examination of Sir Frederick's proposals undertaken by the Achimota Conference.

Yet, on 18 May 1956, when I moved the adoption of the Government's White Paper embodying the constitutional proposals, I had the impression that some people did not fully appreciate how far the Gold Coast had already advanced along the road to independence:

It is now possible for all the legislation required to create in law the independent and sovereign state of Ghana to be drafted, fully scrutinised and passed into law within a matter of a few months. Mr Speaker, in very truth, the moment has come when we are ready to 'step out from the old to the new'; when an old era is dying and a new age is being born; when the soul of Ghana, long suppressed, finds utterance, when we begin to discard the last vestiges of the trappings of colonialism and tribal feudalism and emerge clothed in the pure and shining mantle of sovereignty and independence.

At times we have found the pace of that advance to be too slow; and at times we have had to make it clear that we wished the pace to be quickened, and the goal to be reached without one minute of avoidable delay. The period of waiting is now over.

Our course is clear. Let us take this tide at the flood. It will carry us into our long sought haven. Like many a stout seaman of old, watching wind and weather, and pondering the risks of voyaging across uncharted seas, some Honourable Members may be acutely conscious of the fact that, in preferring 'self-government with danger to servitude in tranquillity' we are accepting risks. We have long calculated these risks and we do accept them. There is a saying attributed to Aristotle: 'The best way of learning to play the flute is to play the flute.' And, Mr Speaker, the best way of learning to be an independent sovereign state is to be an independent sovereign state.

The transitional period under the present constitution is virtually over. It has been a most delicate but nevertheless a most exciting period.

After reviewing the work of my government during the past few years, I went on to deal with our critics:

Shortly after the present Government assumed office, various elements, which had failed to secure the support of the electorate at the election held in June, 1954, began to advocate the adoption by the Gold Coast of a federal form of government and the setting up of a Constituent Assembly. This movement has sought to impugn the validity of the mandate given to my Government by an overwhelming majority of the electorate. It has been at pains to disseminate the idea that it is necessary for somebody other than the Legislative Assembly to make recommendations regarding the constitution of an independent Gold Coast.

Mr Speaker, the Government was not, and never will be prepared to countenance any manœuvre to undermine the authority of this Legislative Assembly. Subject to the slight limitations imposed by the present constitution, the authority of this House is supreme. It would be a sorry day for the Gold Coast – and, indeed, for every non-independent territory in Africa aspiring to full self-government – if the Gold Coast Legislative Assembly or the Gold Coast Government was so misguided as to yield one jot or tittle of its constitutional authority to any *ad hoc* body.

Speaking in this House on such a momentous occasion in Gold Coast – and in African – history, I impose upon myself a measure of restraint, an example which will, I trust, be followed by later speakers on both sides. I consider, however, that the time has come for me to state clearly and unambiguously my views on the tactics pursued by the Opposition and its allies outside this House. By challenging the authority of the House they are – wittingly or unwittingly – taking steps calculated to undermine the whole democratic structure of present day Gold Coast society. They are pursuing courses calculated to set aside the system of parliamentary democracy

which we have established in this country. I fail to see, however, how any democratically elected government can tolerate
any challenge to the democratic authority of a legislature
elected in accordance with traditional parliamentary pro-
cedure. My Government has not yielded – and will not yield
– to any pressure to set up a Constituent Assembly or a national
Constituent Convention – whatever that may mean. Nevertheless the Government has done everything in its power to
ensure that its proposals for a constitution for a sovereign and
independent Gold Coast are based on wide consultation with
the Chiefs and people of the country. If any political party or
other body criticises our constitutional proposals for independence on the grounds that it has not aired its views on
some contentious matter, that party or body cannot with just
cause aver that it was denied an opportunity of stating its case.
The Government's efforts to bring about a Round Table Conference and the obstinate refusal of the N.L.M. and its allies
are known to you all; the deliberations of the Select Committee
appointed by this Assembly on the 5th April, 1955, are known
to you all; the patient adjournments of the Achimota Conference and the gallant but fruitless efforts of the Joint
Provincial Council of Chiefs to secure the participation in the
work of the Achimota Conference of the Asanteman Council,
the N.L.M. and its allies, are known to you all; the invitation
to attend the Achimota Conference is known to you all.

The Government has shown infinite patience and made
every possible effort to ensure that democratic processes were
observed. The country, and the world at large, can see for
itself that it is those who spurned all the Government's efforts
to secure their co-operation who have shown themselves unwilling to compose difference by frank discussion in accordance
with the traditions of parliamentary democracy. But in a
democracy it is the decision of the majority that prevails. The
Secretary of State has also assured me that the last thing he
wanted was that a minority should hold up the implementation of the wishes of the majority of the people of the Gold
Coast.

I spoke of the dispute between the Asanteman Council and
the Brong Chiefs, and said that the Government had accepted in
principle the demand for the establishment of a separate Brong
Region. But it was essential that Ghana should be a unitary and
not a federal state:

Mr Speaker, the Government's proposals for the constitution

of an independent Gold Coast pre-supposes a unitary, not a federal state. Supreme legislative power and supreme financial power must remain at the centre. Nevertheless, the Government acknowledges the need for a measure of devolution of powers from the centre to the Regions and pledges itself to establish Regional Assemblies and Houses of Chiefs in every Region where the majority opinion is in favour of these bodies being created.

As Honourable Members are aware, the plebiscite to decide the future of Togoland under United Kingdom Trusteeship has taken place, and happily the majority of the inhabitants of the territory have opted for union with an independent Gold Coast. Our future plans for regional devolution as they may affect the territory will accordingly be made in the light of this decision of the majority of the people and of the United Nations.

The Government proposes that when the Gold Coast attains independence, the name of the country should be changed from 'Gold Coast' to the new name of 'Ghana'. The name Ghana is rooted deeply in ancient African history especially in the history of the western portion of Africa known as the Western Sudan. It kindles in the imagination of modern African youth the grandeur and the achievements of a great mediaeval civilisation which our ancestors developed many centuries before European penetration and subsequent domination of Africa began. According to tradition the various peoples or tribal groups in the Gold Coast were originally members of the great Ghana Empire that developed in the Western Sudan during the mediaeval period.

For the one thousand years that the Ghana Empire existed, it spread over a wide expanse of territory in the Western Sudan. Its influence stretched across the Sudan from Lake Chad in the east to the Futa Jalon Mountains in the west and from the southern fringes of the Sahara Desert in the north to the Bights of Benin and Biafra in the south. Thus the Ghana Empire was known to have covered what is now the greater part of West Africa – namely, from Nigeria in the east to Senegambia in the west. While it existed, the Ghana Empire carried on extensive commercial relations with the outside world – extending as far as Spain and Portugal. Gold, animal skins, ivory, kola-nuts, gums, honey, corn and cotton were among the articles that writers had most frequently named. It is reported that Egyptian, European and Asiatic students attended the great and famous universities and other institutions of higher learning that flourished in Ghana during the mediaeval period to learn philosophy, mathematics, medicine and law.

It is from this rich historical background that the name Ghana has been proposed as the new name of the Gold Coast upon the attainment of independence; we take pride in the name, not out of romanticism, but as an inspiration for the future.

Mr Speaker, there is nothing revolutionary in the Government's Constitutional Proposals for Gold Coast Independence. They complete the process of the Gold Coast's evolution from non-independent status to independence. They build on the sure foundation which has been laid by this Government. They involve no hazardous venture over uncharted oceans. The ship of state will voyage across seas whose shoals and reefs my ministerial colleagues and myself have come to know during the past five years. The vital difference is that we shall no longer sail to destinations appointed by the Secretary of State along courses set by a Governor and his officials. The Gold Coast Government will be in supreme command and will have to pilot the ship of state through fair weather and foul. Mr Speaker, with God's grace, the Gold Coast Government will measure up to its new responsibilities. It will be a daring pilot in extremity, it will weather whatever storms may be encountered, and will steer the ship of state safely through all dangers into calm seas and safe anchorages.

On 18 September 1956, the Secretary of State announced a firm date for Gold Coast Independence. Two days later I broadcast the good news:

The Gold Coast will attain full Independence on the 6th March 1957. The entire country has welcomed the Secretary of State's announcement that on the one hundred and thirteenth anniversary of the Bond of 1844 the Gold Coast will become a free, sovereign and independent state under the name of Ghana. We are proud that the Gold Coast, which has so long been in the vanguard of the struggle for the liberation of the dependent peoples of Africa, should be the first to attain its independence. Perhaps the most important factor in this struggle has been the fact that my Government, my party and myself have been able to speak for a nation united in its fundamental political aspiration.

The announcement on the 18th September of a firm date for Independence marks the end of an epoch and the beginning of a new era. It also brings to an end a period of political uncertainty. We know now that we must plan and work to a firm dateline. We must press on with the preparations for the celebration of Independence. We must ensure that the ceremonies and festivities that will mark that momentous occasion will be worthy of our country and of our new status among the nations of the world.

An overwhelming majority of the people of the Gold Coast have opted for a unitary form of government. This is politically and financially practicable. I am satisfied that within the framework of a unitary constitution it is possible to insert safeguards which would meet legitimate regional aspirations.

The fixing of a firm date for Independence was a challenge to each one of us to face the realities of the political situation, and to produce a constitution acceptable to all. Great responsibilities lay ahead.

On the transfer of power my Government will assume full responsibility for the affairs of this nation. It will become fully responsible for the defence of Ghana; fully responsible for the maintenance of law and order and for the stability of our currency. The symbols of Independence, the new flag of Ghana and the Ghana coat of arms, have now been approved. In our hour of triumph let us do honour to all the statesmen who down the years have worked and striven to make possible the attainment of Independence. Let us also give thanks to all who in any way great or small, have more recently played their part in bringing our struggle to its close. In this solemn hour let us not merely rejoice because we have reached our goal. Let us not merely make merry because our dearest hope has been fulfilled. Let us think first and foremost of the best interests of our country. Let us put aside petty political controversy and intrigues and lay a firm and stable foundation for the political structure of Ghana.

Good night to you all. May your thoughts, your deeds and your prayers strengthen and sustain the statesmanship of the nation.

Everyone was immensely cheered at the fixing of a definite date for Independence. The long struggle was nearing its end, and the C.P.P. had achieved its first objective – political freedom. Already we were thinking of the next step, economic emancipation, and here we would need the full co-operation of the labour movement of the country.

There has always been strong friendship between the C.P.P. and the Trade Union movement. In 1949 I was made patron of the Trade Union Congress. Seven years later, I addressed the last Annual Conference of the T.U.C. before Independence:

> I know, and you should know, that in our historic struggle for self-government the Trade Union movement of our country has played an important and vital part. And here I wish to express my own sincere gratitude and that of my Government to the Trade Union movement for the part they have played, firstly, in our struggle for freedom and emancipation from a state of subjection, and secondly in opening to us the glorious prospect of a people that know no master but themselves. Now that our political struggle is over, what is the part that the Trade Union Congress can play? I venture to say that the responsibility of the Trade Union Congress to the welfare and well-being of its members and indeed to our people is greater than ever.
>
> We have by our united efforts achieved political freedom – this, as I have said, is a great achievement. What is our next united task? Mr President, our next united task is the achievement of economic justice: freedom from want, and freedom from disease, filth and squalor. Industrial and agricultural development are essential for the achievement of our aim. We as Government are firmly resolved to build an economically strong nation that will improve the standard of living of its people. The future of our country lies in organised labour; labour must be effective and productive. To the successful performance of the great task we have set ourselves, my Government seriously and earnestly dedicates itself. I ask you as leaders of the workers of our country solemnly to dedicate yourselves to this same task. I am confident, Mr President, that my call today to workers of Ghana will not be unheeded.

I spoke of the difficulties facing the T.U.C., particularly the problem of finance, and ended by expressing the hope that the T.U.C. would become the 'Industrial Parliament' of Ghana, prepared at all times to advise the Government on labour questions.

CHAPTER TEN

THE MOTION FOR APPROVAL

The longest, and in some respects the most important speech I made before Independence, was on 12 November 1956, on the motion for Approval of the Government's Revised Constitutional Proposals:

Mr Speaker, I beg to move that this Assembly do approve the Government's Revised Constitutional Proposals for Gold Coast Independence. When Sir Henley Coussey made his opening address to the Coussey Committee he quoted the words of the eighteenth-century English politician and writer, Edmund Burke, who said, 'We are on a conspicuous stage and the world marks our demeanour.'

Never has this been truer than today. How we conduct ourselves when we become independent will affect not only Ghana but the whole of Africa. We have a duty not only to the people of this country, but to the peoples everywhere in Africa who are striving towards independence. If we can make a success of our independence, we shall have made an incalculable contribution towards freedom and progress throughout Africa.

History has entrusted us with a duty, and upon how we carry out that duty will depend not only the fate of the people of this country but the fate of many other peoples throughout the whole of Africa. We must show that it is possible for Africans to rule themselves, to establish a progressive and independent state and to preserve their national unity.

The struggle for self-determination which was started by our forbears is, in our time, coming to a successful end and the prospect of gaining our independence which, through accidents of history, pleasant and unpleasant, was surrendered to a foreign power is indeed exciting. It is most important Mr Speaker, to emphasise that the unity of our country is necessary not only in the interests of our own immediate independence, but as an example to all the other peoples of this vast continent.

According to a leading article in a foremost liberal British weekly journal, the *New Statesman and Nation*, commenting on our recent General Elections: 'In Nairobi, Dar-es-Salaam and Blantyre; in Kitwe, Salisbury and Johannesburg; even in Elizabethville, Beira and Brazzaville, the talk in shanties, in mine compounds and in rondavels has been of Gold Coast liberation. The hopes of African nationalism have been centred upon the achievement of Gold Coast Independence.' Mr Speaker, dare we frustrate this hope?

I then reviewed in some detail the history of the Gold Coast, and the various stages in the struggle for sovereign nationhood. Africans, I said, had never been allowed to participate properly in the work of Government:

The failure to associate Africans with the Government is borne out by the figures of Africans in the public service. In the period up to the Second World War, the public service was the main source of employment in the Gold Coast, and yet Africans were for all practical purposes excluded from the higher posts. Some Governors, such as Sir Gordon Guggisberg saw the evil of this policy and tried to do what they could to remedy it. Unfortunately they were up against a system which made impossible the carrying out of their good intentions. The Africanisation scheme of Sir Gordon Guggisberg of 1925–26 aimed at increasing the number of so-called 'European' posts held by Africans, which in his day was 27, to the modest total of 231 by 1946. As however, there were no adequate provisions made for the training of Africans or for the implementation of the Guggisberg plan it failed completely and by 1946 there were only 89 Africans holding 'European' appointments. The Assembly will realise the degree of change which has been effected in the last six years when I say that today the number of African officers in senior posts is 1,524, and of this number 91 hold super-scale posts, that is to say posts of the rank of Assistant Director or above.

The progress which had been made since the Convention People's Party took office is shown by the fact that in 1952, there were only 520 senior African officers, and of these, only 15 occupied super-scale posts. Today there are three times as many Africans in senior posts and six times as many Africans in super-scale posts.

When the present Government came to power the number of Africans in senior posts was less than 16 per cent of the total; today the figure is almost 60 per cent. Overseas officers are now in a minority in the senior posts of the Civil Service. In the history of very few countries can a parallel be found for such a rapid degree of change-over from overseas officers to those of the country. Independent Ghana will still have need of overseas officers for a period of time but we are entering on our Independence with the problem of the Africanisation of our public service well on the way to solution.

The failure to employ Africans in the public service was matched by the absence of sufficient opportunities for advancement in other ways. This resulted in Africans being almost entirely excluded from almost all sections of commerce and business, including the retail trade. Until recently not only the public service but the commercial and business life of the country was in the hands of strangers and people from overseas. Only in some of the professions, particularly in law, was there any opportunity for Africans to secure advancement. All these things made much more difficult any movement towards self-government. The Gold Coast lacked those classes who, in other countries, had been the spearhead of the nationalist movement. Nevertheless, the speed of our political development in the last six years has been remarkable, and for this, great praise must go to the Convention People's Party.

I spoke of the Opposition and the idea of federalism which the National Liberation Movement favoured. I reminded the House that the Select Committee appointed by the Assembly reported against a federal form of government. So also did Sir Frederick Bourne, the distinguished former Indian Governor, who was sent out to the Gold Coast to consider the constitutional position. The Opposition were unwilling to accept Sir Frederick Bourne's views, so in an effort to reach agreement, the Achimota Conference was summoned. But the Opposition, the Asanteman Council and the Northern Territories Council, refused to attend:

It is hard to imagine what more the Government could have done to try and get an examination of the problems of the constitution in advance of Independence. The Opposition boycotted the Select Committee, they boycotted the debate on its report, they boycotted Sir Frederick Bourne and they boycotted the Achimota Conference. Now their newspapers are complaining that there has been insufficient opportunity for consultation on the constitution.

Finally, in order to resolve the constitutional problem a general election was held. The issues were put very clearly before the people. The Government issued its constitutional proposals in the April White Paper which, incidentally, was accepted by the Assembly without a single dissident vote; the Opposition, as usual, boycotting the proceedings. The Opposition also issued their proposals. The country had before them two rival plans and they voted decisively in favour of the Government's plan and decisively against that of the Opposition.

Before the General Election, the Opposition took the view that they were a national Party and, indeed, the Leader of the Opposition informed the Governor that he would be willing to form a government if he secured fifty-three seats at the election. In other words, before the election, the Opposition took the view that whichever party had a bare majority in the Assembly would be entitled to introduce the particular constitution which that Party favoured.

Since the election, however, the Opposition have produced a new theory which is that no constitution is acceptable unless it is favoured by a majority of the people of every Region into which the Gold Coast is at present divided. And, in order to support this claim, in London and elsewhere, the Opposition have been claiming to speak for various Regions.

Let me just remind the Assembly of what the actual election results show. In Ashanti, the Opposition secured fifty seven per cent of the votes to forty three per cent cast in favour of the Government supporters. It is only in this Region where the Opposition can claim to have had even fifty per cent of the total vote. In the Northern Territories, which the Opposition often declare they represent, the Northern People's Party and their Allies, the Muslim Association Party, failed to obtain an absolute majority of the vote. They only secured some forty nine per cent of the total as opposed to the forty four per cent of the votes which were cast for the Government Party. The balance of some seven per cent was made up by the votes of Independent candidates who were opposing both the Northern People's Party and the Convention People's Party candidates. There were, however, two unopposed returns in the Northern Territories of Convention People's Party candidates and, had there been elections in those two constituencies, it is quite possible that the total Convention People's Party vote would have approached, if it did not exceed, that of the Northern People's Party and its Allies. In Trans-Volta Togoland, the third area for which at one time the opposition delegation in London were claiming to speak, the Opposition were in the minority. Even in Ashanti, which the Opposition and the Asanteman Council claim to represent, there is a powerful group opposed not only to the Opposition's consti-

tutional proposals, but even to inclusion in the Ashanti
Region. I much regret that the Asanteman Council seem to
have been so preoccupied in dealing with national constitutional issues that they appear to have had no time to deal with
the difficulties and disputes which are at the present time
dividing Ashanti. It is essential that between now and
Independence those difficulties are dealt with. It is much
better that they should be dealt with by agreement between
the two parties, and I hope that the Asanteman Council will
make earnest efforts immediately to solve this serious issue in
Ashanti.

The Government particularly welcome the fact that, even
though it was at the eleventh hour, the Opposition and the
Asanteman Council and the Northern Territories Council at
last agreed to sit round the table and discuss their differences
with the Government. This has had one most important result.
It has enabled the issues to be crystallised. The Opposition
wish – and this is really the main issue between the Government and the Opposition – that the Regions should have
powers similar to those possessed by the Parliament of
Northern Ireland. The Government oppose this proposal
because it would penalise the poorer Regions and give undue
advantage to the wealthier areas. I can perfectly understand
this plan being put forward by members from Ashanti because
I think it is at least arguable that in this way Ashanti might
benefit; but if it did benefit under such a scheme, it could only
be at the expense of the Northern Territories. It is for that
reason that I am particularly anxious to hear from the Deputy
Leader of the Opposition, who is, I understand, taking the
place of the Leader of the Opposition, the arguments upon
which he supports the Northern Ireland proposal. It would,
for the reasons I shall give later when dealing with it in more
detail, result in the complete impoverishment of the Northern
Territories. I cannot see how any member from the North,
irrespective of Party, can support such a suggestion. The
question of the powers to be exercised by the Regions is in
reality the essence of the constitutional dispute. It is true that
the Opposition have suggested two other main points upon
which there is no agreement. There is first the Council of
State. For reasons I shall give later, the Government do not
believe that this scheme is workable and will therefore ask the
assembly to reject it, but I do not feel that it involves any great
question of principle which should be allowed to divide the
country. As for the Opposition proposal for a Second Chamber,
the Government have explained that it is only possible to have

a Second Chamber if agreement is reached not to have Regional Houses of Chiefs. Unfortunately at the Constitutional talks neither the Opposition nor the Territorial Council were prepared to abandon the idea of Regional Houses of Chiefs in favour of the idea of a Second Chamber.

I explained that the White Paper which the Assembly was asked to consider had been drawn up as a result of discussions between the Government, the Opposition leaders and representatives of the four Territorial Councils. A number of concessions had been made to meet Opposition views:

It is, however, essential to realise that for a constitution to be a success it must not only meet the views of the minority, it must meet the views of the majority as well. It seems to me that the Opposition sometimes seem to forget that the recent General Election was fought on two proposals for the constitution of this country, and the country decided decisively in favour of the Government's proposals. As I have said before, and, as I emphasise again, the Government have, therefore, a mandate to carry through their proposals. It would be a denial of democracy if the Government now abandoned the proposals endorsed by the country in favour of the Opposition proposals which the country so decisively rejected.

Now let me come to the general principles which, I hope, will govern the country's future constitution. First and foremost, the Government consider that the constitution should be based on the principle that all citizens of Ghana are equal and are all entitled to the same rights.

It is unfortunately true that owing to the facts of history in the Northern Territories, for example, there have been fewer opportunities for education than there have been in other parts of the Gold Coast. But this is no reason why the people of the North should not have exactly the same rights and that their opinions should not have exactly the same weight as those of the people of the South. I entirely repudiate the idea of there being first and second class citizens in the new Ghana. We are determined that in the new constitution provision shall be made so that all the people of Ghana, irrespective of whether they come from the Northern Territories, Ashanti, Togoland or the Colony, have the same rights and the same opportunities. For technical reasons, it will be impossible to include in the Order in Council provision for Gold Coast citizenship and nationality, but a Bill for this purpose is now being prepared and the Government will introduce it at as early a date as possible. In the meantime, the Government have made arrangements with the Government of the United Kingdom for transitional provisions in regard to citizenship to be included in United Kingdom legislation.

I come now to what I believe to be the second great principle which is essential in any constitution of a democratic country. This principle can be expressed by saying that the people of the country must be sovereign. The Convention People's Party has not fought for self-government in order to have a sham form of independence. We are determined not only to see that this country is independent of any foreign country, but also that power passes into the hands of the people and is effectively exercised by them.

The way in which a sovereign people exercise their power is through organs of government which are freely elected by them. These consist of, first and foremost, the National Assembly and next to the National Assembly the various Regional Assemblies and Local Councils which already exist or which it is proposed to set up. All these, the Government believe, should be elected by the people and be responsible to them.

How are we to fashion the constitution so as to see that the people are able to exercise their sovereignty? The first essential is that every act of the Government must be capable of being questioned and queried by the representatives of the people. The Governor General must only do those things which he is advised to do by someone who is responsible to the National Assembly. Parliament must be able to call to account any Minister for the advice which he has given to the Governor General on any subject.

The position of civil servants in Ghana after Independence had to be considered. In the old colonial days the public officer was the representative of the imperial power. He was responsible to the Government of Great Britain and not to the government of the country in which he served. Politics, I said, should not enter into the appointment and dismissal of civil servants:

The Government are most anxious that the public service should be representative of the country as a whole. Just in the same way as there are a proportion of the people in the country who support the Opposition so it would be wrong if there were not a proportion of the civil servants who hold the same views. We believe in personal liberty and this means that the Government should not inquire into, or base any of its actions in regard to a civil servant, on his own personal political views. The sole test of a civil servant's conduct should be his ability to perform the tasks which are entrusted to him. Anything else is entirely immaterial. If, however, this country is not to become a bureaucracy then the actions of civil servants generally must be subject to criticism in Parliament. It is however, very important that this distinction should be made. In every matter of policy, civil servants must be considered to be acting in accordance with the instructions of the Minister who is responsible for the Ministry in which they are employed. It would be entirely wrong for Members of the Assembly to attack the personal conduct of a civil servant. The civil servant cannot reply. He can only speak through the Minister under whom he works. Ministers must, therefore, be assumed to be responsible for all matters of policy and for that reason they must be in a position to answer for the conduct of those who carry out that policy. It would be entirely wrong if, in the independent Ghana, it was possible for the Government to shelter behind the Public Service Commission and say, when the conduct of any particular civil servant is criticised, that his appointment was a matter for which the Government were not responsible. In a democracy, a Minister must be responsible for the action of every official in his Department. He must either defend the official's conduct or, if he cannot do that, he must have authority to see that the official does not continue to pursue the policy with which the Minister is not in agreement.

On the other hand, in a newly developing democracy, it is of supreme importance for the future of the country that there should not be any question of political influence affecting promotion or prospects within the public service. It is for this reason that the Government have decided to retain the system by which all appointments to the public service are made by the Public Service Commission and by which disciplinary questions are referred to that body. The Government think it of the greatest importance that there should be a body such as the Public Service Commission which should guarantee fair opportunity for every one employed in the Government service. Those who enter Government service are entitled, irrespective of whatever Government is in power, to regular promotion and to guarantees against arbitrary dismissal.

The Government's proposal, therefore, means that there will, in fact, be little change in the way in which the public service is run, but the Government will assume full responsibility for the conduct of all civil servants.

Minority rights would be respected. Opposition members in the Assembly would be able to raise questions which seemed to them in the national interest. The Opposition would have a guaranteed proportion of representation on Standing Committees and Select Committees of the Assembly. In matters of grave national importance, I said, a tradition should be established that the Prime Minister of the day could consult with the Leader of the Opposition to secure, if possible, a concerted national policy. I continued:

But questions of minority rights are not only concerned with the Opposition in the Assembly. They affect minorities also in the Regions and it is the duty of the Government to see that in the various Regions of Ghana any minority Party is given fair consideration in the regional machinery of government.

Another principle which I think should be included in all constitutions and which indeed, in itself, contains the very essence of democracy, is that there should be guaranteed free elections. If there is any one matter above all else which I would describe as the first essential of democracy, it is the existence of machinery to provide for impartial supervision of elections. It is, unfortunately, for reasons which I shall explain later, impossible to include in the present Order in Council detailed electoral provisions. It is, however, the intention of the Government to set up a Select Committee of the Assembly to examine, within the framework of the Van Lare Commission Report and the proposals set out in the Government's present White Paper, the most effective means of guaranteeing free and fair elections. From both sides of the Assembly there have been justified criticisms of the up-till-now imperfect methods for the registration of elections. The Government attach the greatest importance to the compilation of accurate registers and to the setting up of impartial bodies to see to it that elections are carried out in a fair and non-partisan spirit. The Government earnestly hope that when the Select Committee on the subject is established, the Opposition will not, as they have done in the past in regard to other Select Committees, boycott its proceedings.

Allied to minority rights and of equal importance are the rights of individuals. The Government believe that the individual citizen of Ghana ought to be guaranteed by law freedom from arbitrary arrest. The Government believe that the individual's home should be inviolate and not subject to arbitrary search, and that his property should not be arbitrarily confiscated and that he should have the right of free speech. The Government believe that any individual should be entitled to join any trade union, political party or other association of his choice. The Government consider that freedom to practise whatever religion a citizen follows should be guaranteed by law; the Government think that it is an essential part of democracy that there should be a free press and that provision should be made by law that any state broadcasting system is as free to put the Opposition's point of view as that of the Government. Above all, the Government believe that the courts of law should be absolutely independent of the Executive and should be a bulwark for the defence of the rights of the individual.

Unfortunately once again, for reasons which I shall explain later, it is impossible to include fundamental rights of this sort in the Independence Order in Council, but it is the Government's intention to include these fundamental rights in the constitution once Independence has been granted.

I next turned to the question of Regional Assemblies. In the Government's April White Paper it was proposed that all Bills, other than those certified (a) by the Minister of Finance as secret until announced in the Budget (b) by the Prime Minister as urgent, or (c) by the Attorney-General as purely formal, should be published at least one month before their first reading in the Legislative Assembly. This was to allow Regional Assemblies and the House of Chiefs to express their views on any proposed legislation before it was discussed in the Assembly. In this way, legislation would be much more thoroughly considered than if the standard practice in other Commonwealth countries was adopted namely, discussion in a Second Chamber. The proposal was a constitutional innovation. 'Nowhere else in the Commonwealth, so far as I know,' I said, 'is there an arrangement by which legislation, before it is introduced into Parliament, is published for the consideration of outside bodies.'

Judges, I proposed, should be appointed on the advice of the Prime Minister after he had consulted with the Chief Justice. I hoped that in the main, judges would be recruited from among practising members of the Gold Coast Bar, though it might be necessary to employ expatriate judges for a time.

The question of electoral law and the formation of constituencies would be studied by a Select Committee of the Assembly. After dealing with plans for the delimitation of constituencies and for the supervision of elections, I came to the proposal that the name of the country should be changed at Independence from the Gold Coast to Ghana:

There are many objections to continuing the name of 'Gold Coast'. It was, in the first place, not the traditional name of the country as a whole but merely the name given in the seventeenth century by the French, and afterwards by the Dutch, to the coastal strip of the present Colony. When we become independent it is most essential that no appearance is given of any one portion of the country dominating any other part and on those grounds alone it would be better to choose a name which was not closely associated with one particular region. Secondly, the name 'Gold Coast' is only the English version of the name. It is translated by different words in each of the vernaculars of the country. There is a similar international difficulty.

I look forward to our country taking its place among the nations of the world. Once again, it is desirable that in every European language the name of the country should be rendered in the same form. The name Gold Coast, however, is internationally regarded not as a name but as a description. It has therefore been the habit for each European country to give to the Gold Coast in its own language not the English title of 'Gold Coast', but a name which in the language of that European country means 'gold coast'. The Government consider it very undesirable that the Gold Coast should begin its independent international life with as many names as there are languages represented in the United Nations.

It seemed to me that the Opposition sometimes criticised simply for the sake of causing disagreement. I spoke about Opposition proposals for the method of appointing judges and also about the powers and position of the Attorney-General. I looked forward, I said, to hearing Opposition spokesmen explain their views to the House. My Government was always ready to consider suggestions.

There was happily no dispute between the Government and the Opposition about the need for some degree of decentralisation of the police force. The boundaries of areas of police administration should be related to the area of regional and local government administration. But for practical reasons the best police organisation for the country would be a unified central police force.

On the Opposition proposals for a Council of State and a Second Chamber I spoke at some length. It seemed to me that both suggestions were undemocratic and unacceptable. I reminded the House, that the suggestion of a Second Chamber was carefully considered by a Select Committee some time ago, and they reported decisively against it. The Opposition had asked that the House of Chiefs in each Region should act as Second House to the Regional Assembly:

> Such a proposal is, of course, quite inconsistent with the Government's proposal which has been accepted by the three Territorial Councils that the Regional Councils should work, roughly speaking, in the same way as do County Councils in England. This would mean that the executive authority of the Regions would be exercised through various Standing Committees dealing with the different powers transferred to the Regions. County Council government in England would be quite impossible if there was a House of Lords in each county. Regional Government on the County Council model would be equally impossible with a House of Chiefs.
>
> In the Government's view, the function of the House of Chiefs is quite different. Its object is to safeguard the institution of chieftaincy in the Region concerned. The House of Chiefs would be the Government's Regional adviser on all matters connected with the chieftaincy and in regard to all questions of customary law and practice. The House of Chiefs would, therefore, have quite different functions from those of the Regional Assembly. The Government believe that the suggestion that the House of Chiefs should be a Second Chamber of the Regional Assembly should be rejected.

I ended by apologising for speaking longer than I had ever done before, but the debate was of supreme importance. The Government would take careful note of everything said in the discussions which followed. Democracy consisted in free discussion, and all members had a duty to express their view freely and frankly:

> We shall soon become masters of our own country and for that reason a very great responsibility rests upon us all. We must show the world that Africans can give a lead in justice, tolerance, liberty, individual freedom and in social progress. The basis of our coming Independence rests in the character and condition of our people. The source of our prosperity, the

cocoa industry, was not developed for us by the British or by any expatriate commercial interests. The first cocoa was brought to the Gold Coast by an African, Tetteh Quarshie, and the industry has been in the hands of Africans throughout. The diamond industry, which in other parts of Africans is exploited by expatriate capital is, in the Gold Coast largely in the hands of African diamond miners. Even our timber industry has not been entirely monopolised by foreign interests. It is no chance that George Arthur Grant[1] was a leading African timber merchant. The political forces in this country and the demand for Independence are based upon agriculture and industry which have been established by the people of this country without outside foreign help.

Mr Speaker, when we stand on the verge of Independence, it is only right that we should pay tribute to those who have made that Independence possible. I have spoken in my speech of the very great part played by the Convention People's Party, but I, and the Party, realise the debt we owe to the work which was done by other individuals and other parties. Though we have had deep political differences, it would be wrong if I did not also pay a tribute to those who, while not agreeing with the Convention People's Party, have nevertheless made their contribution towards attaining Independence.

I believe the whole Assembly will agree with me in saying that when we come to part with British rule and control we will do so with the utmost goodwill towards the people of Britain. We are glad to remain within the Commonwealth and while our experience has led us to realise the difficulties and evils of the colonial system which we have shaken off, we have nevertheless great respect for many British officials who have devoted their lives to the service of Africa. In particular, I should like to mention Sir Gordon Guggisberg. I have referred earlier to the failure of the Africanisation policy which he inaugurated. This was due, not to lack of goodwill on his part, but to his being faced by a system of colonial administration which was too powerful to be overcome by the goodwill of any Governor. I should like also to mention Sir Alan Burns. Like Sir Gordon Guggisberg, his work largely came to nothing but he devoted himself to the service of the Gold Coast. He too was defeated by circumstances too strong for him. Finally, I wish to say one word about our present Governor. It has fallen to his lot to be Governor throughout the period when the Gold Coast was preparing itself for Independence.

[1] 'Pa' Grant, first President of the United Gold Coast Convention.

I believe that when the history of these days comes to be written, it will be realised that this country owes a far greater debt to Sir Charles Arden-Clarke than is generally realised.

Mr Speaker, the hopes and fears of the future of this country are all crowded into this occasion. But I know that the future will be bright; and I hope that some day, somewhere, we also may be able to say with William Wordsworth:

> '*Bliss was it in that dawn to be alive,*
> *But to be young was very heaven!*'

CHAPTER ELEVEN

ON THE THRESHOLD OF INDEPENDENCE

I have always believed that the trade union movement is of the utmost importance not only in Ghana, but in the development of Africa as a whole. When I was a student in America, I worked as a steward aboard one of the passenger ships of the Clyde Mallory Line, and I belonged to the National Maritime Union. I have practical experience, therefore, of trade union membership.

On 14 January 1957 I spoke at the inauguration ceremony of the All African Regional Conference of the International Confederation of Free Trade Unions It was fitting that Accra should have been chosen for an international Trade Union Conference, since the Gold Coast was then on the threshold of independence:

The Gold Coast Government believes that the trade union movement is of the utmost importance in the development of Africa as a whole and I can assure you that my Government will give all the support which it can to the establishment and maintenance of independent and free trade unions in the new state of Ghana.

It would be a mistake, however, if trade unionists were to consider that their duties in regard to Africa consisted merely in helping the established trade unions. It is essential that the trade union movements throughout the world understand and take into account the political and economic developments which are taking place in Africa. I should like to outline to you the position as it affects the Gold Coast because what has happened here and what will happen in the future is, I hope, a prototype of the development which we may expect to see taking place in other parts of Africa. It is of the utmost importance for trade unionists to realise that the nature of the movement for economic, social and political freedom among African peoples is bound to be deeply affected by the attitude of the rest of the world.

Let me illustrate this by the example of the Gold Coast. This country, like many other African and Asian colonial territories, is of immense importance to the far more industrialised countries of America and Europe in which the trade union movement has its greatest strength. Unfortunately wealthy industrial countries often fail to realise that the source of their prosperity is bound up with progress and economic development in the less fortunately situated countries who produce the primary products and from which come the raw materials essential to modern industry. Trade unionists throughout the world have in fact a direct interest in the well-being of the countries which are the source of raw materials.

We need to be more aware than we are at present of the interdependence of the sectors of world economy. The relationship between urban and rural communities in individual countries is now extended to the relationship between industrialised and raw material producing countries. The banking systems of the world, as they operate between industry and agriculture, have aided capital formation in Europe and America. The idea of a World Bank and an International Monetary Fund is in fact formal recognition of an established pattern of world economic relations. World trade unionism, therefore, is a necessary complement to this new form of industrial and financial network which covers the whole world.

Countries like the Gold Coast have realised that the standard of living can be raised if agriculture is improved and diversified and industries are developed. It is for this reason that we seek foreign investment and technical assistance. Investment in underdeveloped territories aids the circulation of world resources. Loans and other forms of financial assistance create facilities for the exploitation of natural resources, increase the volume of world trade and widen the sphere of prosperity.

Many countries like the Gold Coast have been too dependent on agriculture, and in some cases, on a single crop. This situation has rendered us extremely vulnerable to fluctuations in world prices for our dominant crops. These fluctuations have had unsettling effects on long term plans and crippled attempts to raise the standard of living. In order to keep up with the times, it is necessary to develop heavy industries in this country. The Volta River project, for example, is designed for such a purpose. The scheme envisages a partnership between the Government of the Gold Coast, the United Kingdom Government and Aluminium Limited of Canada. Its object would be to develop new bauxite mines and to construct a dam on the Volta to provide power for smelting the aluminium. The planning of such an operation has to be most carefully co-ordinated if the economy of the country is not to be adversely affected in other ways. And here I would like to point out that we have been able to finance our developments, such as that of the construction of Tema harbour, out of development revenue and not by borrowing. Our external public debt is very small indeed compared with other countries. The financial reserves of our Government for development and of the cocoa Marketing Board for maintaining a stable cocoa price are adequate. The basis for a developing economy exists to an extent which is not at present found in other territories.

Take our agricultural economy, for example. Delegates from abroad may note our good weather and see the luxurious vegetation of our country and may be inclined to think that the problems of tropical agriculture are simple and that it is merely a matter of deciding what crop to grow. On the contrary, the introduction of new crops is an extremely difficult technical question and involves considerable expenditure for experiments and for pilot schemes. Agriculture in the tropics, if it is to be more than mere subsistence farming, requires far more planning and state assistance than does the development of agriculture in the temperate zones.

Let me now re-state the reasons why under-developed territories require foreign assistance. Development requires planning over a long period and therefore aid is necessary as a form of insurance to make it certain that the development plan can continue despite fluctuations in the prices of raw materials. In order to create a climate of opinion necessary for foreign investment, it is essential that development projects are limited to those which are immediately revenue-producing. Nevertheless, it is essential that certain projects which will only ultimately be revenue-producing should be undertaken. In such cases, outside aid may also be necessary.

After brief reference to the special needs of the Northern Territories, I ended by considering the narrower aspect of trade unionism in the Gold Coast:

We welcome the creation of trade unions and we welcome help from trade unions from abroad in assisting our unions to organise and to expand. But it is essential that trade unionism in Africa takes into account the particular conditions of Africa. It would be fatal if it was thought that trade unionism can be established merely by copying what has been done in Europe and America.

I believe that the trade union movement in Africa has a great part to play and has far wider tasks to perform than merely the safeguarding of the conditions and the wages of their members. Ultimately the problem of all developing countries is the problem of increased productivity. In the Gold Coast we have, as in so many under-developed countries, the paradox of high labour costs and low wages. This does not seem to me to arise from any inherent lack of skill on the part of our workers. I believe that they are capable of handling the most intricate machines with the same ability as workers from the most developed countries who have a long tradition of industrialism behind them. All of you as trade unionists will know the stock suggestion that labour is inefficient because the workers do not work hard enough. It is a charge brought against workers everywhere and I do not believe it is any more true in the Gold Coast than it is elsewhere. Nevertheless the problem of increasing the productivity of labour remains and it is a problem which it is the duty of the trade union movement to assist in solving.

There is no doubt that it is in the field of human rights that trade unionism in individual African territories, and as a world movement, will encounter its greatest challenge. In Africa, the attitudes to labour will have to undergo radical examination and radical changes as well. In the traditional society, there can be no dependence on slave, serf, or forced labour and in the multi-racial societies the gulf that makes it difficult for ordinary human sympathy to be extended to the worker must be bridged. We intend to encourage in Africa not only the dignity of labour in workers' movements, but the dignity of man whose needs constitute the ultimate end of all productive enterprise. We intend to demonstrate that the exploitation of man by man must cease. We also intend to demonstrate that a man is entitled to the fruits of his labour. The trade union movement as I see it in Africa is one of the important spearheads for economic and social progress. Trade unions in Africa are therefore expected to play an active role in the struggle against colonialism. They must work for the ultimate political freedom and emancipation of their territories.

I hope that this present conference will be merely one of the first to be held here in Accra. Now that our country is becoming a free, sovereign and independent state it will, I hope, become a centre for conferences of this sort. We welcome here in the Gold Coast discussion and frank exchange of views. We believe in democracy all over Africa by welcoming here without distinction of race, colour or origin all those who care to come and discuss among us their problems and ideas.

I wish you all a successful conference and a pleasant stay in our country.

Just over a month later, on 24 February, I spoke at Saltpond to the last conference before Independence of the National Delegates of the C.P.P. I reviewed the work of the Party and urged members to continue to maintain a disciplined organisation:

At long last what we have all sacrificed and fought for is now in sight. Exactly ten days from today, that is, on the 6th March, 1957, this country, under its new name of Ghana, will be a free, sovereign and independent state. All the legal documents concerning this great event have been completed and now we await the arrival of that great day – the 6th March, 1957.

Are you ready? Are you ready for that great day? Are you ready to celebrate this momentous event with all due grandeur and ceremony befitting the occasion? I hope that by now you have all completely changed your hearts, attitudes and minds and have realised that you are no longer a colonial but a free and independent people of a free and independent nation.

Fellow Ghanaians and friends: in this happy mood, generated by the sweet thoughts of this country attaining its independence and freedom on the 6th March, I salute you and bid you welcome to this Emergency Delegates' Conference of our dynamic Party. It is most fitting that on the eve of independence we should meet to review the past and plan for the future.

I spoke of the years of struggle which lay behind, of Positive Action, and of the victory of the C.P.P. in the General Election which ushered in the Tactical Action phase. I went on to speak of the temptations of office:

When I addressed the first Easter Delegates' Conference at Saltpond in 1951, a month after we had come into office, I warned Party leaders, Assemblymen and Ministers against being spoiled by the sweets of office and against bribery and corruption. I have always considered that bribery and corruption are social evils which must be completely uprooted from our social fabric, and I am determined to see that these evils are rooted out. It is to this that the Party inspired a country-wide anti-bribery and anti-corruption campaign to assist the police to bring offenders to be dealt with by the law. I hope that both Party members and non-Party members alike, in fact every citizen of the new State of Ghana, will henceforth help to kill this social evil wherever it may be found.

You will know too well how hard our political opponents have tried – though in vain – to discredit the leaders of the Party. You know how hard they have tried to discredit the C.P.P. Government. You know how hard and how often they have tried to bring about the collapse of the Party. We have survived all their vicious and treacherous manœuvres because we have worked with faith and honesty. As long as we tread that path, comrades, we have nothing to fear. I must frankly say, however, that the performance of some Party members has not been up to the mark. I therefore counsel you all very earnestly that as we enter the new status of sovereignty in the new Ghana, all Party members, indeed all citizens of this new state, should make new resolutions to make Ghana not only a prosperous and peaceful country, but also a nation of clean and honest citizens.

I have dwelt at length on this question of bribery and corruption because I hold the view that there can be no true progress while our society is plagued with these evils.

One of the reasons why our adversaries have failed to undermine the Party is that the C.P.P. is a disciplined organisation. The discipline among the leaders and the rank and file has been remarkable. And here I take this opportunity on behalf of the National Executive and the Central Committee to congratulate you all for this wonderful achievement.

But I must warn you: the difficulties in the post independence period are likely to tax your sense of discipline even more. The common fight against imperialism contributed in no small measure to the unity of purpose and the exemplary display of discipline among you. Let us therefore all harness these qualities against the new adversaries – deceit, debauchery, dishonesty, superstition and greed, want, disease, illiteracy and economic ills besetting our country, so that we may build the new Ghana of our dreams fit for free men to live in.

I reminded members of the countless unknown people who had contributed to the success of the Party, without any hope of reward. To build the new Ghana, more such valiant people would be needed. I went on to consider future policy:

With national independence won, where do we go next? Countrymen, I need not tell you that this embraces matters of great urgency. 'Seek ye first the political kingdom and all things will be added to it' we often said. What are the other things? it may be asked. Before I answer this question I must make one important observation, and that is this – now that we have gained our freedom, the first and most important thing we must do is to guard that independence very jealously. May I remind you of the inscription that will adorn the Independence Arch on Christiansborg Road, Accra: '*Let this memorial hold sacred in your memory the liberty and freedom of Ghana. The liberty and freedom which by our struggle and sacrifice the sons and daughters of Ghana have this day regained. May this independence be preserved and held sacred for all time.*'

I shall now attempt to answer the vital question, 'After Independence, what next?' The answer is simply this: the attainment of political independence will be followed by a period of national reconstruction, the first instalment of which will be embodied in our second Development Plan to be presented to the new Ghana Parliament for approval within one year of the attainment of independence. The Plan will deal mainly with social and economic reconstruction and have as its main objectives full employment and the development of the whole country, though projects of national importance will be given their due emphasis wherever they may be sited. In addition, secondary and technical education must be more widely spread over the whole country.

Fellow countrymen, I myself have often been appalled at the extremely bad water which some of our people are compelled to use. I am determined to see to it that water supplies are given due priority in our next plan. Development of water and electricity services, construction of more feeder roads, provision of more mail and telephone facilities and more and more houses for the people are some of our next objectives. With independence attained we hope to take up the question of whether or not to proceed with the Volta River Project and, when a satisfactory agreement has been made, we shall go ahead with it with the approval of our Parliament.

Finally, with regard to the period of national reconstruction after Independence, I must say this with all the emphasis at my command: if Government must provide work, then it is incumbent upon the people to work. Some people, even though unemployed, hanker after clerical jobs and will not take up manual labour. That sort of attitude must stop. Allied with this last point is the fact that independence imposes a great responsibility on all of us to work harder. No more can we say that P.W.D. work, Electricity Department work or Government Office work is white man's work, with all the attendant sloppiness or neglect that is often witnessed. Now all can see that these jobs are really for us and we must therefore work harder to help implement the plans for national reconstruction. We must not only work harder, but also aim at efficiency and excellence in our work so as to increase our productivity for the good of all. The socialist pattern of society which we envisage for Ghana can only be constructed upon a high level of productivity, of education, of civil responsibility and a spirit of enterprise and service.

This is the time when we must harness the dynamism of workers by hand and brain, the farmers and the progressive intelligensia into a tri-partite alliance under the direction of our Government in order to develop the productive resources of the country. The emphasis of the struggle has now shifted from the anti-imperialist phase to the internal one of the struggle against the enemies of social progress; that is, against poverty, hunger, illiteracy, disease, ignorance, squalor and low productivity. These social enemies can be compared to land-mines left on the battlefield by a vanquished army of imperialism. Before we gain occupation of these recovered lands and have the best use of them for a higher standard of living, we have to remove all these land-mines and clear the scars of battle. Therefore every citizen of Ghana must mobilise himself for the next phase of the struggle. Are you ready?

We are now entering the second phase of the bloodless revolution and since you, Party members and countrymen, who have provided the driving force and made it possible for independence to be achieved, are looking forward to a better social and economic future, I enjoin you all to get ready for the task ahead. Again, I ask, are you ready?

You remember our previous slogan was 'SELF GOVERN-MENT NOW' or simply 's.G. NOW'. Now it is 'FREEDOM'. Let the old slogan give us a new one, namely 'SERVE GHANA NOW'. Thus, if you are greeted with shouts of 'FREEDOM' the response should be 'SERVE GHANA NOW'!

After Independence, I went on, the possibilities of achievement were much greater. The standard of living, particularly in rural areas, must be raised. Ghana must be an inspiration to the rest of Africa:

To achieve this we must have a short period of consolidation; to pause, look back awhile, assemble our wits and energies and get ready to forge ahead in confidence to the second victory. During this period of consolidation, however, the

C.P.P. Government will continue with greater zeal and drive to provide these rural areas with basic amenities such as water, electricity, communications – including roads, postal services and radio facilities – schools and houses.

There is hardly any country of our size and stage of development with its economy as strong as ours. We have financed all our development of several million pounds from our own resources; we have even paid some of our overseas debts; moreover, between the Government, the Cocoa Marketing Board and other public bodies, our total assets now amount to over £200 million.

We are not by any means bankrupt, but the sudden catastrophic fall in the price of cocoa has made us go slow with expenditure until we can take our next bearing. We have already taken steps which are directed to the effective consolidation of our finances and against waste, so that in the era of independence we can vigorously tackle our task of national reconstruction. Our opponents can and will keep on telling lies about us; these lies will be meaningless, now that their aim for so doing cannot be achieved. I know that your faith in the leadership of the C.P.P. and our Government is such that our political opponents will soon realise that they are playing a losing game. Our Party knows its job and understands its mission. While our opponents are busily engaged in their campaign of lies against us, let us work to maintain our Party's organisation and solidarity.

Our Party set out to achieve freedom and independence under a unitary form of government and has won a resounding victory over those who advocate a federal form of government. Thank goodness that federation, secession and 'Mate Mehu' have been completely destroyed once and for all in this country.

I then spoke of Party organisation. The National Association of Socialist Students' Organisation (NASSO for short), which was the ideological wing of the Party, and the Youth League, were organising themselves into effective units within the Party. It would be necessary to build a new headquarters for the Party, and I hoped to deal with the matter that year. I ended:

Comrades, we have completed the first of our jobs – that of political emancipation from colonialism and imperialism. The next objective is that of the social and economic reconstruction of our new nation. You have fought a good fight and won the first battle. Are you prepared for the second battle?

Are you ready? Then let us rejoice! Let us celebrate our victory! Our C.P.P. is unconquerable. Forward we march in the service of Ghana's freedom, in time with our motto: 'FORWARD EVER, BACKWARD NEVER'. Let us therefore organise our Party as never before and strengthen our country against those who may dare to make a farce of our freedom and independence.

As you leave this conference, I, as your chosen leader, take the opportunity to wish you Godspeed back to your homes, and a happy celebration of the victory we won by our toil and sacrifice. And may we, countrymen, take this opportunity to remember those who are no more but whilst they lived helped the cause of freedom.

CHAPTER TWELVE

GHANA IS BORN

During the last few crowded days before Independence, Accra became rapidly filled with visitors. Scores of aircraft arrived bringing delegations from fifty-six nations. But the visitors to Accra were by no means all foreigners. Men, women and children from every part of the country flocked into the capital to join in the celebrations. No one who was there during that week will, I think, ever forget the gaiety and the colour of the occasion.

Perhaps the most formal of the many brilliant functions which took place at this time was the state dinner at the Ambassador Hotel. The Duchess of Kent, who was representing the Queen, and members of all the foreign delegations attended. In my speech of welcome, I took the opportunity to declare our foreign policy:

It is my pleasant task to welcome, on behalf of the Government the overseas guests who are here today and who have come to celebrate with us our independence. We consider it a great tribute to our country that no less than 56 nations should have sent delegations, many of them led by statesmen of world renown. It is a great pleasure to us to welcome these delegations because we realise that their presence here is not only a tribute to our country but is a mark of the importance which world opinion attaches to the emergence of an independent state in Africa.

It is particularly gratifying to us that so many nations are represented because it will be the policy of the Government of Ghana to develop the closest possible contacts with all other parts of the world. We are most anxious to establish friendly and cordial relations with all countries and we hope that it may be possible for us to play our full part in the United Nations, whose official representatives we are honoured to have amongst us.

Our country is not a stranger to world affairs. Through our connection with the United Kingdom we have been to some degree already in touch with the Commonwealth. In two days time our colonial relationship with Britain will end, but we

part with the warmest feelings of goodwill. With the ending
of the old relationships we shall establish our new position as
a fellow member with the United Kingdom of the Commonwealth. It affords us much pleasure, therefore, to have with us
not only the delegation from Great Britain, but also the delegations from all the other countries of the Commonwealth.
We hope this will be the beginning of a much closer association.

After emphasising the traditional links with the Commonwealth I went on to speak of our friendship with other countries:

While our connections in the past have been in the main with
the United Kingdom and the Commonwealth, we have had
links with many European countries. France is our neighbour
in Africa and along our coast are forts built at some stage in
our history by Portugal, Sweden, Denmark and Holland.
From Switzerland and from Germany came the famous Basel
and Bremen Missions. It is right at these celebrations that we
should remember these countries whose nationals introduced
many of our crops and in a number of other ways contributed
to our culture.

In another way, we have a strong link with the new world.
There exists a firm bond of sympathy between us and the
Negro peoples of the Americas. The ancestors of so many of
them come from this country. Even today in the West Indies,
it is possible to hear words and phrases which come from
various languages of the Gold Coast. I am glad also that we
have with us other nations with whom up till now we have had
little or no contact. I hope our meeting on this happy occasion
will be the beginning of a lasting friendship.

I then explained the origin of the new name of 'Ghana'.
Although many pronouncements concerning its origin had
already been made, there were always those who were quite
clearly learning for the first time of the existence of the ancient
African Empire:

It is our earnest hope that the Ghana which is now being
reborn will be, like the Ghana of old, a centre to which all the
peoples of Africa may come and where all the cultures of Africa
may meet. It is for that reason that I welcome so gladly at this
gathering the many representatives of the nations of Africa.
We believe that throughout the world there is understanding
of our problem and goodwill towards us in the task upon

which we are about to embark, and that your presence here is a token of that goodwill.

Your Royal Highness, as you may know, our womenfolk in this part of Africa exert a special influence on our lives. Some say that they exert a dominant influence, but so far I myself have managed to survive as a bachelor! But there is no doubt of their very special position, and we therefore naturally feel that it is most appropriate that we should have you with us this evening as our most distinguished guest. If I may say so, we feel that it is even more appropriate that it should be you who represents Her Majesty the Queen, the Head of the Commonwealth family into which we are now entering.

A more comprehensive statement of foreign policy followed on the eve of Independence, when with excited crowds gathering outside the building, and gradually covering the Old Polo Ground opposite, I spoke to a crowded House on the new status of our nation:

This is a decisive moment in our history and it is fitting that we, as representatives of the people, should assemble here in Parliament on the eve of Independence to take stock of our present position, to take a peep into the future and to declare boldly to the world what, in broad terms, our domestic and foreign policy will be when, one hour from now, we join the other independent states of the world as a free and sovereign nation.

In the modern world, independence also means inter-dependence, for such is the technological and scientific advance in this age that the world appears to be smaller than its own prodigious size. What happens in one country may have repercussions – both favourable and otherwise – in another country. This naturally leads to the very important subject of Ghana's foreign policy after Independence. Our foreign policy shall be based on three words: Dignity, Peace and Friendship.

Before I go on to discuss the foreign policy of the Government, I would like to inform Honourable Members that on the attainment of independence, I, as Prime Minister, propose to take over the Portfolios of Defence and External Affairs. As Ghana achieves independence, it observes a world torn and divided in its political relationships. The Government of Ghana therefore, feels that at this stage the country should not be committed in any aspect of its foreign policy and that it should not be aligned with any particular group of powers or political bloc. The Government of Ghana does not intend to follow a neutralist policy in its foreign relations, but it does intend to preserve its independence to act as it sees best at any particular time. The Government hopes that Ghana may become a member of the United Nations as soon as possible, and looks forward to maintaining friendly relations with members of the Commonwealth and with all freedom loving nations.

In pursuing its independent policy the Government of Ghana will have regard, first and foremost, for the interests of the people of Ghana: in particular, their continued economic and social progress. Every step in the Government's power, both internally and in its external relations, will be taken to further the development of the nation's resources for the common good. Foreign investment will be encouraged and the Government's policy in this respect, which was first stated by me on the first of March, 1954, will be implemented in accordance with the principles of the constitution.

The Government of Ghana will direct its efforts to promote the interests and advancement of all African peoples in their pursuit of freedom and social progress. The sacrifices made by the people of Ghana in their struggle for independence are only the first stage in the common advancement of their brothers all over Africa. The Government hopes that, as a free, sovereign and independent state, Ghana can become the centre for the discussion of African problems as a whole and that, with the co-operation of all other African territories, we shall be able to foster a common attitude to local problems and world problems which will ensure that problems peculiar to Africa will receive the attention which they have not had for so long. Our aim is to work with others to achieve an African personality in international affairs.

A brief review of our domestic problems and our economy confirmed that internationally we were able to stand on our own feet:

While the new state of Ghana will not have a big population, we shall be as large as quite a number of countries in Europe, Asia and South and Central America. Our position, perhaps, can best be judged by looking at our national income per head. The wealth produced in Ghana each year averages just over £50 per head of the population. This may be small as compared with the United Kingdom where the national income

per head is over £300. But compared with other countries in
Africa and Asia our average national income is high. It is two
and a half times that of Tanganyika. Our national income per
head of population exceeds those of India, Pakistan and
Ceylon, even though, on account of our much smaller population, our gross national product is nothing like as large as
those countries.

Nevertheless, we are the sixth largest producer of gold in
the world and the fourth largest producer of manganese.
Cocoa, of which we are the largest single producer in the
world, comes from farms which are entirely African owned
and therefore, in regard to this – by far the most important of
our exports – we are in no way dependent upon foreign capital.
The amount of our public debt is very small and much of our
development, such as the building of Tema Harbour has been
financed out of development funds and not, as in other
countries, by borrowing.

Since the Convention People's Party came into power, we
have always been able to maintain a budget surplus and a
favourable balance of external trade. Even more notable has
been the extent of public saving which has enabled us to undertake substantial development and to create new capital in the
community without a corresponding increase of private
wealth. In 1953–54, for example, 10% of our gross national
product was saved. In other words, the Government put aside
for public development £1 out of every £10 worth of wealth
produced. The corresponding figure for public saving in the
United Kingdom in the same period was just over 3% of the
gross national product and in the United States just under 2%.

It is important for it to be realised that the material basis
for the independence of Ghana exists. We can stand on our
own feet. The foreign policy of Ghana will not, therefore, be
dictated by the need for us having to seek assistance from
other countries. I mention this because during the debates
both in the House of Commons and in the House of Lords on
the Ghana Independence Bill, there was considerable discussion on the future of aid to Ghana and to other territories
likely to attain independence. For this reason it is, I think,
desirable that I should make plain the position of the Government.

I pointed out that we did not seek continuing aid as a gift
from the richer members of the Commonwealth. When spending
£124 m. during the course of our Five Year Development Plan
we had received £1½ m. in aid from Colonial Development and

Welfare Funds. It was not a large proportion and we had in return made our contribution to the gold and dollar resources of the sterling area:

The Gold Coast has contributed, on an average, 25% of the net dollar earnings of the British colonial territories, and, taking into account our contribution of around £9 million a year in gold, in the five years from 1951 to 1955 in which the Convention People's Party have been in power, the Gold Coast contributed a net positive balance of £153 million to the gold and dollar reserves of the sterling area. It will be seen therefore, that though the Gold Coast is small and, by Western standards, not a very wealthy country, it has made a significant contribution to maintaining the stability of the sterling area.

In recent years, however, our economy has become distorted and we have devoted ourselves largely to producing dollar cash crops like cocoa and other commodities which are dollar earners. Because the price of cocoa so varies on the world market, we have the greatest difficulty in planning our development because we never know what revenue we may have available and therefore we cannot undertake those large schemes of not immediately productive development which are absolutely essential for the Northern Territories and for other under-developed parts of the country. For that reason we think we would be justified in entering into negotiation with other members of the sterling area for a scheme by which we are insured against any prolonged depression in the price of cocoa and other dollar producing commodities in exchange for an undertaking on our behalf to continue to manage our economy so as to produce gold and dollar earnings for the sterling area. The cost to the Commonwealth countries who benefit from our dollar earnings would not be large and, in fact, under the scheme we have in mind, even under the most unlikely event of the whole of the insurance guarantee being called upon, the total involved would only be £30 million spread over ten years.

It would be wrong, however, for us to consider our membership to the Commonwealth in purely economic terms. The Commonwealth association is of value to us because it unites us to countries who have the same system of law and the same system of Parliamentary government as we have. One crucial problem, which the world must face, is how colonial territories can emerge as free, equal and independent nations without having to experience the violence of armed revolt and those material losses which always accompany violence. The Commonwealth can, I believe, become a pilot scheme for developing the most effective methods by which colonialism can be ended without revolution or violence and under conditions in which the former colonial territory still retains a close and friendly association with the former imperial power.

We value the Commonwealth link also because we believe through it we may be able to make our own distinctive contribution to Commonwealth, and, indeed, to world relations. One of the spurious axioms of colonialism is that those who carry out the policy of the colonial power, however well intentioned they may be, almost always subconsciously seek a solution to the problems of the colonial territory in the terms of a solution which was applicable to the so-called mother country. In our view we must seek an African solution to the problems of Africa. This does not, of course, mean that we reject Western influence as such, nor that we think that all Western techniques and methods are not applicable in Africa. It does, however, mean that in Ghana we must look at every problem from the African standpoint.

I explained for example, how tropical diseases, including malnutrition, had held back the productivity of the African. There was obviously no inherent defect in African people. The problem was not one of race but of environment:

We can only begin to plan when we accept the limitations of our situation and realise that a European solution may not be possible. For example, we have to face up to the fact that the cow and the horse, the traditional source of food and of motive power in the Western world, may never be able to play a decisive part in our economy. The effect of the tsetse fly on our history has been to make us perhaps more dependent on mechanical means of transport than practically any other nation. Seeking an African solution, therefore, means that once we abandon the traditional method of porterage by head loading we are compelled by the tsetse fly to rely upon the internal combustion engine. If we are to rely upon this successfully, we cannot afford the waste of vehicles ruined by bad roads, or by bad driving, or by lack of maintenance. In Europe it is sufficient for a farm to be served by a cart track and for a farmer to have a horse to draw his cart and his plough. In Ghana we must have feeder roads capable of carrying motor vehicles and our farming, if it is to be done otherwise than by hand, must be done by mechanical means. An

African solution for our farming problem, therefore, is that not only must we have a high standard of roads, but also that our whole educational system must be geared to producing a technically minded people. Because of the limitations placed on us, we have to produce, of necessity, a higher standard of technical education than is necessary in many of the most advanced countries of the Western world.

At first sight it might seem that the problems of an adequate educational system are beyond the resources of the country. I do not think they are, provided we approach our problems in a strictly realistic manner.

Institutes of tropical agriculture and of tropical medicine could now be established with international support, and in conjunction with our own University. Other problems, too, awaited solution:

Excessive heat is one of the factors which hinders our development. It presents difficulties in the storage of meat, milk and other foodstuffs. It prevents the worker from obtaining sufficient rest and it interferes with efficiency in the workshop and the office. In the Western world, these conditions are dealt with by refrigeration, air conditioning and fans, and, of course, to some extent these provide a solution for the problem in Ghana. But they cannot be a complete solution unless there is country-wide distribution of electric power on a scale which is probably far beyond our present resources. We can, however, develop the use of one source of energy which we have in abundance – the heat of the sun. Already in Accra and in other towns architectural designs have been evolved which make use of the sun to produce draughts of air, which, by flowing over the surface of the roof and walls of the building, keep it cool. We propose to continue experiments of this sort, combining the work of the Building Institute, which already exists, with that of the University.

Yet another example is the problem of language. One of the most obvious difficulties which face Africa south of the Sahara is the multiplicity of languages and dialects. Everyone of us in this Assembly today has to conduct his parliamentary business in a language which is not his own. I sometimes wonder how well the House of Commons in the United Kingdom, or the Senate in the United States, would manage if they suddenly found that they had to conduct their affairs in French or in Spanish. Nevertheless, we welcome English as not only providing a common medium for exchange between ourselves, but also for opening the door to us to all the heritage of the world. At the same time, however, it is essential that we do consider seriously the problem of the language in Africa. At present, such is the influence of Europe in our affairs, that far more students in our University are studying Latin and Greek than are studying the languages of Africa. An essential of independence is that emphasis must be laid on studying the living languages of Africa, for, out of such a study will come simpler methods by which those in one part of Africa may learn the languages of those in all other parts.

I believe that one of the most important services which Ghana can perform for Africa is to devise a system of education based at its University level on concrete studies of the problems of the tropical world. We have the resources to undertake this and I believe that we should not lack support from the rest of the world.

It will be the policy of the Government to turn the University College into a full-fledged university. The University will be the co-ordinating body for educational research, and we hope that it will eventually be associated with research institutes dealing with agriculture, biology, and the physical and chemical sciences.

We are very proud that today in a country of less than five million inhabitants[1] there should be nearly half a million children enjoying primary education. We must however, provide further outlets for these children and give them an opportunity to learn something of engineering, tropical agriculture and of the problems of tropical medicine and hygiene. Only with a population so educated can we hope to face the tremendous problems which confront any country attempting to raise the standard of life in a tropical zone.

These problems, of course, cannot be solved by education alone. We must reshape our machinery of government in order to deal with them. It is essential that we co-ordinate at every level government activity. It is no use devising a method of dealing with an agricultural problem unless we possess means by which we can explain to the people how to apply the solution. No issue is simple. Agriculture is very often a problem of civil engineering, of preventing soil erosion or providing water. Whether or not to irrigate may in itself be a medical problem as to what waterborne diseases may be thus introduced or spread. The extent of the risk of spreading diseases may depend on the power of mass education to persuade the

[1] A recent census has raised the figure to seven million.

population to take effective precautions against the diseases involved. It is therefore the intention of the Government to set up a central planning and development commission which will attempt to co-ordinate all the aspects of development.

A re-examination of the needs of Ghana however, cannot stop short at merely planning development. Quite clearly one of the first things which must follow from independence is that citizens of Ghana must play a far bigger role in the commercial and industrial life of the country than they do at present. We must examine the root causes of why it is that someone who comes from abroad seems able to succeed in commerce and industry in a way in which our own people often do not. No doubt in part this is due to our own lack of experience which time and education are likely to cure. But this is, I think, only a part of the reason. It is also due to a shortage of African capital. When Europe began its development, commerce and industry were financed by the surplus capital of the farmer. Our farmers are, however, very often prevented from putting their wealth to good use by the nature of our land law. One effect of colonialism has been to alter our ancient methods of administering and transmitting property in land and yet not, on the other hand, substituting for it a wholly British system of land tenure. Once again I think an African solution is possible. It seems to me that it is possible for us both to conserve the essentials of our own land law which affects and influences the whole of our social system and at the same time to provide that security of title which will enable land owners to raise capital in the same way as is done in more developed countries and thus to finance commerce and light industry in the rural areas. Clearly, however, this problem cannot be solved merely by land reform. We must make use of the funds accumulated by public saving to assist to finance the endeavour of our own people. That is why the Government attaches such importance to the state providing credit for African agriculture, commerce and industry.

Nevertheless, whatever we do to increase African participation in industry and commerce and however wisely we deploy our own resources, it is clear that for some time to come Ghana will require the investment of foreign capital. It is of course essential that no foreign cartel or trust is allowed to dominate the economy of the country, but the present economic position of Ghana is such that there is no risk of this happening. Here again is a problem to which we should seek an African solution.

The bringing of foreign capital to the country was essential,
I continued, and we would have to reconsider commercial and
company law and fiscal policy to make sure that conditions were
sufficiently attractive for investors. We would have to prove ourselves credit-worthy:

While it is most important for us to attract private investment,
it is equally important that we prove ourselves credit-worthy
to national and international financial organisations. It is,
among other things, for this reason that the Government propose that immediately after Independence there shall be a
period of financial and economic consolidation. During this
period of consolidation we would avoid committing ourselves
to any major project which might interfere with some other
form of development which, after a study of our situation, we
might come to consider to be preferable in the national interest.
The Government is conscious of the great – and perhaps
decisive – contribution which the Volta project could make
to the diversification of the economy, and to reducing our
dependence on the basic cash crop, cocoa. We observe that
the world demand for aluminium is increasing at a remarkable
rate, and we know that the Volta scheme is technically and
economically sound. We therefore intend to do everything in
our power to ensure that two of our greatest natural resources,
hydro-electric power and bauxite, are exploited before they
lose their real value. The government also observes that no
major source of aluminium has yet been developed in the
sterling area. The capital sums involved in this vast project
are inevitably very large, and are directly related to the matter
of foreign investment to which I have already referred. The
Government intends to hold further discussions about the
project with the British Government, the International Bank
for reconstruction and development and the aluminium
companies.

I ended with a short reference to the consequences of our
success or failure upon other African territories. We must not
fail:

The success or failure of our efforts to make Ghana into a
prosperous and happy state will extend far beyond the frontiers
of Ghana itself. A failure on our part would have tragic consequences for other African territories striving towards independence. We must not fail. We shall not fail.

I am sure all sections of the House have this in view. Let us all co-operate to make this new state a success. Whatever our political differences, whatever our political affiliations or persuasions, let us all unite to work selflessly for the progress and prosperity of our new state of Ghana and her peoples. We have fought and won the battle for freedom. We must now assail the ramparts of all the social and economic evils that have plagued our country all these years, and to win this second battle of economic and social reconstruction, I rely on the unqualified support of all sections of the community. Let us march forward together.

From the House I drove the short distance to the Polo Ground where a crowd estimated at 100,000 was waiting to hear the midnight pronouncement of Independence. As I mounted the rostrum, together with senior members of my Government, a great cry of welcome arose. I looked around over the vast crowds and waited for a few moments until the stroke of midnight. Slowly the Union Jack was lowered, and amid terrific excitement the red, green and gold flag of Ghana was raised. Then I began to speak:

At long last the battle has ended! And thus Ghana, your beloved country, is free for ever. And here again, I want to take the opportunity to thank the chiefs and people of this country, the youth, the farmers, the women, who have so nobly fought and won this battle. Also I want to thank the valiant ex-servicemen who have so co-operated with me in this mighty task of freeing our country from foreign rule and imperialism! And as I pointed out at our Party conference at Saltpond, I made it quite clear that from now on, today, we must change our attitudes, our minds. We must realise that from now on we are no more a colonial but a free and independent people! But also, as I pointed out, that entails hard work. I am depending upon the millions of the country, the chiefs and people to help me to reshape the destiny of this country. We are prepared to make it a nation that will be respected by any nation in the world. We know we are going to have a difficult beginning but again I am relying upon your support, I am relying upon your hard work, seeing you here in your thousands, however far my eyes goes. My last warning to you is that you ought to stand firm behind us so that we can prove to the world that when the African is given a chance he can show the world that he is somebody. We are not waiting; we shall no more go back to sleep any more. Today, from now on, there is a new African in the world and that new African is ready to fight his own battle and show that after all the black man is capable of managing his own affairs. We are going to demonstrate to the world, to the other nations, young as we are, that we are prepared to lay our own foundation.

As I said in the Assembly just a few minutes ago, I made a point that we are going to see that we create our own African personality and identity; it is the only way in which we can show the world that we are masters of our own destiny. But today may I call upon you all; at this great day let us all remember that nothing in the world can be done unless it has the support of God. We have done with the battle and we again re-dedicate ourselves in the struggle to emancipate other countries in Africa, for our independence is meaningless unless it is linked up with the total liberation of the African continent.

Let us now, fellow Ghanaians, let us now ask for God's blessing, and in your tens of thousands, I want to ask you to pause for one minute, and give thanks to Almighty God for having led us through obstacles, difficulties, imprisonments, hardships and sufferings to have brought us to the end of our trouble today. One minute silence – Ghana is free forever! And here I will ask the band to play the Ghana national anthem.

Here the Ghana national anthem was played.

I want simply to thank those who have come from abroad to witness this occasion. Here I wish I could quote Marcus Garvey. Once upon a time, he said, he looked through the whole world to see if he could find a government of a black people. He looked around, he did not find one, and he said he was going to create one. Marcus Garvey did not succeed. But here today the work of Rousseau, the work of Marcus Garvey, the work of Aggrey, the work of Casely Hayford, the work of these illustrious men who have gone before us has come to reality at this present moment. And so we thank all of you and I am going to ask the band to play again, because it must sink in and make us realise that from today, we are no more a colonial people. This time, the national anthem is going to be played in honour of the foreign states who are here with us today to witness this occasion and I want you all, those who have hats on, to take off your hats and let the band play our national anthem. And from now on that national anthem is the national anthem of Ghana to be played on all occasions.

The national anthem was played, and played again amid cries of *Freedom! Freedom! Freedom!*

The National Assembly of Ghana met the following morning. Chiefs in their rich robes mingled with distinguished guests in the visitors' gallery. In this colourful and crowded atmosphere the Duchess of Kent read the Queen's speech to the House. I then rose to move 'That a Humble Address be sent to Her Majesty the Queen on behalf of this Assembly':

To Her Most Excellent Majesty Queen Elizabeth the Second, may it please Your Most Gracious Majesty: We, the Speaker and Members of the National Assembly of Ghana, in Parliament assembled, beg leave to offer Your Majesty our sincere thanks for the Gracious Speech with which the First Session of our Parliament has been opened.

Normally speaking the moving of an Address in reply to the Speech from the Throne is an occasion for a general review of the policy of the Government. While on this occasion it is not appropriate for us to have a long debate on the contents of the Speech, nevertheless it would be wrong for me, as the first member of Parliament to speak in the National Assembly of Ghana, not to say something of our hopes and aspirations.

We are today a fully sovereign and independent state subservient to no other nation. This is in itself a great achievement and it is right that we think on those who made independence possible. It would be impossible to give a long list of names of those who have materially assisted us in reaching our goal. Without the self-sacrificing work of many Members of this Parliament, we might not be having these celebrations today. In all parts of the country there are men and women who, by their devotion and sacrifice, have made this day possible. We should not forget also those who, though not citizens of Ghana or even resident here, have assisted us in our struggle for independence. I am glad that some of those who helped us in the days when our prospects seemed darkest are here with us today as guests of an independent Ghana.

The achievement of freedom, sovereignty and independence is the product of the matter and spirit of our people. In the last resort we have only been able to become independent because we were economically, socially and politically able to create the conditions which made independence possible and any other status impossible.

We part from the former imperial power, Great Britain, with the warmest feelings of friendship and goodwill. This is because successive Governments in the United Kingdom recognised the realities of the situation in the Gold Coast and adopted their policy accordingly. Thus, instead of that feeling of bitterness which is often born of a colonial struggle, we enter on our independence in association with Great Britain and with good relations unimpaired. We are proud that we are the first colonial territory in Africa to gain its freedom and to enter into the Commonwealth. We value the Commonwealth link because it brings us closer to other nations who practise the same type of democracy and have the same system of laws which we have established here. Particularly we value it because it brings us into association with the newer Commonwealth countries of Asia whose problems are so akin to our own. We have maintained the ceremonies which have marked the opening of this Parliament because they are common to the countries of the Commonwealth and because they emphasise a common approach to the problems of democracy.

We should be under no delusion about the difficulties of the task which we must undertake at Independence. I am sure that we can surmount all obstacles. Within the lifetime of people now present in this House today our country has been changed out of all recognition. Fifty years ago there were no harbours, scarcely any roads, and life was as primitive as in almost any part of the world. Today we enter on our independence with all the machinery of a modern state. By our own exertions, and almost entirely through finance deriving from the Gold Coast, we have built a fine system of communications, and new roads and bridges have opened up the country. We already possess one excellent port and a great new harbour is under construction. Out of a population of under five million[1] we have today over half a million children at school. We have developed social services and a sound system of finance. Many commercial firms from abroad are investing in our country and we are developing our own light industry. That all this could have been achieved under tropical conditions in so short a time is a tribute to the genius of our people.

Independence is, however, only a milestone on our march to progress. Independence by itself would be useless if it did not lead to great material and cultural advances by our people. In pressing on with these advances we shall be doing more than merely benefiting Ghana. If we in Ghana can work out solutions to the problems which beset the tropics, we shall be making a contribution to Africa and to the world as a whole. By the knowledge and methods which we must develop, if we

[1] See footnote, p. 103.

are ourselves to succeed, we shall aid very materially other territories and enable them the sooner to reach conditions under which they may become independent.

Nevertheless, our most important contribution to the movement for the independence of colonial people will be the force of our example. If we can make a success of our endeavours, it will be demonstrated to the world that a former African colonial territory is as able and capable of conducting its own affairs as any country in the world. This will be an event of tremendous significance. If on the other hand we fail, if we show ourselves disunited, inefficient or corrupt, then we shall have gravely harmed all those millions in Africa who put their trust in us and looked to Ghana to prove that African people can build a state of their own based on democracy, tolerance and racial equality. In striving to create a modern state dedicated to freedom and justice, we shall have many enemies to fight against. Our first task must therefore be to make certain that there is a strong and resolute public opinion which condemns, as anti-social, idleness and neglect; carelessness, which destroys valuable crops or machinery, and corruption which undermines the basis of a sound commercial life. I regard this National Assembly as the most important single body for creating this climate of public opinion which will make possible our progress. If we are to have true democracy it must be based on a free and vigorous Parliament.

We have had parliamentary disputes over the form of our constitution. It would be quite extraordinary if on a matter so important to us all it had been possible to obtain uniformity of opinion. But I consider that the way in which we have met together and in the end reached an agreed compromise solution shows that Ghana has achieved political maturity. Nevertheless, a heavy responsibility rests upon every Member of this Parliament. By our actions the whole future of Africa must be affected. When I spoke in this House in regard to the constitution, I began by quoting the words of a great English politician of the 18th century, Edmund Burke, 'We are on a conspicuous stage and the world marks our demeanour.'

These words are very true of Ghana today. I believe that this House and country will be worthy of the responsibility history has entrusted to us and that we will not disappoint those millions of people in other parts of the world to whom our success or failure will mean so much.

CHAPTER THIRTEEN

BUILDING A NEW NATION

With the achievement of Independence, the main theme of my speeches changed. I began to concentrate on the long-term objectives; economic freedom for Ghana, and African emancipation and unity.

At the end of July 1957, I opened the Bank of Ghana. This was the foundation on which the superstructure of our economic independence would be built. I emphasised the importance which the Government attached to the new bank:

In the modern world, a central bank plays a very important and decisive role in the life of a country. Our political independence will be meaningless unless we use it so as to obtain economic and financial self-government and independence. In order to obtain this, it is of absolute and paramount importance that a central bank should be set up by the Government.

Although we are a small country, and compared with some other countries, not a wealthy one, we have nevertheless accumulated considerable savings. It is therefore right and proper that at this ceremony I should pay a tribute to the men and women of Ghana who have accepted in so responsible a way the Government policy of putting aside as public savings and reserves, money which might otherwise have been devoted to private spending. We owe a duty to the people of this country not only to see that these savings are wisely invested so that they do not depreciate in value, but also to see that they are invested in such a way as to assist in the development of Ghana. There are two ways, and two ways only, by which Ghana can be developed. In the first place, savings accumulated in other countries by governments or by companies or by private individuals, can be invested in Ghana and used to finance our development schemes and projects. Secondly, development can be financed from our own public and private savings. I hope that our development will be financed in both these ways.

In regard to investment from abroad, it would be ungenerous if we did not acknowledge the great value to Ghana of the investments already made here by foreign companies and individuals. It is the intention of my Government, and the wish of the country, to do all we can to encourage such investments, to protect the interests of those who have already invested, and to attract new investors. In this the Bank of Ghana can, and must, play a most important role in assisting to maintain confidence in our own financial system. However, we should be very foolish if we were to depend solely on outside investment to finance our development. In the long run our progress must depend upon the proper utilisation of our own resources. And in this connection the Bank of Ghana must play an even more vital role. In the early days of the development of any country, very naturally local savings were largely invested in Government funds of the imperial or colonial power and in foreign enterprises. But I believe the time has come when it is as safe for the investor to invest in a harbour on the coast of Ghana as it was for him, twenty or thirty years ago, to invest in the docks of Liverpool or London.

We can not expect a foreign investor to put his capital into Ghana if Ghana itself invests all of its own capital outside its boundaries. Whatever may be a country's political relationship to the world, it still, for all practical purposes, remains a colony if the whole of its hard earned savings are invested in some other more developed country. In the narrower field of using our own resources to finance particular commercial enterprises, the Commercial Bank of Ghana and other banks in the country have done most valuable work. The Government now looks to the Bank of Ghana to carry on that work in the wider national and international sphere. In the mobilising of our national resources for the use of the nation, the Bank has a really vital role to play.

I am particularly glad that our national banking institution has been built up in such close co-operation with the Bank of England. We are very fortunate indeed to have secured the expert assistance from the Bank of England and to have established such close ties with them. But, because we have established and will, we hope, maintain this close link with the Bank of England, let no one be in any doubt about the complete independence of our new Bank. That is exactly what it is and we intend the Bank of Ghana to be just what its name says it is – THE BANK OF GHANA. It is essential to our own independence that we have a government owned central bank and that the central bank follows a policy designed to secure our economic independence and to foster the general development of our country.

And now, I feel I must, on behalf of the Government, offer

BUILDING A NEW NATION

my very heartiest congratulations to all those who have been closely concerned in bringing about this great event, and to wish those concerned with the conduct of the Bank, all possible success in this momentous enterprise.

World interest in the affairs of Ghana has been continuous ever since Independence. This is understandable since our development has a direct bearing on the rest of Africa. We in Ghana are now well used to living under a spotlight, but from time to time I find it necessary to get quite away from the centre of affairs to rest, reflect and plan. On these occasions there is always a certain amount of speculation about where I have gone, and why.

In September 1957, I spent three weeks at Half Assini,[1] the first real break that I had enjoyed in seven years. On my return to Accra I broadcast to the nation on the criticisms of the Ghana Government which had appeared in some sections of the world Press as a result of the deportation of Alhaji Osman Lardan and Alhaji Amadu Baba:

I feel that some of the comments have shown an understanding of our problems, and a genuine desire to help. There have been other examples, however, where criticism has been ignorant or malicious – in some cases both – and clearly intended to embarrass the Government of Ghana and to make our task still more difficult. Unfortunately, the net result of all this has been to make some people, particularly abroad, lose all sense of proportion, and to lose sight of the main issues. I am convinced that nothing would be gained by holding a post mortem on past events. What I want to do is to clear the air and remove misunderstanding.

The first duty of a Government is to govern. Hence the preservation of our internal security is paramount. It is imperative. I wonder if those abroad who have criticised us, fully appreciate this problem in Ghana where we have to deal with a complex relationship of feudal, tribal and other factors and where we have to fight against inspired rumours and vicious misrepresentations. It is obvious that we are dealing with conditions quite unlike those in many other countries. Thus we must adopt methods appropriate to the problems we have to solve and still preserve the basic rights of the individual. As to the deportations which led to all this controversy, I have this to say:

[1] A village in Nzima near my birthplace.

May I remind you that the section of the Deportation Act, 1957, under which action was originally taken was not questioned by members of either side when debated in our Parliament. That section simply renewed the powers previously possessed and exercised by the old colonial government. Parliament thus recognised that these powers of deportation are still necessary under existing conditions in Ghana. It has been rumoured that the Government has a list of people it intends to deport. This is not so. But I emphasise again that Government is determined to preserve law and order, and will not tolerate subversive activities in any form. My Government will not hesitate to act if unlawful or subversive – and I repeat the words unlawful and subversive – methods are used to undermine it.

I went on to say that the Government had kept the public fully informed. There was no question of a miscarriage of justice:

The judiciary is unfettered. The most recent African appointments to the Bench include two former politicians who were very active members of the Opposition parties. The latest appointment to the Ghana Appeal Court is an English Queen's Counsel who was a former member of the General Council of the Bar in the United Kingdom.

When the international press and radio comment on our affairs I hope that they will keep facts such as these in mind. I hope that they will constantly strive to increase their understanding of our problems. I also hope that they will appreciate the responsibilities which face us, a new nation, working in an almost blinding limelight of world publicity. And I renew a plea which I made publicly to the world press in London a few weeks ago: do not apply to us standards of conduct and efficiency which are often not attained in your own countries. It is this form of hypocritical criticism which, I believe, does more to arouse anger and resentment than anything else.

It took ten years of concentrated effort to win our political freedom. All our problems could not be settled at once. But as each month passed, there were new and heartening signs of progress and development.

On 17 December, the flag of Ghana was raised for the first time on an ocean-going merchant ship, the s.s. *Volta River*, of our own Black Star Shipping Line. I was at Takoradi to welcome the ship to her home port on that historic day:

It is natural, as we stand here today, that we should think of other nations who, in days gone by, had set out to build up their own maritime fleets from modest beginnings. I recall Henry of Portugal, who was called the Navigator, and in whose vessels Vasco da Gama sailed to these shores and even further south to discover the Cape of Good Hope and the way to the East. We now follow in the footsteps of these early pioneers.

s.s. Volta River will not be sailing in uncharted seas for today sea routes are well defined: she will, however, carry not only Ghana produce and goods, but, also our goodwill to places far away. As she enters foreign ports all will know by her distinctive funnel, and the flag she flies, that she comes from Ghana and that she is Ghana's own. This is one of the small and humble beginnings we are undertaking in order to shape the destiny of this country. I am glad that *s.s. Volta River* will shortly be joined by five chartered vessels. This will enable the Black Star Line to provide a regular service to and from Ghana and other parts in West Africa to the United Kingdom and Europe and, as occasions arise, to other countries. We hope in the very near future to organise a special service linking all the countries and territories in West Africa. Our ships will then ply along the West African coast and carry goods and passengers to all the West African ports.

The building up of a national shipping line cannot be done overnight, especially as it is our aim and desire that our ships are manned as soon as possible by Ghanaians. Training to be captains, engineers and navigators of necessity takes time; the examinations required for these positions are exacting, but they are in themselves a challenge to the young men of Ghana who want to see their country advance and who I know will be willing to join this venture of the seas. Service in the Merchant Navy has long been recognised in other nations as one of the most valuable ways to serve one's country. The possibility of establishing a regular Chana Navy is being considered, and this will offer further opportunities for service to Ghana. And when the Ghana Navy comes to be supported by a Ghana Air Force, then surely we are on the way to progress.

I thanked all those who had helped to establish the new shipping line, and said that I hoped young men would consider seriously a career in the Merchant Navy. The opportunities were boundless, the rewards considerable. We looked forward to the day when the *Volta River*, or some other Black Star ship would enter Takoradi under the command of a Ghanaian master. After brief reference to our foreign policy, which I said was based on economic and cultural co-operation with all countries, I officially inaugurated the Black Star Shipping Line.

Just over a week later, I addressed the first meeting of the Internation Missionary Assembly in Accra. Representatives of thirty-five different countries attended. I welcomed them and told them that their conference could do immeasurable good if they faced squarely the moral challenge of emergent Africa, and brought to it the vision and steadfast service shown by their brave predecessors in the missionary field. I hoped that they would take back with them a message and a challenge:

You see Africa. You see the ambitions and hopes of millions of Africans who, so far, have had the crumbs of civilisation falling from the rich tables of the Western world. The Africans of today are only at the beginning of their adventure. They need education. They need advancement. They need capital without which no progress to the higher opportunities of life is possible. Yet what do we Africans see when we look abroad? We see wealthy nations pouring out their vast treasure on sterile arms. We see powerful peoples engaged in a futile and destructive armaments' race. We see the precious capital that might help to raise up Africa and Asia flung away to potential destruction. What has this to do with the Christian charity proclaimed by the West? Or the human brotherhood we hear so much about from the East? Seen from the angle of Africa's needs and hopes, the Great Powers' rivalry looks like one thing only – a senseless fratricidal struggle to destroy the very substance of humanity.

So I would say that the unity that you represent here and the further unity which you seek in these talks, are symbols of the whole world's profoundest need. We salute your efforts. We are proud that Ghana should be the scene of your deliberations and we pray that the values you stand for and the hopes you represent may prevail in your hearts, in the development of this young country and in the great family of mankind.

On Christmas Eve I broadcast to the nation. The year 1957 is now indelibly written into the history of Ghana for all time as the year of our freedom and independence. I spoke of the already substantial development of the country, and of my Government's plans for the future:

My first objective is to abolish from Ghana poverty, ignorance and disease. We shall measure our progress by the improvement in the health of our people; by the number of children in school, and by the quality of their education; by the availability of water and electricity in our towns and villages, and by the happiness which our people take in being able to manage their own affairs. The welfare of our people is our chief pride, and it is by this that my government will ask to be judged.

At the present stage of Ghana's economic development the whole community must act in the national interest. In fact most of our development so far has had to be carried out by the Government itself. There is no other way out, for our people lack the capital and technical know-how to embark on great industrial undertakings. We cannot agree with those who say that such state participation is a denial of democracy. We have only to look at Sweden, Britain, Australia and many other countries to prove such a statement to be false. For our own part we are sure that, hand in hand with political and economic democracy, there will be plenty of scope for free enterprise to flourish throughout Ghana. Again and again I have emphasised that we welcome foreign investment and will protect it. In our foreign relations we do not forget that we are a part of the Commonwealth. And we do not need to mention our good relations with Great Britain. But at the same time we wish to maintain good relationships with all other countries.

The world, I said, was divided into ideological blocs feverishly arming for mutual annihilation with atomic and hydrogen bombs, and inter-continental missiles. Yet mankind wanted peace:

You may ask what we, in this small defenceless country, can contribute towards world peace? What can we say to the statesmen and leaders of the great powers? Is it not simply this? That we should plead with them to turn their swords into ploughshares and to use their vast scientific and technical resources for the common good of mankind. God knows that we in Africa are sick and tired of war and strife, for our continent has been for centuries the scene of tribal conflicts and foreign exploitation. Today we have a vested interest in peace, for only in a peaceful world will we in Ghana be able to realise our aspirations and make our contribution to the happiness and prosperity of mankind. Therefore, as we in this country gather around the family circle to celebrate once again the birthday of our Lord and Saviour, I want on behalf of not only the people of Ghana but of all Africans, to appeal to the statesmen and leaders of the great powers – East and West – to try and resolve their differences and ambitions by peaceful means and thereby save the world and civilisation from destruction. In pursuit of this supreme objective of peace, Ghana will give her fullest and unqalified support.

Thus, our Christmas message from Africa to the leaders in the West and in the East, inspired by the teachings of Christ, is simply this: 'We pray that you will meet in the coming year and make a supreme effort to resolve at least sufficient of your differences to let you start disarming and thus free the peoples of Africa from some of the fear which you have thrust into our lives. Next consider jointly how the vast resources now wasted in the production of frightful atomic and hydrogen weapons of destruction could best be used to remove the poverty and sufferings from the lives of hundreds of millions of peoples in Africa and Asia. Then, and only then, will fear be banished from our continent and true respect and lasting friendship be the basis of our dealings with each other.'

This is no time for hatred and recrimination. We in Ghana are prepared to forget the past and to make any sacrifice of our national sovereignty towards the attainment of world peace. So, as we say farewell to the closing year, let us hope that 1958 will bring with it a lessening in the present tension between the great powers and better understanding between nations and peoples regardless of race, tribe, colour and creed.

CHAPTER FOURTEEN

THE SECOND DEVELOPMENT PLAN

The first two years after Independence, from 1 July 1957 to 30 June 1959, was set aside as a period of consolidation. A Second Development Plan was prepared to cover the period. During that time we intended to complete certain projects which had been started during our First Development Plan; to undertake additional works which merited priority, and to reach a decision about the Volta River project.

On 20 February 1958, I stated in the Assembly my Government's policy for national development. I emphasised three fundamental points. First, we were determined to achieve economic independence. Second, we intended to develop our resources so as to produce a strong, healthy and balanced economy. Third, we hoped to reduce our economic vulnerability by lessening our dependence on a single crop, cocoa. I spoke of the Second Development Plan, and of important work to be done in the spheres of education, medicine and communications. There were plans for new schools, hospitals, roads, and buildings of all kinds. More towns and villages would enjoy the benefits of a piped water supply:

Work on the preparation of the Second Development Plan started some weeks ago and Ghana is fortunate in having at its disposal experts of recognised international standing now engaged in the preparation of this new plan. It is impossible to be precise, at this stage, as to the magnitude of expenditure over the five year period, but we should like to achieve a rate of development of the order of twenty million pounds annually. The new Plan will thus require one hundred million pounds, over five years. We envisage this expenditure as the sum total of a carefully calculated and planned operation.

Having achieved independence, my Government's primary objective must be to maintain and consolidate that independence. And this is no less important in the economic sense as in its political meaning. We are determined to maintain, and if possible to increase, the momentum of our development effort. As I have remarked, the problem of manpower is already receiving very careful consideration. It is the intention of my Government to save manpower wherever possible by simplifying administrative, financial and legal procedures. A start on this has already been made and we have established an Organisation and Methods Division which has been reinforced by expert assistance provided by the United Nations. We intend to pursue our present policy of Africanisation to the limit consistent with efficient government, and simultaneously to make up our shortages of administrative and technical personnel by additional recruitment from the world market.

We will do everything in our power to build up and maintain a government machine which will be capable of conducting efficiently the ordinary business of government, and simultaneously of playing its full part in the execution of our development programme.

I expressed the hope that the Second Development Plan would be completed in sufficient detail within the next six to nine months, so that the House would be able to debate it before the end of the year. We intended at all times to consult regional and local authorities.

Both the Agricultural and the Industrial Development Corporations would have a most important part to play in putting the Plan into operation. If the plan was to succeed, substantial investment was necessary:

In order to stimulate development in the private sector of our economy, my Government is now considering new measures designed to encourage overseas investments in Ghana, and also to assist our local investors. We have recently brought to this country several experts in the field of foreign investment, and we hope that we will gain materially from their suggestions.

It is my Government's intention to stimulate overseas investment by establishing an Industrial Promotion Division. If it is to be successful it must have at its command the services of a person with international experience of such work, and with a standing sufficient to command respect in commercial and industrial circles. Steps are about to be taken to find such a person, and the necessary staff to support him in his task. Members will recall that we have now established an Interim Investment Board and we hope that this will facilitate the handling of enquiries and proposals from private investors.

I have dwelt at some length on industrial development, for

many of our hopes for Ghana's future are directly related to it. Industrial development demands the availability of good services – communications, power, water. In the new plan, we shall continue to pay special attention to communications – the improvement of our roads, which are already a credit to our country; the maintenance of good rail and air services; the provision of first class port facilities; and the expansion of our new shipping operation, the Black Star Line.

Electric power is essential. The Government's intention to build a big new steam power station at Tema has already been announced, and this is directly related to our plans for industrial development. Rural electrification will also receive special attention in the new plan.

I went on to say that education, as in the past, would continue to remain one of the main pillars, if not *the* main pillar, of the Government's effort in the Second Development Plan. We hoped to produce a balanced programme which would continue to improve the general standard of education of all our young people:

Health and sanitation will also receive particular consideration, for their importance to the well-being of our entire population is well recognised. We shall do our best to expand existing services and to provide new facilities.

We intend to examine carefully the possibilities of building up a tourist industry.

Nor do we intend to forget the Arts. I hope very much that we can build a National Cultural Centre where our own musicians and singers, and artists of international repute can perform.

In preparing the new plan we shall keep the problem of employment constantly in mind. Clearly one of our ultimate objectives must be an expanded and diversified economy which offers plenty of opportunity for all our people to work, especially the younger ones with their new skills and training. As an immediate measure, we believe that the new Builders' Brigade will have much useful work to do in the next plan, in addition to the mass education and community development efforts.

Many other factors will also need to be taken into consideration, but I do not intend to enumerate them here except to emphasise that we shall ensure that our national security is maintained, and indeed strengthened. This means a strong and efficient police force, and the maintenance of our army in first class condition. The new plan will provide the necessary facilities for these vital services which are one of the essential safeguards of our independence.

I referred to the technical assistance which we were receiving from the United Nations and from the governments of the U.S.A., the United Kingdom and Israel. Experts and technical advisers specialising in agriculture and health had already arrived, and a research programme was in full swing.

The Volta River project had next to be considered. I explained some of the reasons for the delay in proceeding with it:

Since Independence, we have been examining various ways in which the necessary capital might be raised. This has proved to be an exceedingly difficult task. We have encountered many difficulties. Let me tell you some of them.

First of all, the attitude of other Governments which might be interested in participating in the project has been that we should first come to a satisfactory arrangement with the aluminium companies. On the other hand, the aluminium companies have adopted the attitude that they wish to be assured of certain things in advance, for example, the cost of power. The cost of power, however, is dependent upon the conditions under which other Governments might lend us money and you can thus see easily how a vicious circle of negotiation has been created. A further difficulty has been the recession which is now so evident in the dollar and sterling areas. This has meant that the other parties interested in the Volta scheme would prefer to defer taking a decision at this time. This may be understandable, but Ghana cannot endlessly accept a situation where under boom conditions she is told that the Volta scheme would take too long to bring into production, and then in a phase of recession is told that the necessary capital cannot be raised. Another major factor which has increased our difficulties has been the decision of the British authorities last September to increase the bank rate to 7%. I cannot see how the Volta scheme, or indeed any important Commonwealth development can be carried out entirely from sterling sources with such a crippling rate of interest. Some weeks ago I came to the conclusion that we must seek to break this apparent deadlock. I therefore approached President Eisenhower personally. The President has replied to me emphasising the interest of the United States in Ghana and its future development. While noting the very real difficulties which exist in undertaking so great a scheme as the Volta River project, the President has offered to use the good offices of the United States Government in examining possible ways under which the scheme might be started.

Naturally, my Government has gratefully accepted this offer from President Eisenhower, and has informed the British Government and Aluminium Limited accordingly. But before taking any further steps with the United States Government, my Government wishes to have a general review with Aluminium Limited, the company which has so far been principally concerned with this scheme, and which holds the bauxite concessions in the Aya-Yenahin area. I anticipate that this review will take place shortly.

It is my strong belief that the Volta River project provides the quickest and most certain method of leading us towards economic independence. We appreciate that the magnitude of the scheme increases the initial difficulty of raising the necessary capital. On the other hand, my Government sees no satisfactory alternative way of resolving this basic problem of political economy, and therefore intends to strive energetically in co-operation with those Governments which we have already approached and with other interested parties, to bring the project into operation.

Such are our achievements and our plans for the development of our country. We have done much in the past, but much more remains to be achieved in the future. Development is not an end in itself, but a means to an end. In this sense I cannot do better than to repeat something which I said in the course of my Christmas Eve broadcast: 'My first objective is to abolish from Ghana poverty, ignorance and disease. We shall measure our progress by the improvement in the health of our people; by the number of children in school, and by the availability of water and electricity in our towns and villages, and by the happiness which our people take in being able to manage their own affairs. The welfare of our people is our chief pride, and it is by this that my government will ask to be judged.'

At the fourteenth Annual Conference of the Trade Union Congress, I invited delegates to co-operate fully in the Development Plan. I suggested that they joined with the United Ghana Farmers' Council, the Co-operative Movement, and my Government, to form a united team:

We need you as much as you need us. For we are dedicated

to the same cause – the industrial development of our country and the economic emancipation of our people. With your support I have absolute confidence in our future.

What we need is unity and tranquillity at home and peace abroad. Today, peace is not only indivisable but the supreme and universal need of mankind. For the first time in history, the world is threatened with total destruction. Our dreams and hopes for a better and richer life now hang on the balance and that is why I have appealed to the statesmen of the Great Powers to turn their backs upon war and the preparation of war, and to think and work for peace. Small and insignificant as we are, Ghana is prepared to make any sacrifice towards the attainment of a lasting world peace. Sometimes I wonder whether it would not be helpful if we in Ghana, and all other like-minded nations, established a separate Ministry of Peace as opposed to ministries of defence and war, which could devote itself exclusively to considering ways and means by which international tension could be reduced and under-standing between the peoples of all nations increased. This would inspire us all to dedicate our national energies and resources to the cause of universal peace and to the total happiness of mankind.

Imagine what we in Ghana could do with only an infini-tesimal part of the monies squandered by the great powers of East and West upon atomic and hydrogen bombs, inter-continental missiles and other weapons of mass destruction? With such financial resources we would fight the only war worth fighting in the modern world, the battle against poverty, disease, illiteracy and superstition.

CHAPTER FIFTEEN

THE 'AFRICAN PERSONALITY'

Shortly after the Independence celebrations in 1957, I invited all the independent states in Africa to attend a conference in Accra early in 1958 to discuss questions of mutual interest. For months, the ambassadors of those African nations with representation in London met to prepare the ground for the Conference. Two missions from Ghana visited Cairo to consult with the Egyptian government. Then a delegation, headed by our Minister of Justice, visited the capitals of all the other participating nations. Plans and arrangements were completed, and a few days before the Conference opened I broadcast to the nation to explain its importance:

For the first time, I think, in the history of this great continent, leaders of all the purely African states which can play an independent role in international affairs will meet to discuss the problems of our countries and take the first steps towards working out an African contribution to international peace and goodwill. For too long in our history, Africa has spoken through the voices of others. Now, what I have called an African Personality in international affairs will have a chance of making its proper impact and will let the world know it through the voices of Africa's own sons.

At this conference, we shall exchange views on political, economic, social and cultural matters of common concern to all participating countries and hope thereby to establish a basis for future co-operation in these fields. We shall not forget our brethren in many parts of Africa who unfortunately do not yet enjoy the freedom we have won. Not only shall we hope to work out means by which freedom so dearly won will be preserved, but we shall also be concerned to give encouragement and hope to all not yet free to their destiny. The success of this conference and the sense of responsibility with which we approach our discussions will, I believe, be a measure of the readiness and ability of all Africans to manage their own domestic and international affairs.

It is unfortunate that this conference is restricted to only eight independent, truly African states. The participating countries jointly decided that it would be impracticable at this stage to invite countries which are unfortunately not yet able to speak for themselves internationally. We regret this omission, which further underlines the urgency of freeing this continent of foreign domination. I sincerely hope, however, that very shortly the opportunity will occur for making the voices of all these other dependent countries in Africa heard.

I believe that the fact that eminent leaders of political thought and action of the free states of Africa can come together to discuss matters of mutual interest is in itself momentous. During the next ten days, the whole world will be turning its eyes to Africa. By our concerted action, we have a chance of proving that we have a positive and constructive contribution to make to the work of the international communities to which we belong, whether it be the Commonwealth, the Afro-Asian community or the United Nations. I believe we shall not fail.

Two days later, on 15 April, I welcomed the representatives of Ethiopia, Libya, Tunisia, Morocco, Egypt, Liberia and the Sudan to the Accra Conference. This first conference of independent African states was, I think, the most significant event in the history of Africa for many centuries:

This is a memorable gathering. It is the first time in history that representatives of independent sovereign states in Africa are meeting together with the aim of forging closer links of friendship, brotherhood, co-operation and solidarity between them.

As we look back into the history of our continent, we cannot escape the fact that we have for too long been the victims of foreign domination. For too long we have had no say in the management of our own affairs or in deciding our own destinies. Now times have changed, and today we are the masters of our own fate. This fact is evidenced in our meeting together here as independent sovereign states out of our own free will to speak our minds openly, to argue and discuss, to share our experiences, our aspirations, our dreams and our hopes in the interests of Mother Africa.

What is the purpose of this historic Conference? We are here to know ourselves and to exchange views on matters of common interest; to explore ways and means of consolidating and safe-guarding our hard-won independence; to strengthen the economic and cultural ties between our countries to find

workable arrangements for helping our brothers still languish-
ing under colonial rule; to examine the central problem which
dominates the world today, namely the problem of how to
secure peace. And, finally, to send out an appeal to the great
powers of the world to do whatever they can to save the world
from destruction, and humanity from annihilation. As we
watch the efforts being made to convene a Summit Conference,
we would ask the great powers to make a supreme effort to
resolve their differences. In any case, we appeal to them to
live in tolerant and peaceful co-existence, and to leave us to
live our own lives. These objectives constitute the main
purpose of our conference.

I outlined the past history of Africa and spoke of the two great
dangers which still threatened large parts of the continent –
colonialism and racialism:

We have learnt much about the old forms of colonialism. Some
of them still exist, but I am confident they will all disappear
from the face of our continent. It is not only the old forms of
colonialism that we are determined to see abolished, but we
are equally determined that the new forms of colonialism
which are now appearing in the world, with their potential
threat to our precious independence, will not succeed.
    Similarly with racialism. Many of the advocates of
colonialism claimed in the past – as some of them do now –
they were racially superior and had a special mission to
colonise and rule other people. This we reject. We repudiate
and condemn all forms of racialism, for racialism not only
injures those against whom it is used but warps and perverts
the very people who preach and protect it; and when it
becomes a guiding principle in the life of any nation, as it has
become in some other parts of Africa, then that nation digs
its own grave. It is inconceivable that a racial minority will
be able for ever to maintain its totalitarian domination over
an awakened majority.
    We, the independent states of Africa, seek to eliminate
racialism by our own example of a tolerant, multi-racial community reflecting the freely expressed will of the people based
upon universal adult suffrage. Within our own countries we
must try to practise goodwill towards individuals and
minorities, and we must also endeavour to demonstrate the
same attitude in our relations with other nations. In this way,
we who in the past have had unhappy experiences with
racialism, will be in a position to make a new and positive

contribution to the elimination of racialism based on tolerance and goodwill, which can serve as an example to other parts of Africa and to the world.

Colonialism had often in the past caused tension between European countries. I spoke of the way in which colonies had been used as pawns in the game of power politics. We ought to give every possible encouragement to freedom fighters throughout Africa, who were trying to free their countries from foreign rule:

> Africa is the last remaining stronghold of colonialism. Unlike Asia, there are on the continent of Africa more dependent territories than independent sovereign nations. Therefore we, the free independent states of Africa, have a responsibility to hasten the total liberation of Africa. I believe that there are lessons from the past which will help us in discharging this sacred duty.
>
> If I have spoken of racialism and colonialism it is not, as I have said, because I want to indulge in recrimination with any country by listing a catalogue of wrongs which have been perpetrated upon our continent in the past. My only purpose in doing so is to illustrate the different forms which colonialism and imperialism old and new can take, so that we can be on our guard in adopting measures to safeguard our hard-won independence and national sovereignty. The imperialists of today endeavour to achieve their ends not merely by military means, but by economic penetration, cultural assimilation, ideological domination, psychological infiltration, and subversive activities even to the point of inspiring and promoting assassination and civil strife. Very often these methods are adopted in order to influence the foreign policies of small and uncommitted countries in a particular direction. Therefore we, the leaders of resurgent Africa, must be alert and vigilant.
>
> We, the delegates of this Conference, in promoting our foreign relations, must endeavour to seek the friendship of all and the enmity of none. We stand for international peace and security in conformity with the United Nations Charter. This will enable us to assert our own African personality and to develop according to our own ways of life, our own customs, traditions and cultures. In asserting our African personality we shall be free to act in our individual and collective interests at any particular time. We shall also be able to exert our influence on the side of peace and to uphold the rights of all people to decide for themselves their own forms of government

as well as the right of all peoples, regardless of race, colour or creed to lead their own lives in freedom and without fear. This inalienable right was emphasised and endorsed in the five principles, recognised at the Bandung and other conferences, which are now well known, namely, non-aggression, non-interference in each other's internal affairs, equality, mutual benefit and peaceful co-existence. I am confident that we, the representatives of free independent states of Africa here assembled, will re-affirm our support for these principles.

˙ In the past, the economic pattern of our countries was linked with the metropolitan powers of Europe and we have been accustomed to look to them for the maintenance of our markets and sources of supply. As independent states, it is in our mutual interest to explore trade possibilities between our respective countries while at the same time enlarging our trade with the rest of the world. In this connection we should exchange trade missions among ourselves. While doing all we can by our own efforts to develop our economies, and so strengthen our political independence, we should at the same time welcome economic assistance offered through the organisations of the United Nations, such as the proposed Regional Economic Commission for Africa. We shall also welcome other forms of economic aid from outside the United Nations, provided it does not compromise our independence.

The independent African states, I said, must co-operate to improve the standard of living of their peoples. Most African governments faced the same sort of problems. Education and health were of major importance. I then went on to speak of cultural co-operation, and of foreign policy:

Addressing ourselves to the cultural aspects of our relationship, we must also examine ways and means to broaden and strengthen our association with one another through such means as the exchange of students and the visits of cultural, scientific and technical missions, both governmental and non-governmental, and the establishment of libraries specialising in various aspects of African history and culture which may become centres of research. There are no limits to ways in which we on this African continent can enrich our knowledge of our past civilisations and cultural heritage through our co-operative efforts and the pooling of our scientific and technical resources.

The goals which we have set before us require a world of order and security in which we can live and work in tran-

quillity towards their realisation. That is why we have a vested
interest in world peace. Our foreign policies must therefore
be such as to contribute towards the realisation of that fundamental objective. As free and independent nations we must
also endeavour to follow the policy of positive non-alignment
so as to enable us at any time to adopt measures which will
best suit our national interests and promote the cause of peace.
It is only by avoiding entanglement in the quarrels of the
great powers that we shall be able to assert our African
personality on the side of peace in conformity with the Charter
of the United Nations.

At the present time the great powers are spending astro-
nomical sums of money on piling up stocks of the most
destructive weapons that have ever been contrived; weapons
which, if employed, will wipe out mankind and leave this
earth barren and desolate. If these great powers can be persuaded to divert a small fraction of this precious capital, which
they are now using for destructive ends, to finance the
economic and social programmes of the under-developed
countries of the world, it will not only raise the standard of
living in these countries, but will also contribute greatly to
the general cause of humanity and the attainment of world
peace.

Like hundreds of millions of people all over the world we
appeal to all the powers concerned to cease the testing of
nuclear weapons. Radioactive winds know no international
frontiers and it is these tests – in a period of so called peace –
which can do more than anything else to threaten our very
existence. But what do we hear? At the very moment when a
Summit Conference is being contemplated it is reputed that
plans are being made to use the Sahara as a testing ground for
nuclear weapons. We vehemently condemn this proposal and
protest against the use of our continent for such purposes. We
appeal to the United Nations to call a halt to this threat to our
safety.

It was essential, I said, that we should demonstrate our ability
to settle our own problems in Africa:

We must leave no stone unturned in our endeavours to lessen
tensions in Africa no less than elsewhere, as every success which
we are able to achieve in resolving issues like frontier disputes,
tribal quarrels and racial and religious antagonisms, will be a
step forward in the bringing about of world peace. To the
extent that we are able by our own exertion and example, to

maintain peace and friendship within our own states and on our continent, will we be in a position to exert moral pressures elsewhere and help to quench the flames of war which could destroy us all.

Today we are one. If in the past the Sahara divided us, now it unites us. And an injury to one is an injury to all of us. From this Conference must go out a new message: 'Hands off Africa! Africa must be free!'

The Conference resulted, as indeed I hoped it would, in a great upsurge of interest in the cause of African emancipation and unity. Day to day news of the discussions and of the decisions reached were broadcast from the studios of our own Radio Ghana.

I opened the new Broadcasting House of Radio Ghana just over a month before the Accra Conference. On that occasion, I spoke of Ghana's unique position of responsibility, especially in relation to the dependent territories in Africa. 'We are taking steps,' I said, 'to investigate the possibilities of external broadcasting for Ghana as a means of projecting ourselves further in Africa and overseas. The Ghana Broadcasting Service has already achieved a high standard; but we intend to develop it further and to make our broadcasting service one of which every Ghanaian will be justly proud.'

The listening public in Ghana, as indeed in the rest of Africa, is increasing all the time. People are better informed than ever before. I frequently broadcast when I have something important for the whole country to hear. It seems a long time since the early days, when I had to reach the people through mass meetings, or through the columns of newspapers.

On 5 July 1958, on my return from a tour to the seven countries which took part in the Accra Conference, I broadcast a report. I explained that there were fifteen men in our party, and our purpose was to convey to the heads of states and governments, many of whom were unable to attend the Conference personally, the good wishes of the government and people of Ghana:

Everywhere we went our goodwill mission was enthusiastically received, not only in official circles, but also by the common folk. In fact, we were often embarrassed by the spontaneous demonstrations of the people, such was their joy in having us as their country's guests.

Fortified by your prayers and good wishes, we set off from

Accra aboard the special chartered 'Ajax' B.O.A.C. plane in the early morning of May 29th. By the time we returned in the afternoon of the 28th June, we had travelled over 20,000 miles and had been in the air for 70 hours.

Despite the strenuous nature of the tour, and the full programmes prepared for us (we seldom had a free moment for ourselves) I am pleased to report that we all stood up well under the strain. I am equally happy to say, that I could not have wished for more pleasant companions.

Messrs Krobo Edusei, Padmore and Tachie-Menson were the life of our party. To all of them I want to express my thanks for their loyal support and devotion to duty and for their pleasant companionship which contributed to lighten my heavy burdens and to make the tour an outstanding success.

We went first to Ethiopia, where we were received by His Imperial Majesty Haile Selassie I, the father of the young Prince who headed his country's delegation to the Accra Conference. Then we flew to the Republic of the Sudan, and from there to the United Kingdom of Libya. Leaving Libya, we flew to Tunisia, where we were received by my old friend President Habib Bourguiba. In view of the tension then existing between Tunisia and France over the Algerian war, our visit was deeply appreciated as a true expression of our solidarity with them when they needed the moral support of their friends.

From Tunisia we proceeded by sea to Morocco, where we were entertained by King Mohammed V. Then from Casablanca we flew non-stop to Cairo. It was the longest hop of our tour, and lasted thirteen hours:

In Cairo, we were received by President Nasser who welcomed me and my party at the airport. As Head of State it was an expression of friendship which I greatly appreciated. The President and myself rode together in an open car through the main streets of Cairo where we were almost mobbed by enthusiastic crowds.

Our stay in Egypt was the longest of the tour. It provided me with an opportunity of seeing much of the industrial, agricultural, scientific and educational activities sponsored by the Government since the revolution and to visit historic places of interest such as the Pyramids and other ancient ruins like the Sphinx.

From Cairo we flew across the Sahara desert to Liberia by way of Kano in Northern Nigeria. In Monrovia we were

welcomed at the airport by my old and esteemed friend
President William Tubman, who you will remember headed
his country's delegation to the Accra Conference. There we
spent a most pleasant three days. Then we returned home to
our families and friends on the afternoon of June 28th. You
can imagine our delight at this reunion. Our homecoming
welcome surpassed our greatest expectations, for which I want
to express my heartfelt thanks and appreciation to all the
people of our dear country.

Let me now try to sum up my impressions of the tour.
Politically, I consider that our mission was a complete success.
Apart from making new friends and renewing old friendships,
the visits to the various capitals enabled me to exchange views
with the Heads of States and Governments on international
developments since the Accra Conference. I was also able to
discuss ways and means of further strengthening ties of friendship between our respective countries and improving economic and cultural relations. The steps agreed upon to
implement these objectives were embodied in a series of com-
muniques. In addition to these matters the tour also provided
me with an opportunity to discuss with other African statesmen a problem very close to my heart, namely, the speedy
liberation of all dependent territories in Africa from colonialism, imperialism and racialism.

Long before we achieved our independence, I made it quite
clear that Ghana's freedom would be meaningless if it was not
linked with the total liberation of the entire continent of
Africa. One of the main objectives of the Accra Conference
was therefore to explore all conceivable avenues to see to the
complete termination as soon as possible of the degrading
system of imperialism and racialism from our countries. But
in order to be of assistance to those who look to us for inspiration and leadership, we must jealously safeguard our hard won
independence, sovereignty and territorial integrity.

In this connection, I want to say with all the emphasis at
my command that as long as I am responsible for the peace
and security of Ghana I shall not allow myself to be influenced
by anyone in neglecting to adopt any means necessary to safeguard our hard won freedom and independence against the
machinations and intrigues of those who openly or sub-
versively try to undermine our national unity and rob us of
our independence. One only has to look around the world
today to see evidence of the tragic consequences which have
overtaken many of the recently independent Afro-Asian
nations because their leaders failed to take timely precau-

tionary measures against those who will not shrink from using undemocratic methods to undermine and overthrow democracy. Countrymen and countrywomen, I shall not fail in the fulfilment of my duty and I expect your loyal support.

Let me remind all of you irrespective of your colour, creed, race, or tribe that a great responsibility lies on us all, and that we can only succeed in shouldering this great and honourable responsibility by closing our ranks and uniting our efforts in the service of our motherland. I appeal to you all to develop further and re-activate our sense of national pride and patriotism which made it possible for Ghana to achieve political independence in a record time. I shall make known to you at the appropriate time our next five year plan. The implementation of that plan will testify our indomitable confidence in the future. I further appeal to you to mobilise all your energies to enable us to achieve as speedily as possible the economic emancipation for our country and the liberation of all dependent territories in Africa.

CHAPTER SIXTEEN

VISIT TO AMERICA

My visit to America arose out of an invitation from President
Eisenhower, extended through Vice President Nixon at the time
of Ghana's independence ceremonies in March 1957. For more
than a year I looked forward to going to the United States in my
official capacity as Prime Minister of the newly independent
Ghana. It would, in a way, be the fulfilment of the hopes and
dreams of my student days at Lincoln University, and would
provide an opportunity to renew old friendships.

Personal and sentimental reasons alone, however, would not
have been sufficient to take me away from Ghana during that
troubled summer of 1958. But tension was still high in the Middle
East, following Suez, and American troops had landed in the
Lebanon. Arab-Israel relations could hardly have been worse.
There was trouble on the borders between Egypt and the Sudan;
serious unrest in Algeria. For these reasons it seemed a good time
to discuss problems of common interest with American
leaders.

I had domestic as well as world problems in mind. The
economic and social development of Ghana, particularly the
Volta River project and the second five year development plan
were both subjects I wanted to discuss. I hoped also for the opportunity to explain to the American public the significance of
recent events in Ghana, including the Accra Conference, which
foreshadowed the emergence of a distinctive 'African personality'.

My eagerness to undertake this visit was heightened by an
invitation from Mr Diefenbaker and his government to pay a
short official visit to Canada before going on to Washington. I
had met the Canadian Prime Minister at the Commonwealth
Prime Ministers' Conference in London in 1957, and I was glad
of the opportunity to renew the friendship.

We flew from Accra to Montreal by way of Lisbon and after
a day in Montreal we travelled by road to Ottawa. On 21 July
I addressed the House of Commons and Senate in Ottawa:

We in Ghana have a strong feeling of pride in our Commonwealth membership. . . . On attaining our independence, we chose to become a member of the Commonwealth of our own free will. We enjoy the same institutions of parliamentary democracy and the same climate of politics and public morality as the other members; we have the same respect for tradition and the same regard for ceremonial; we place the same value on the human individual and appreciate the dignity of restraint; we accept the sovereignty of Law and the sanctity of the pledged word.

I spoke of Canada's role as founder of the Commonwealth. Canada had provided a shining example of the way in which different racial groups can live and work together in a spirit of tolerance and mutual confidence. 'Just as you in Canada,' I said, 'have given the world the benefit of your experience and views . . . so we in Africa hope that we shall also be able to contribute fresh views and knowledge for the common benefit of the community of nations.' I reminded them of the Accra Conference:

We are endeavouring to establish among ourselves in Africa a fundamental unity of domestic and foreign policy which could be of special significance to the role of the African nations in international affairs. We are determined to work together in the political, economic, social and cultural fields with the object of raising the standard of life of our peoples, and of making a distinctive African contribution to international discussions and the achievement of world peace.

There was nothing incompatible with Ghana's effectiveness as a member of the United Nations and the Commonwealth and with our 'African' objectives. On foreign affairs, I explained that basically we pursued a policy of non-alignment and positive neutrality. We hoped to see an end of nuclear tests and some degree of general disarmament. With regard to developments in the Middle East, I said:

We believe that any attempts to pass judgment on what has passed would at this stage simply heighten tension, and that the task now is to secure a workable solution for the future. This, we suggest, could be based on three principles – the substitution of a United Nations force for the American troops now in Lebanon, the holding of free elections in that country under United Nations supervision, and the subsequent establishment of Lebanon as a free and independent state with a status of neutrality internationally guaranteed on the analogy of Austria.

Finally, I spoke of our domestic development, emphasising our desire to start the industrialisation of our country at the same time as we increased the productivity of our agriculture. The development of resources in less developed countries had an important bearing on more advanced industrial nations. Western economies were dependent on adequate supplies of raw materials. Everyone wanted to see the maintenance of a high level of employment and the expansion of world trade. 'In recent years,' I concluded, 'I believe that this common interest and identity of purpose between the wealthier nations and the less developed areas has not been adequately recognised.' I expressed the hope that greater attention would be paid to the political implications of economic development.

I was most impressed with the industrial development that I saw during my brief visit to Canada, and my one regret was that I could not stay longer and see more of that great country. Work was nearing completion on the St Lawrence Seaway and I had the opportunity of inspecting a part of this enormous project when we motored from Montreal to Ottawa.

In Ottawa my party and I were accommodated in the Château Laurier. This imposing hotel, with its strong Victorian atmosphere, was a complete contrast to the ulta-modernity of the new Queen Elizabeth Hotel in Montreal where we had spent the previous night. But the solidness and warmth of the place stuck me as being more typical of the Canadians than the impersonal internationalism that clings to plastics, formica and chromium plate.

I was fascinated by the Canadian Mounted Police who provided an escort for me throughout my stay in Canada. What I admired most about them was that not only were they smart and picturesque, but they were outstandingly efficient at their job.

After four days in Canada, I flew south to Washington to begin my visit to America. Our official visit to the United States began at 11.30 a.m. on 23 July, when our plane landed at Washington Airport. Members of my party included the Minister for Trade and Industries, the Hon. Kojo Botsio, and Mrs Botsio, and the Minister for Information and Broadcasting, the Hon. Kofi Baako. Mr A. L. Adu and Mr Enoch Okoh also travelled with

us. Our ambassador to the United States, His Excellency Daniel
Chapman and Mrs Chapman completed the party.

We were met by an impressive array of American leaders.
Vice President Nixon was at the airport, and so were the Chief
of Staff of the Army and the Dean of the Diplomatic Corps.
There were representatives of the nations of the British Commonwealth and other officials. We were given full military honours.

After a short speech in reply to Mr Nixon's address of welcome,
we drove to the President's guest house. There we just had time
to change and get ready for the luncheon given in my honour
by President Eisenhower, at the White House.

President Eisenhower had, shortly before my visit, been suffering a good deal from ill health, and I must say that I was fully
prepared to find, if not a rather sick man, then certainly one who
was having to take things easy. I was surprised when I was
greeted by a cheerful, rosy-cheeked man whose warmth, gaiety
and alertness of mind exuded health and well-being. We had
most interesting discussions during lunch and I was happy to
find how well-informed he was about Ghana and her problems.
I was impressed by his well-ordered mind and his direct
approach, qualities which one would, of course, expect to find
in a man who had such a distinguished military career.

In the afternoon, I placed wreaths on the Tomb of the
Unknowns and on Washington's tomb at Mount Vernon. Our
first day ended with an enjoyable dinner given in our honour by
the Vice President and Mrs Nixon.

The American Press was giving a lot of publicity to our visit
and I was glad that a meeting with the National Press Club
had been arranged for the second day. It gave the opportunity
I wanted to answer some of the questions uppermost in the minds
of American journalists. Some members of the Press Club had
been in Ghana at the time of Independence; others had attended
the Conference of independent states. They had been interested
then; now they wanted to know more.

I did my best to explain the policy of my government, particularly the economic policy. We had seen only too well the
effect of dependence on a single cash crop, cocoa. It made us far
too vulnerable to fluctuations in world prices. The recent trade
recession, I told them, had already affected our economy. We
wished to develop other crops and industries. For this it was
essential to obtain cheap power from the Volta River. Only then

would our great deposits of bauxite and other minerals be properly utilised.

The American Press must be well used to foreigners asking for financial aid. Since World War Two, the United States Government has spent millions of pounds helping to restore the economic balance in Europe and to assist the development of dependent countries. I wanted to make clear at the outset that we had not come to beg:

Let me emphasise one point. I have not come to the United States asking for direct financial aid. What we want is for you to co-operate in the economic and profitable development of our resources. This means that if either your government or your investors put money into our country we want it to go into sound projects and schemes, which will ultimately lead to the repayment of the initial investment.

The questions which followed my short address covered a wide range of topics.

Question: *Is there a Communist element in Ghana, and if so, would establishment of a party be permitted?*
Answer: So far as I know, I don't think there is any Communist element or group as such, but you can never tell what goes on in the minds of individuals. We in Ghana have no fear. I might even go further and say that our better institutions and the like which we have there, do not allow the ideology to have any fruitful set-up in our country.

Question: *Friends of Ghana are disquieted by your government's new preventive detention Bill. It empowers the government, I believe, to keep citizens in prison up to five years on vague charges of relations with other nations. Isn't that a bad omen for democracy in Africa?*
Answer: I wish we had more time to go into the details of this. I personally think that it is not a bad omen. Rather, in the initial stages of this new emerging state, something like that temporarily had to be adopted. . . . If we had not tried to be a little firm our independence would have fallen to pieces within three months.

A burst of applause followed. Then came the next question:

Question: *Mr Prime Minister, are the stories of racial tensions and disturbances in the United States criticised in Ghana, and what is the reaction?*

I replied to this at some length. Racialism, I said, wherever it existed, obviously should be abolished. It seemed, however, that the racial question in the United States had often been exaggerated deliberately by those who hoped to bring the country into disrepute.

There were many other questions; one of them about Ghana's call to Israel for commercial assistance and the setting up of the Black Star Shipping Line:

Question: *How far do you intend to develop your relations with Israel, and is there objection to this from other African governments?*
Answer: There is not, and there can never be any objection from any other African government. . . . I remember when I was in Cairo I was never even asked the question.

Question: *Sir, how serious do you consider the threat of Ashanti separation?*
Answer: We have had our little difficulties, but that is by now all settled for good. . . . So there is no problem there now.

Question: *What is the Ghanaian reaction to the landing of American troops in the Lebanon?*
Answer: . . . Ghana feels that the United Nations should really be there. . . . I would like to see the whole of the Middle East quarantined – that is the only way. . . . When I was in Libya I talked to the Prime Minister. In Libya they are trying to find oil and I think they have discovered it now. So the Prime Minister was almost in tears, very, very sorrowful that they have discovered oil. . . . He said wherever oil is discovered there is always trouble.

One journalist wanted to know how far Ghana supported the policies of the United Arab Republic. I answered that, broadly speaking, Ghana looked at problems from the point of view of the African continent. For example, we supported the Algerian people in their efforts for freedom and self-determination 'because Algeria is on the African continent'.

Before the final question was put, one of the Press Club members presented me with a 'certificate of appreciation'. This, he said, was awarded in recognition of meritorious service to correspondents in the nation's capital. As an old journalist myself, I value this award highly. The meeting ended on a light note:

Question: *How would you compare cocoa with the beverages served in the National Press Club?*
Answer: My natural reaction to this is, that you are not drinking enough cocoa in this country.

How important it is to have a sense of humour. Without it political discussions so often become either heated or tedious. I am glad that visitors to Ghana are usually struck by the lively sense of humour of the people. One of the best things about Ghanaians is that they are able to laugh at themselves; they have a natural gaiety. That is why we would never tolerate dictatorship or any other abuse of power. After political freedom, our main concern is for peace and a higher standard of living for all. I emphasised this last point when addressing the Senate of the United States, on the afternoon of 24 July:

Like you, we believe profoundly in the right of all people to determine their own destinies. We are therefore opposed to all forms of colonialism old or new, and we want to see all nations and their peoples genuinely independent and seeking a higher standard of life. In this respect, we have a special concern for those of our fellow Africans whose countries are not yet independent.

I went on to say that our foreign policy was one of non-alignment. We supported the United Nations fully and earnestly hoped for general disarmament and the relaxing of world tension. Ghana needed American investment, both government and private, but only for projects which could stand on their own feet, and which could ultimately repay the original capital with reasonable interest. Some of these points I repeated to the House of Representatives in an address the following morning. I wanted to be sure that no one misunderstood the purpose of our visit or the policy of my government.

Probably the most comprehensive speech I made during the American tour was to the Council on Foreign Relations, when I did my best to describe the staggering political and economic developments which had taken place in Africa since the war. In these developments there were, I said, three factors common to all emergent Africa:

The first is our desire to see Africa free and independent. The second is our determination to pursue foreign policies based upon non-alignment. The third is our urgent need for economic development. There is no area in Africa today where these three points are not on the agenda of politics. There is no need to underline for American readers the reason for Africa's rejection of colonial status. We believe, as do Americans, that to be self-governing is one of the inalienable rights of man. In Africa, if peoples are to be truly independent, their governments must reflect the fact that, in all parts of Africa, the overwhelming majority of the population are native-born Africans. Even in countries of considerable European settlement, such as Southern Rhodesia, 90% of the people are African. When, therefore, at our recent African conference, we called for an end to colonialism, we were doing no more than stating our belief that the fact of a vast African majority should be accepted as the basis of government in Africa.

There were obvious difficulties. Differences in race, speech, colour and religion had to be faced. In certain parts of Africa, notably Kenya and the Rhodesias, the European minority still had virtually a monopoly of education, skill and resources. That was why, at our African conference, we proposed a *phased* political transfer of power:

We asked for the fixing of definite dates for early independence and called upon the administering powers to take rapid steps to implement the provisions of the United Nations Charter and the political aspirations of the people, namely, self-determination and independence. These steps should, in my view, include a greatly accelerated and enlarged programme of education and technical training, the opening up systematically of new opportunities for Africans in agriculture and industry and a rapid growth of African participation in the country's political life. Such timetables would restore what, we believe, is most lacking in Africa's plural societies – and that is the element of confidence and hope on the part of the African majority.

The determination of Africans to achieve freedom, did not necessarily place them in opposition to the West. Africa's foreign policy was based on the principle of non-alignment.

Non-alignment can only be understood in the context of the present atomic arms race and the atmosphere of the cold war. There is a wise African proverb: 'When the bull elephants fight, the grass is trampled down.' When we in Africa survey the industrial and military power concentrated behind the two great powers in the cold war, we know that no military or strategic act of ours could make one jot of difference to this balance of power, while our involvement might draw us into areas of conflict which so far have not spread below the Sahara. Our attitude, I imagine, is very much that of America looking at the disputes of Europe in the 19th century. We do not wish to be involved. In addition, we know that we cannot affect the outcome. Above all, we believe the peace of the world in general is served, not harmed by keeping one great continent free from the strife and rivalry of military blocs and cold wars.

But this attitude of non-alignment does not imply indifference to the great issues of our day. It does not imply isolationism. It is in no way anti-Western; nor is it anti-Eastern. The greatest issue of our day is surely to see *that there is a tomorrow*. For Africans especially there is a particular tragedy in the risk of thermo-nuclear destruction. Our continent has come but lately to the threshold of the modern world. The opportunities of health and education and a wider vision which other nations take for granted are barely within the reach of our people. And now they see the risk that all this richness of opportunity may be snatched away by destructive war. In any war, the strategic areas of the world would be destroyed or occupied by some great power. It is simply a question of who gets there first – the Suez Canal, Afghanistan and the Gulf of Aquaba are examples.

On this great issue, therefore, of war and peace, the people and government of Ghana put all their weight behind the peaceful settlement of disputes and seek conditions in which disputes do not become embittered to the point of violence. We are willing to accept every provision of the United Nations Charter. We go further and favour every extension of an international police force as an alternative to war. One of the most important roles of the smaller nations today is surely to use their influence in season and out of season to substitute the peaceful settlement of disputes and international policing of disturbed areas for the present disastrous dependence upon arms and force. For this reason, at our African conference, we underlined our demands for controlled disarmament, we deplored the use of the sale of arms as a means of influencing other nations' diplomacy and we urged that African states should be represented on all international bodies concerned with disarmament.

Thus it is not indifference that leads us to a policy of non-alignment. It is our belief that international blocs and rivalries exacerbate and do not solve disputes and that we must be free to judge issues on their merits and to look for solutions that are just and peaceful, irrespective of the powers involved. We do not wish to be in the position of condoning imperialism or aggression from any quarter. Powers which pursue policies of goodwill, co-operation and constructive international action will always find us at their side. In fact, perhaps 'non-alignment' is a mis-statement of our attitude. We are firmly aligned with all the forces in the world that genuinely make for peace.

I went on to speak of Ghana's membership of the British Commonwealth:

Some Americans have expressed surprise that Ghana, after emerging from colonial status, should choose of its own free will to remain within the Commonwealth and thus – amongst others – in partnership with the United Kingdom which, the day before yesterday, was still colonial overlord. But we believe that the evolving form of the Commonwealth is an institution which can work profoundly for peace and international co-operation. It is the only organic world-wide association of peoples in which race, religion, nationality and culture are all transcended by a common sense of fellowship. No policies are imposed on it from above. It does not even seek unity of policy. But it provides a unique forum in which men of different culture and different approach can sit down together and see what can be done to lessen tensions and to increase the economic and social well-being of themselves and their neighbours. This is not a bloc. It is not a power grouping. It is a club or family of friends who see their continuing friendship as a strand of peace in a troubled world. It is because the Commonwealth is this kind of association that Ghana was happy to become its first independent African member on the basis of free association and unfettered sovereignty.

As a result of the old colonial link, I said, many of our economic ties were with Europe; and provided independence and equality were recognised in time, there was no need for those ties to be broken. Every responsible African leader knew the extent to which Africa needed outside economic assistance. Rapid

economic improvement had to follow quickly upon Independence. We in Ghana were not in such great need as other
countries. But nevertheless, we were short of teachers and technicians of all kinds. The Western powers had an opportunity to
play a new and vital role in Africa.

I told the Council of the steady increase in African productivity. Ghana's imports had nearly doubled in little more than
five years. Although not on so great a scale, American trade and
American interests had also steadily increased in Africa since the
war. This was a trend, based on reciprocity and equality, which
all African leaders wished to extend. It was the surest guarantee
of permanent friendship between Africa and the West.

The hopes and ambitions of the African people have been
planted and brought to maturity by the impact of Western
civilisation. The West has set the pattern of our hopes, and by
entering Africa in strength, it has forced the pattern upon us.
Now comes our response. We cannot tell our peoples that
material benefits and growth and modern progress are not for
them. If we do, they will throw us out and seek other leaders
who promise more. And they will abandon us, too, if we do not
in reasonable measure respond to their hopes. Therefore we
have no choice. Africa has no choice. We have to modernise.
Either we shall do so with your interest and support – or we
shall be compelled to turn elsewhere. This is not a warning or
a threat, but a straight statement of political reality.

And I also affirm, for myself and I believe for most of my
fellow leaders in Africa, that we want close co-operation with
our friends. We know you. History has brought us together.
We still have the opportunity to build up a future on the basis
of free and equal co-operation. This is our aim. This is our
hope.

Our stay in Washington was not wholly taken up with speech-
making and political engagements. There was a busy social
round, also. Our ambassador and Mrs Chapman gave a reception in my honour at the Sheraton Park Hotel; we were entertained to dinner by the Secretary of State and Mrs Dulles. On
another occasion, I met the Chiefs of Mission of Liberia, Sudan,
Morocco, Tunisia, Libya, the United Arab Republic and
Ethiopia. I also remember well a luncheon party given by the
New Zealand ambassador, where I met ambassadors of the other
Commonwealth nations.

Before we left Washington, President Eisenhower and I issued a joint statement. In it, we said that we had discussed the Volta River project and the five year plan. It was agreed that private American intersts should continue to explore the aluminium manufacturing phase of the Volta project, and at the same time examine proposals for other manufactures. Engineering reports which had been prepared in 1955 were to be brought up to date, and the cost shared. With regard to the five year plan, the United States Government would consider particular fields of activity in which it might be able to help through technical co-operation and development loans.

The statement recorded our agreement that the United States should withdraw its forces from the Lebanon as soon as a United Nations force could act effectively there. The statement ended:

> The President noted with deep interest the Prime Minister's explanations regarding the development of a distinctive 'African Personality', emphasising in this connection the sincere interest of the government of the United States in the orderly political, economic and social advancement of the peoples of the African continent.

In many ways we were sorry to leave Washington. But we looked forward to the next stage of our American tour, to Harrisburg, Philadelphia and New York.

The flight from Washington to Harrisburg took only one hour. We were met by the Governor of the State and taken straight away to see the buildings and plant of the Hershey Chocolate Corporation. On arrival at the Hershey factory, the sight of a red carpet and a reception committee brought a smile to my lips. 'The last time I visited your factory,' I announced, 'I was looking for a job! Not only was there no red carpet then to smooth my way: there was no job either!'

From there we drove to the Penn-Harris Hotel where we were entertained to lunch by Lincoln University. This was a real get-together of old classmates, teachers and friends. The speeches that were made were from the heart, filled with personal feeling and well spiced with stories and anecdotes that could only be understood by those who were members of that fraternity. My schedule was so tightly packed that I had to leave immediately after lunch and there was no time to sit and chat about old times with all the many familiar faces that I picked out in that crowded room.

We left New Cumberland Airport, Harrisburg at three o'clock in the afternoon and forty-five minutes later we landed in Philadelphia. The American people are so air-minded that they think nothing of travelling huge distances with very little respite in between. The late Mr Dulles was an outstanding example of such a traveller. I sympathise with those who find the time-table arranged for them in the States rather a crowded one.

In Philadelphia, we visited the Independence Hall and the University of Pennsylvania, where I received a citation. After a reception at the Centre for International Visitors, we were driven once more to our aeroplane and took off for the third time that day, this time for La Guardia, New York.

We spent the next three days in New York; my suite at the Waldorf-Astoria a sharp contrast to the lodgings I had twelve years before when I was a poverty-stricken student in the city. Mr Ralph J. Bunche, speaking at the reception given to me by the Harlem Lawyers' Association, reminded me of those early days:

> I know that you need no reminder that you are in Harlem. Nor do you, as one who found for an important if difficult period of your life, a second home in this land, need to be told anything about this particular community, its people, its problems and its spirit. . . . We are glad, very glad that you have come to be with us here, for we greatly admire both you and your country.

Mr Bunche was in Ghana at the time of Independence. He referred to this, and went on:

> We salute you, Kwame Nkrumah, not only because you are the Prime Minister of Ghana, although this is cause enough. We salute you because you are a true and living representation of our hopes and ideals, of the determination we have to be accepted fully as equal beings, of the pride we have held and nurtured in our African origin, of the achievement of which we know we are capable, of the freedom in which we believe, of the dignity imperative to our stature as men.

The spectacular and spontaneous welcome given to me by the people of Harlem remains one of the happiest memories of the whole tour, and I publicly thanked them in a speech which I made at the civic luncheon given by the acting Mayor of New York. On that occasion, I also referred to the cosmopolitan character of the city:

> The future world which we seek to build, and for which we in Ghana are prepared to give every assistance in our power, must be one in which, like New York City many people of different racial origins and religious beliefs will be able to live and work in peace, freedom and dignity.

Later in the day I spoke about Ghana's cocoa industry at the New York Cocoa Exchange. About the time of my visit, Ghana was slowly recovering from a setback to cocoa production due principally to the inroads of Swollen Shoot in the cocoa farms. This was a particularly virulent disease and the pessimists declared that the whole industry would be wiped out in twenty years. They were wrong, as I explained to listeners at the Exchange. In Ghana, resolute steps were taken. Diseased trees were cut down; farmers were compensated and helped to plant again:

> Today I am happy to be able to say that the worst is over. . . . The government is encouraging the expansion of cocoa throughout the country. You gentlemen in the trade, therefore, can be confident for the future, and can reasonably expect our farmers to supply you in the future with better grades of cocoa in ever increasing quantities.

I congratulated the Ghana Gocoa Marketing Board for its far-sighted policy, and for the way it had financed the building of roads, hospitals and schools. I ended:

> As I have said, we are ready to supply you with greater quantities of cocoa in the future. I am sure that you, for your part, will be prepared to sell whatever we produce. . . . We hope you will do everything in your power to advertise our products and advise the great American public to drink more cocoa and eat more candy!

The next day was one of the busiest of the tour. After lunching with the National Foreign Trade Council, I visited the United Nations Headquarters. Only a year before, at Independence, Ghana had been admitted to full membership of this organisation. My government strongly supported the Charter and I was glad of the opportunity to meet the Secretary-General of this great organisation, and to see round the building which housed it. In a recording made there I said:

> All of us in Ghana, government and people alike, pledge ourselves to do everything in our power to help this great organisation to achieve that lasting peace which is the highest ideal of all mankind.

Force alone is no longer a decisive factor in world affairs, thanks to some extent to the part played by U.N.O. I told a meeting of the Afro-Asian group that the African and Asian communities had an important contribution to make. All powers, great and small, are sensitive to world opinion and take it into account when deciding their policies:

> We represent a large segment of world opinion and herein lies our strength. Ours is a force which cannot be applied coercively. It can only be employed persuasively; but it is nevertheless an effective force.
> We can perform a very useful function by using our strength in trying to help bridge the gulf which separates the world into ideological blocs. . . . Our task as a group in the United Nations, it seems to me, is to use our strength wisely and objectively on the side of peace.

During my American tour I had to speak to many different types of audience. I tried on each occasion to talk to those who had come to hear me, as informally as possible. I spoke to the Press as 'an old journalist'; to the House of Representatives as 'a fellow politician'; and to the students as an 'ex-student'. But when the Foreign Trade Council invited me to lunch I could hardly claim to be a business man. Instead, I said that I would try to imitate them by being business-like; I would not waste their time with a lengthy speech.

I think they appreciated this, for they listened intently as I outlined briefly my government's plan for the economic development of Ghana. We wanted Americans to invest in industrial projects in Ghana, but not to provide direct financial grants.

I repeated these points when addressing the National Confectioners' Association in Chicago. I added:

> Independence has created the right political atmosphere for a real effort of national regeneration. Agricultural development

has been given greater impetus, new industries have been introduced or planned: first class roads and other means of communication are rapidly opening up the country: hospitals and
health centres, schools and colleges and social centres are
springing up: community development is bringing a better
way of life to the rural areas; and the right climate is being
created for the attraction of foreign investment to stimulate
further the economy of the country. The story of Ghana, and
other territories in Africa which now enjoy independence,
demonstrates that the first objective to work for is political
freedom which, on attainment, is bound to stimulate economic
and social development which others would like to place first.

Unfortunately, we only had time for one full day in Chicago.
We would have liked to see more of the city and its people. We
left on 1 August to fly to Ghana by way of New York and
London.

As our plane gathered height over La Guardia Airport, I felt
thankful that our busy schedule of engagements had been fulfilled without a hitch. We had, I think, achieved the main
purpose of our visit, as the joint statement issued by President
Eisenhower and myself testified. Ghana-American friendship
had been strengthened. We had learned more about American
policy and ideals, and at the same time we had, by our visit,
made the American public more aware of the vast changes
taking place on the African continent.

CHAPTER SEVENTEEN

POSITIVE NEUTRALITY

On 3 September 1958, I explained to the National Assembly the foreign policy which had guided the government in its international relations since Independence:

The aim of the Government has been to follow an independent foreign policy, that is, a policy that is not committed ideologically or militarily with any particular power or political bloc. This policy of non-alignment we have interpreted to imply that the Government would act as it sees best on any issue in the light of the country's obligation to the United Nations Charter, our position in relation to the African continent and the Commonwealth, our adherence to the principles enunciated at the Bandung and the Accra conferences and our determination to safeguard our independence, and sovereignty. As a result of pursuing a policy of non-alignment, Ghana has been able to make a positive and constructive contribution to the easing of the latest international tension in the Middle East.
   The basic aim of our foreign policy must be seen against the background of the following considerations, namely, Ghana's position in relation to the United Nations, the Commonwealth and the African continent; and the continued economic and social progress of our people.

I proposed to deal with each of the considerations in turn:

Ghana regards the faithful adherence to the principles of the United Nations Charter as an integral part of her foreign policy and we shall continue to co-operate fully in the activities of the United Nations and its specialised agencies. It is a matter of crucial importance to us and to our sister African nations that the United Nations Organisation should become an effective instrument for the preservation of world peace. Let me repeat what I have always emphasised: Ghana has a vested interest in peace; our constant concern is national security, in order that we may get on with the job of economic and social reconstruction in an atmosphere of peace and tranquillity.

With regard to the position in the Middle East, I had this to say:

> We are particularly concerned that the approach to the Middle East problem should be governed by two principles (a) the need to keep power bloc conflict out of the Middle East, and (b) the recognition of the independence and territorial integrity of each Middle East state by all the other states in the area. Happily, an acceptable approach towards a solution to these problems has been arrived at by the Arab states of the Middle East themselves. In our opinion the resolution which has been unanimously adopted by the United Nations Emergency General Assembly takes great strength from its reference to the basic principles of respect for the territorial integrity and the sovereignty of all states as well as non-aggression and non-interference in the internal affairs of other states. Those principles enunciated at the Bandung Conference have been solemnly restated by the Accra Conference of Independent African States and constitute a permanent basis of our policy.

I then spoke of our membership of the Commonwealth in the same terms as I had used to explain to Americans our continued partnership with the United Kingdom. It is, however, mainly in Africa that Ghana's foreign policy lies. I reminded Members that the Conference of Independent African States established a fundamental unity of outlook on foreign policy, which was of deep significance to the role of the African nations in international affairs. Ghana made no secret of the fact that she rejected colonial status for any part of Africa, and that she desired to see all Africa free and independent:

> When we say that we reject colonial status for any part of Africa, and desire to see all Africa free and independent, we do not mean that we intend to resort to subversion to achieve our purpose. We feel confident in being able to inspire our fellow Africans still under foreign domination to achieve their freedom by ourselves making a success of our own freedom, firstly, by maintaining an effective, stable and democratic government, and in creating economic and social conditions which will enable our people to attain a high standard of well-being; secondly, by co-operating with the other independent African states, within and without the United Nations, urging that the administering powers respect the Charter of the

United Nations and take rapid steps to implement the political aspirations of the people, namely, self-determination and independence; thirdly, by giving all possible assistance to our brothers still under colonial rule in their struggle to be free; and fourthly, by bringing to the conscience of the world their burning desire to be self-governing, which is one of the inalienable rights of man.

In Ghana, the hazards and excitements of the political struggle were behind us. Ahead lay the battle for economic independence. Political independence created the right atmosphere for national regeneration:

Mr Speaker, we in Ghana believe that the only kind of government which can do the most for the peoples of Africa is the type which exercises complete and independent sovereignty over its territory. This is so because the maximum welfare of any people can never be achieved unless they have the right to decide, in full freedom, the nature of their needs and how they can best be satisfied. The welfare of one people cannot be given in trust indefinitely to another people, no matter how benevolent the governing power might be. The whole of the recent history of Ghana is living proof of this truth. When, therefore, we welcome the proposal to hold an all African Peoples Conference in Accra, it is not because we desire to dictate to our fellow Africans what constitutions they must adopt if they are to be free, but rather to develop our African personality and reach a greater understanding among ourselves so that we can build together the basis of co-operation for the fuller, richer and more progressive future of our peoples within the framework of an African community.

This statement, taken with previous statements made in the House and elsewhere on previous occasions, presented the record of our efforts to give significance to our independence, and to make our contribution towards the creation of an African outlook and personality in international affairs. 'It was to be hoped,' I said, 'that our efforts would help to bring a ray of hope of a brighter future not only to our own people, but to all in other parts of Africa who looked to us for inspiration in their struggle to be free.'

CHAPTER EIGHTEEN

INDIA, AND AFRO-ASIAN UNDERSTANDING

I had for a long time wished to visit India, but there always seems to be so much to occupy me that the only steps I took towards fulfilling this wish, were promises to do so each time I met Mr Nehru or his sister, Mrs Pandit. When Mr Nehru sent me an official invitation to visit India, therefore, I was delighted to accept. It was arranged that I should leave Ghana on the 20 December 1958, and fly to India via Rome.

My task in India was twofold. I wished to learn all I could about India, to discover how she had tackled economic as well as political problems during the eleven years of her independence, and with what results. At the same time I wanted to take every opportunity to explain my policy for Ghana, and my belief in the eventual liberation of the whole African continent.

On arrival in Bombay, I was given a lavish reception in the Kamala Nehru Park. The Park and the adjacent hanging gardens were brilliantly lit by multi-coloured lights. In reply to the Mayor's address of welcome, I spoke of the emergence of an 'African personality'. At times it was difficult to make myself heard for the bursts of cheering which punctuated my speech.

I have particularly happy memories of my visit to Bombay. It was our first port of call in India, and as Mr Mirajkar, the Mayor, reminded me, I was the first African statesman of an independent African country to visit the city. This memorable welcome came not only from the city fathers but from the ordinary folk who lined the streets to cheer as I was driven to see the atomic energy establishment at Trombay, and later the state-owned Aarey Milk Colony.

From Bombay we flew to New Delhi where Jawaharlal Nehru welcomed us at the airport. He referred to the renaissance of Asia, and said that many people had been surprised by recent developments in Africa, 'They suddenly realised that something big was happening in Africa.' He welcomed me not only as Prime Minister of independent Ghana, but as the symbol of the hopes of the people of Africa as a whole. India and Africa, he said, had a common background of colonial rule, 'so inevitably they come closer to each other, to learn from each other and, where possible, to help each other'.

'Although I have never visited India before,' I said in my reply, 'India has in a real sense been always known to me. I have been influenced in much that I have been able to carry out by the ideas of that great man, Mahatma Gandhi, and your own superb and humane example.'

One of the highlights of my stay in New Delhi was the ceremony at the University when an honorary Doctorate of Letters was conferred on me. Students from Ghana and from other parts of Africa are found in most of the Indian Universities. I was glad to have the chance of thanking these institutions for their help in training so many of our young men.

The next day I was given an impressive civic reception in New Delhi. I told the Mayor and members of the corporation that I had for a long time wanted to visit India:

I have come not only to congratulate the people of India on their noble fight in the cause of freedom and the unique role India is playing in world affairs, but also to observe for myself the successful manner in which you are consolidating the freedom and independence which you fought for and won some eleven years ago.

I said that although there was much in common between the struggles for independence in Ghana and in India, there was one significant difference. In India, the struggle was so protracted that by the time the British left the country, Indianisation was practically complete. In Ghana, however, the change was comparatively sudden. Africanisation in government administration and in education had scarcely begun. After independence, we had had to start almost from scratch to manage our own affairs. In fact, independence came as such a surprise to some sections of the British press that they had not been able to recover from the shock.

From the first day of our independence, the world press has kept Ghana under close examination. Our smallest acts have been analysed in detail, and the policies of my government have often been criticised. I do not mind criticism, provided it is based on fact. But sometimes the press in Britain and elsewhere has published criticism based on nothing more than loose or malicious speculation. Those who work for the press and radio have a great responsibility and even a moral obligation to report facts as they are, and not as they would like to see them.

Indian newspapers gave wide and friendly publicity to my visit. I have vivid memories of a lively press conference in New Delhi on 29 December. Questions fired at me there were searching and on the whole constructive. Here are some of them:

Question: *May we have your views on how far the Western parliamentary democracy could be adapted to conditions of emergent Africa?*
Answer: Of course. The basic principles of parliamentary democracy are two: the first that there should be a periodic election, general election – and that there must be universal adult suffrage.

I explained that both these principles had been applied in Ghana. Then followed questions about my economic policy, about tribalism in Ghana, and about the strength of the National Liberation Movement. Then came the expected questions on the Accra Conference:

Question: *The Accra Conference decided to work actively for a final assault on colonialism and imperialism in Africa. I imagine that one of the Powers exercising colonialism in Africa is Great Britain, and you are a member of the Commonwealth. . . . How far is your membership of the Commonwealth consistent with the objective of liberating Africa from Western colonialism?*
Answer: I do not see any incompatibility at all in that. . . . After all, you know the composition of the Commonwealth. . . . It is a free association of sovereign independent states. . . . We look at it almost like a family, but that does not mean that each does not have its own interests and its own internal and external policies to follow.

Question: *How exactly do you propose to work for the final assault on colonialism and imperialism in Africa? What exactly is in your mind?*
Answer: It is organisation. Let the very territories in Africa organise.

Question: *Have you any information that the deliberations and decisions that took place at the Accra Conference have reached those sections of Africa which are shut off from the outside world, like the Belgian Congo, etc.?*

Answer: Even those who are shut out were represented. The Belgian Congo and Angola were represented, and we have set up a secretariat in Accra which, I think, is in touch with all these groups.

Question: *You have said that your object is that ultimately all countries in Africa will join in an African commonwealth or union. Is there already, to your mind, any popular sentiment in favour of a federation of African states, or is this an intellectual concept at the level of the top African leadership?*
Answer: I do not think it is only an intellectual concept. The only way I can answer that is to say that the movement is spreading; in the African Peoples' Conference the majority of opinion supported this view.

In answer to another question I made it clear that we were not concerned with starting subversive movements. 'All that we are asking for is that in Africa the majority should form the basis of government,' I said. As far as our foreign policy was concerned, I told them that Ghana did not want to join either of the big power blocs. We were trying to steer clear and to have friendly relations with everyone.

At the time of my visit to India there were only nine independent truly African states, Ethiopia, Guinea, Liberia, Libya, Morocco, Sudan, Tunisia, the United Arab Republic and Ghana. The rest of Africa was divided and partitioned among five European powers: Belgium, Britain, France, Portugal and Spain. There were also countries, such as Algeria, Rhodesia and South Africa, where a European minority had settled and formed governments at the expense of the African majority. Wherever I went in India, I explained the magnitude of the task which still lay ahead of us. The Indians, of course, understood well what I meant by non-violent positive action and passive non-co-operation. In their own struggle for independence they had used these very weapons.

In a speech to the Indian Council of World Affairs on 26 December, I again stressed Ghana's role in the African liberation movement. I then went on to reply to certain criticisms in the world press about happenings in Ghana since Independence:

The government of Ghana has often been criticised by a section of the western press for adopting what they have called 'undemocratic methods'. It would have been more helpful in creating a better understanding if these critics had first carefully considered the reality of our situation. As a new and young government, our first responsibility has been to preserve the independence and security of our state. . . . In our case the criticism has been that we have not proceeded in precisely the same way as the old Western democracies. . . . In this connection I want to emphasise two fundamental points in relation to our approach to democracy. First, Ghana society is by its own form and tradition fundamentally democratic in character. For centuries our people gave great powers to their chiefs, but only so long as they adhered to the rules and regulations laid down by the people; the moment they deviated from these rules, they were deposed. In our recent history we have inherited a parliamentary system of the Western type which, as you know so well in India, is a subtle and sophisticated type of administration full of balances and checks. This, by its very nature, is a very difficult and cumbersome system to apply to our traditional pattern of government.

I believe that this process will not in any way prejudice our democratic way of life so long as two basic principles are always accepted, namely, universal adult suffrage, which ensures that every adult man and woman has one vote; and regular, free and unfettered elections. . . . I have no doubt that in time we in Africa will evolve forms of government rather different from the traditional western pattern but no less democratic in their protection of the individual and his inalienable rights.

Certain disloyal and subversive elements in Ghana had had to be dealt with firmly, because they prejudiced our very existence as a free and independent state. There had been plots and various attempts to exploit tribal and regional loyalties. Obviously, steps had to be taken to preserve our internal security. I expressed the hope that in future our critics might carefully consider the reality of our situation.

Turning to the subject of foreign policy, I said that Ghana valued her membership of the United Nations:

Whatever may be its merits and demerits, it permits smaller nations to work together and to make their voices heard in a way which would never be possible if this forum did not exist. . . . The position which Ghana has adopted in the United Nations on various issues reflects our foreign policy of non-alignment and positive neutrality.

I should perhaps make it clear that this attitude of non-alignment which Ghana still adheres to, does not imply indifference to the great issues of our day. We view with fear and apprehension the arms race between the great powers and the terrible weapons of destruction at their disposal. Our own continent of Africa has become a testing ground for atomic explosions. With all the wonderful new fields of knowledge and with power at our disposal as never before to command the natural resources of the world man has so far shown himself capable only of increasing his own fear of the future. I earnestly hope that there may be effective control of nuclear weapons and general disarmament before it is too late.

The day before we left New Delhi I took formal leave of the Indian Prime Minister. 'We have enjoyed ourselves immensely,' I said, 'and we carry back with us to Ghana and for that matter, to Africa, sweet memories of our visit. . . . I hope it will not be long before you will make it possible to visit Ghana and some other parts of the African continent.'

Mr Nehru replied, 'Your coming here has been very welcome. . . . I cannot at the present moment say when I will be fortunate enough to visit Ghana, but I can tell you this, that I am anxious and eager to go there, and I hope to go there.' It has not yet been possible for the Prime Minister to come to Ghana, but I hope to see him here one day.

I broadcast on the all-India radio on the same day on which I bade farewell to Mr Nehru. I spoke of the great welcome I had been given, and of the bond of friendship between our two countries. It was a full day, that 2 January 1958. From the broadcasting station I went to the reception arranged by the Indo-Ghana Cultural Association. This association was set up in New Delhi in 1958 and there were already branches in several other Indian cities. Its purpose is to assist culturally in the resurgence of Afro-Asian 'family' and to strengthen the bond of friendship between India and Ghana. In his address of welcome, the President, Rana Jang Bahadar Singh declared: 'Long live Nkrumah–Nehru principles.'

At the reception, the Goldsmiths' Union presented me with a gold medal as an 'exhibition of the fraternal affection of men of the same profession'! I thanked them and said, 'Yes, it is true. My father was a goldsmith!' This was the second gift I received that day. Earlier, the Minister for Scientific Research and

Cultural Affairs had presented me with a bronze sculpture entitled 'the Voice of Africa'. It was by the Indian sculptor, Ama Nath Sehgal.

From Delhi we travelled by train to Nangal in the north of India where the Bhakra Nangal Dams are being built. This, of course, was of particular interest to me in view of our own Volta River project. I was interested also in visiting the new town of Chandigarh with its modern architecture. In some cases, 'futuristic' would more aptly describe the designs. I spent a most memorable day with the Indian Army at Jhansi, I went aboard the navy's prize battleship, the *Mysore* and spent an enjoyable morning with the Air Force.

Before leaving India I spent a few days of relaxation in Bangalore. His Highness the Maharaja of Mysore arranged a tiger shoot for me. We did not succeed in shooting a tiger, but we got more excitement than we bargained for when we were suddenly charged by a rogue elephant!

We spent only a short time in India, but I think our visit was a great success. I had many informal and friendly talks with Mr Nehru. We discussed international problems as well as other matters of mutual interest. I felt that India-Ghana friendship had been strengthened, and with it, Afro-Asian understanding.

CHAPTER NINETEEN

THE TENTH ANNIVERSARY OF THE C.P.P.

On the tenth anniversary of the founding of the C.P.P., I addressed a large gathering of Party members in the Accra Arena. I said that the twelfth of June 1949, the date on which the C.P.P. was founded, marked a focal turning point in the history of our country's struggle for freedom and self-determination. It was fitting that we should remember all those who had given their lives in Ghana's cause, and the Central Committee of the Party had decided to have a monument built to commemorate them:

Comrades, it is no idle boast when I say that without the Convention People's Party there would be no Ghana, and that without political independence there would be no hope of economic salvation. The Convention People's Party is Ghana. Our Party not only provides the government but is also the custodian which stands guard over the welfare of the people.

Before speaking of the record of our Party and its achievements over the ten years of its existence, it is necessary first of all to place it in its historical perspective. History shows us that from the time of the signing of the Bond of 1844, which gave to Great Britain the means of imposing her political control over our country, there have been repeated efforts from patriotic citizens at various times to loosen the grip of alien domination. In this connection we are proud to remember the early political pioneers in our country's history, those patriotic intellectuals, for example, associated with the Aborigines' Rights Protection Society and the West African National Congress. Names enshrined in the history of our people are, among others, those of Casely-Hayford, Mensah Sarbah, Atto Ahumah and Dr Aggrey.

These men, judged in terms of the society and time in which they lived, did all they possibly could for their country. They were sincere and dedicated men. I traced the struggle for freedom from the signing of the Bond of 1844 with Great Britain, to the founding of the C.P.P. and the attainment of independence.

Our many sacrifices were rewarded. We were now the masters of the citadel. The flag of imperialism was lowered and over the ramparts we proudly hoisted our national flag, symbol of our hard-won freedom and the banner of the hope of Africa's total redemption. Our Party flag has a rightful place beside this symbol of our nationhood, for it was under the red, white and green banner that the battle for freedom was fought and won.

Before we took over complete political power we were able, despite the many constitutional problems which we had to surmount on the political front, to make certain significant advances on the economic and social fronts.

During the period when we shared office with the British imperialist civil servants, the Party was able, through its majority representatives in the Cabinet, to institute a Five-Year Plan which enabled us to make up some of the leeway against the social neglects of British imperialism during the preceding hundred years. I do not think I am exaggerating when I say that we have been able to achieve in the past ten years very much more than the imperialists did in the century when they were absolute masters here. Therefore, we reject the carping of those critics who judge us merely by the heights which we have achieved and not from the depths from which we started.

In the past two years since we have become the absolute masters of our fate, we have been able to complete and consolidate the first Five-Year economic and social development programme and to plan on a more ambitious scale for the tasks ahead. Today we stand on the threshold of the Second Development Plan which will usher in the economic revolution.

Before I address myself to the new task before us, let me once again emphasise that without the first revolution – *the political revolution* – we should never have been in a position to plan the future. The history of these past ten years has shown indubitably that political power is the inescapable prerequisite to economic and social power. With the political power vested in the people, we are now in a position to launch an offensive against the remnants of economic imperialism which have entrenched themselves in our country over the past hundred years under the benevolent protection of British political power. It is no accident that trade follows the flag.

Foreign vested interests used to have a free hand, and could if they wished, act contrary to the economic and social interests of the people. The government had already taken steps to remedy this state of affairs. The Cocoa Marketing Board, for example, handled the profits of the cocoa industry, and used them in the best interests of the nation as a whole.

I then went on to examine certain weaknesses in the Party, and to suggest future policy:

Though we emerged victoriously from our fight against imperialism and colonialism, we made many mistakes in the course of the battle. I want us to examine seriously some of those mistakes, for the task ahead is even more formidable than the one which we have overcome, and now that we stand on the threshold of the second revolution, it becomes necessary for us to re-group our forces and plan our strategy and tactics for the future. The task of self-criticism is therefore obligatory. For we must see that our forces are well and truly steeled for the economic battle on which we shall now be engaged. Our Party must be disciplined and well led and fortified with an African socialist ideology which will reinforce the invincibility of our Party. We must examine our organisational structure, improve our method of day-to-day work, raise the moral quality of our members and the ideological education of our comrades.

The Convention People's Party has developed from a small organisation to a nation-wide movement, embracing within its ranks and among its sympathisers the overwhelming majority of our nation. The composition of the Party has become socially quite heterogeneous and there is the danger that our socialist objective may be clouded by opportunistic accommodations and adjustments to petit bourgeois elements in our ranks who are unsympathetic and sometimes even hostile to the social aims to which the Party is dedicated.

These aims embrace the creation of a welfare state based upon African socialist principles, adapted to suit Ghanaian conditions, in which all citizens, regardless of class, tribe, colour or creed, shall have equal opportunity, and where there shall be no exploitation of man by man, tribe by tribe, or class by class, our party also seeks to promote and safeguard popular democracy based upon universal suffrage – 'One man, one vote'.

In order to carry out the great economic programme, the C.P.P. must put its own house in order. I explained that the Central Committee of the Party had agreed upon a number of measures to strengthen, discipline and improve general methods of work. Local branches would be rebuilt into more compact and active units, so that they could provide local leadership in their respective committees. Even the smallest village ought to have a Branch, so that the political education of the people could be improved. There was no room in the Party for the racialist or tribalist:

> We intend to take drastic steps to expurgate all these and other reactionary tendencies, and we shall not hesitate to expel from our ranks anybody who propagates or spreads in the slightest degree, racial and tribal chauvinism. In our Party all are equal regardless of their race or tribe. All are free to express their views. But once a majority decision is taken, we expect such a decision to be loyally executed, even by those who might have opposed that decision. This we consider and proclaim to be the truest form of *Democratic Centralism* – decisions freely arrived at and loyally executed. This applies from the lowest to the highest level. None is privileged and no one shall escape disciplinary action. For the strength of our Party depends upon its discipline. Up to now there has been too much loose-ness, and from now on we intend to tighten up on all echelons of the Party, from the Central Committee down to the humblest Branch.

Members called 'Vanguard Activists', drawn from the most politically educated section of the Party, would be trained at special courses to explain the aims and objects of the C.P.P. to those who did not clearly understand them. The Activists would live and work among the common people:

> They are the salt of the earth. We, the so-called educated members of the Party, must learn from them. That is why I say:
>> 'Go to the people
>> Live among them
>> Learn from them
>> Love them
>> Serve them
>> Plan with them
>> Start with what they know
>> Build on what they have.'

Let this wise Chinese advice be a constant guide in our day-to-day Party work among the humble masses.

The fact that the Convention People's Party has become a great force is due primarily to the trust which these common people reposed in us and because of our past close contact with them. We must never lose this contact, but rather we must constantly deepen and strengthen it. For if we turn away from the mass of workers and farmers, we shall lose the support which has enabled us to reach the heights we have attained and our chance to 'Serve Ghana Now'.

In the coming period of reconstruction through our Second Development Plan, we shall need more than ever before the confidence of the masses and the solidarity of all workers, by hand and by brain, if we hope to achieve our goal of making Ghana a modern state and of giving our people a higher material of life and a richer spiritual and cultural existence.

I warned Party leaders against opportunism and arrogance. They must gain the respect and trust of the masses, for 'without the masses there would be nothing for them to lead.'

The Convention People's Party is, above all, a dynamic Party with a clear-cut social goal and political ideology to guide it. We aim at creating in Ghana a socialist society in which each will give according to his ability and receive according to his needs. We are not therefore, a mutual admiration society of frustrated and disgruntled intellectuals out to destroy what they cannot build. We can only attain our aims by discipline and hard work and study.

All of us need to go back to the Party school from time to time to re-learn some of the things we may have forgotten in the hustle and bustle of our daily routine. Week-end seminars will help to stimulate our thinking and stir up our ideas. None of us is too old in the political struggle not to gain something new from periodic educational courses. Our branch secretaries especially should be educated in political consciousness and understanding of the political objectives of our Party, for how else can they interpret them to our rank and file members and to the great mass of Party sympathisers? But, neither will it do harm for Ministers, our Parliamentary Secretaries and our Members of Parliament to attend courses at our Party school. In fact the Central Committee intends making such a course of study in Party ideology obligatory upon them.

Having dealt at some length with the structure and inner life of the C.P.P., I passed next to the Second Development Plan. Its purpose was, I said, to reorganise the national economy and

to raise the standard of living in Ghana. The Party had entered
into an alliance with the T.U.C. and with the Ghana Farmers'
Council. This 'Grand Alliance' would guarantee the success of
the Plan, but temporary sacrifices would have to be made. The
farmers had shown that they were prepared to make certain
sacrifices: it was up to others to follow suit:

> It is my pleasant duty to tell you that, stimulated by the un-
> selfish gesture of our farmers, the Central Committee of the
> Convention People's Party has decided that all Party
> Ministers, Ministerial Secretaries and certain others, shall give
> up to the nation ten per cent of their salary. We consider it
> only fair that sacrifices should come from the top as well as
> from below, since the fruits of our Development Plan will
> benefit all sections of the community.
>
> Although I am here speaking as the leader of the Conven-
> tion People's Party, it will not be out of place for me to address
> an appeal to the nation and to call upon all the citizens to give
> us their unstinting support so that the whole population of
> Ghana can march forward shoulder to shoulder for a one
> hundred per cent fulfilment of the targets which we have set
> ourselves within the framework of the Five Year Development
> Plan.
>
> A fact which we must assimilate is that we are now working
> for ourselves. That is, we are Ghanaians working for Ghana,
> regardless of our party affiliations. We are not any more work-
> ing for colonialism. The Government will see to it that any
> sacrifices which the workers, whether by hand or by brain,
> and the farmers may make, will not rob them of the fruits of
> their labour. The Government will ensure that these sacrifices
> will be made in the benefit of all the people and not merely
> to enrich a minority section of the population, foreign or
> native. For this would be doing violence to our fundamental
> socialist principles.

We planned to encourage the growth of industries, and we
needed all the technical and administrative talent we could lay
our hands on. This led me to consider the work of the University
College and the Kumasi College of Technology.

> It pains me to have to say that these institutions are not pulling
> their weight. The returns which we are getting for the money
> poured into these institutions is most discouraging. I have
> already aired my criticisms on another occasion about the

Kumasi College of Technology. Let me here look at the University College. Over 90% of the student body is being maintained by Government scholarships. It costs us more to produce a graduate at Legon than in many other Universities abroad. We have provided with unparalleled lavishness all the facilities necessary. It is a common opinion that our students are 'feather-bedded'. And what is the result? With few exceptions University College is a breeding ground for un-patriotic and anti-Government elements.

But the students are not alone to be blamed. The staff bears a heavy responsibility for the anti-Government atmosphere which prevails. We are not fools. We know all that is happen-ing and we can pinpoint those elements, both native and foreign, around which this unhealthy state of affairs revolves.

I want my present observations to serve as a warning. We do not intend to sit idly by and see these institutions which are supported by millions of pounds produced out of the sweat and toil of the common people continue to be centres of anti-Government activities. We want the University College to cease being an alien institution and to take on the character of a Ghanaian University, loyally serving the interests of the nation and the well-being of our people. If reforms do not come from within, we intend to impose them from outside, and no resort to the cry of academic freedom (for academic freedom does not mean irresponsibility) is going to restrain us from seeing that our University is a healthy University devoted to Ghanaian interests.

Finally, I put the development of Ghana in its African context, and spoke of Pan-Africanism and the emergence of an African personality in international affairs:

As I have often emphasised, the freedom and independence of Ghana is meaningless unless it is linked up with the total liberation of Africa. As the international platform of the Con-vention People's Party programme states: The Party seeks to establish fraternal relations with, and offer guidance and sup-port to, all nationalist, democratic and socialist movements in Africa and elsewhere which are fighting for national inde-pendence and self-determination on the one hand and whose programmes are opposed to imperialism, colonialism, racialism, tribalism and religious sectarianism and all other forms of national, racial, tribal and religious chauvinism and oppression, on the other. We are working towards making this policy a reality. That is why we insist that in Ghana in the higher reaches of our national life, there should be no reference to Fantis, Ashantis, Ewes, Gas, Dagombas, 'strangers', and so forth, but that we should call ourselves Ghanaians – all brothers and sisters, members of the same community – the state of Ghana. For until we ourselves purge from our own minds this tribal chauvinism and prejudice of one against the other, we shall not be able to cultivate the wider spirit of brotherhood which our objective of Pan Africanism calls for. We are all Africans and peoples of African descent, and we shall not allow the imperialist plotters and intriguers to separate us from each other for their own advantage.

I had spoken longer than usual, but there were so many topics to cover. I ended by referring to the Ghana-Guinea Union, and the need for continual Party vigilance. Then I called for three cheers:

> 'Long live the Convention People's Party!
> Long live the Ghana-Guinea Union!
> Long live African Independence and Unity!'

CHAPTER TWENTY

BUILDING A WELFARE STATE

Our second Five Year Development Plan was officially launched on 1 July 1959. I called it 'D' Day in the battle for the economic emancipation of Ghana. In a broadcast on the eve of 'D' Day I explained the nature of the Plan, and asked the people of Ghana to support it:

If this campaign is to succeed it will require an all-out effort from every man and woman living throughout the length and breadth of the land. You, the farmers, the fishermen, the masons, the lawyers, the doctors, the labourers, the business men, the engineers, the architects, the traders, the teachers, the students, the whole people of Ghana, whatever your occupation or status, have a vitally important part to play in making this campaign a resounding success. You are the troops who will make the assault and sustain it through the next five years and who will in the end break through to a wider and fuller life for our nation.

No campaign can succeed unless it is well planned; and after many long months of careful thought the Government drew up and presented a Five Year Development Plan to Parliament. On the 5th March your freely elected representatives approved the Second Development Plan and authorised the Government to implement it. The Plan envisages an expenditure of some three hundred and fifty million Ghana pounds. Some people have said that a plan of this magnitude is over-ambitious. When presenting the Plan to Parliament I stated that the Government was convinced that this was the very time for us to be ambitious; without ambition nothing can be achieved. When we began to organise our struggle for national independence ten years ago, we demanded 'self-government now'. In the circumstances then prevailing, many people considered this to be an impossible target, but if our political target had been 'self-government in 1957' I assure you that we would still be a colonial territory merely crawling towards independence. Just as 'self-government now' expressed the earnest desire of everyone of us during the years of our political struggle, so does this ambitious Plan give expression of the will and determination of the people to break through the barriers of economic backwardness on the broadest possible front and to make possible a great increase in national productivity, especially in the fields of agriculture and industry. It is only from the surpluses of increased productivity that a higher standard of life for the whole nation can be achieved, and I and my Government are determined to lead the nation to this goal in the shortest possible time.

Though we are ambitious, we are also realistic; every plan of campaign sets out limited objectives which must first be secured before the troops can move forward and continue the assault. Our first and minimum objective is to execute a programme carefully selected from the plan which, in the first place, will involve an expenditure of just over one hundred and thirty six million Ghana pounds. I wish to emphasise, however, that this is only our first objective.

The details of the Development Plan and of our first objective have been widely published and an abridged version, now being printed both in English and in our Ghana languages, will be distributed to reach every home in the country.

I said that the Government intended to exert every effort to build up the national momentum to carry the Plan through. A National Consultative Development Committee, under my Chairmanship, had been established on which political organisation, the T.U.C., the Ghana Farmers' Council, the Co-operative Movement, Benevolent Societies, Women's, Youth and other organisations were represented. It was the task of the Committee to organise and direct the national effort.

A Development Publicity Committee had also been set up to keep the whole country informed about the working details of the Plan. Everyone had a vital part to play:

As I said earlier, you are the troops who will carry out this assault; what then is expected of you? Your basic contribution will be in the performance of your normal employment by making every effort to improve the standard of your work and the amount of work you do in each day. At the close of the day as you go home to rest, you should think back over your work and ask yourself *How have I merited?*:

Did I go all-out to produce an extra effort for the development of my country?

Did I waste time unnecessarily?

Did I waste materials by carelessness or poor work?
Did I apply all my skill and ingenuity and produce a first-class job?
And, having answered these questions honestly, make up your mind to do a better day's work and when tomorrow comes, see to it that you improve upon the previous day's performance. Many workers take a short-sighted attitude in this matter. *Why*, they say, *should we work harder to profit someone else, for the harder we work the sooner the job will be done and the sooner will we be unemployed.*
This is indeed short-sighted, for the greater our productive effort as a nation the greater will be the surplus of goods and services to increase the standard of living for all.

Both workers and employers must pull their weight, I said. They had an equal responsibility to maintain industrial peace:

Just as the worker must make an all-out effort to give of his best, so must the employer and his managerial staff see to it that fair remuneration is given for work done and, above all, that the work is efficiently planned to ensure that the maximum productive effort is made. The worker who wants to get on with his task must not be frustrated by bad organisation on the job, inadequate tools, and bottlenecks in the supply of materials. The employer has a vital part to play in this campaign; he can expect profits to reward him for his efforts but these profits must be reasonable and must be justified by efficient organisation and greatly increased output.

I spoke of rural development, and of the great contribution which the University College and the Kumasi College of Technology could make to the new Ghana:

We should like to see the products of the University College of Ghana and of the Kumasi College of Technology playing an increasingly important role in the development of our country. Upon the shoulders of these students rest the future progress of our dear land and it is our hope that both the staff and the students will avail themselves of the existing facilities in these institutions to prepare themselves for the task ahead – namely, the social and economic reconstruction of Ghana. The Government look to lecturers and professors of our University College and the College of Technology to assist the nation in the successful implementation of the programme which we have outlined in our development plan.

Already the University College has been playing an important role in the public life of the country. During the recent
drought in Accra the University College helped in saving the
cattle industry on the Accra plains by making water available.
We are also happy to note the excellent research undertaken
by the Physics Department in connection with the recent
International Geophysical Year and the work they have done
in tracking the satellites. The assistance of the staffs of the
Economics, Sociology and Geography Departments is also
being enlisted for the forthcoming census.

I asked everyone to save as much as possible:

We have at the moment only sufficient funds to finance a part
of the Second Development Plan. I am confident that further
finance can be raised abroad but we must, in the first place,
see what we can do here in Ghana. Just as the farmer must
save some of his corn to plant a bigger and better crop next
year, so must the nation save some of its income for the pur-
chase of tools and machines, the building of roads, ports and
schools, which will increase productivity in the years to come.
There will be employment for everyone in this broad-fronted
development assault, and considerable sums of money will be
released locally to pay for the labour and materials required
during the campaign. If this money is spent straight away on
imported luxuries and non-essential things, we as a Nation
will get little benefit and the increased flow of money will
result in a sharp rise in prices. How much better if a large part
of the funds released for local spending is saved and lent to the
nation to further our development.

As soon as possible, the Government intends to establish a
money market in Ghana which will absorb savings and direct
them to productive use but, in the meantime, the same end
can be achieved by saving through the Post Office Savings
Bank, the Commercial Banks and the Ghana Building Society.
We must achieve the capital formation needed to launch and
sustain major productive efforts and as a nation, we must
cultivate the habit of saving from our earnings and of investing our savings where they will be secure for the future, and,
like the farmers' corn, can be used to plan out next year's crop.

An efficient and impartial Civil Service was essential, if the
Plan was to succeed. Civil servants, particularly those in the
higher grades, should maintain a political neutrality and give

completely loyal service to the duly constituted Government, regardless of its political complexion:

We, the Government, are animated by a sense of urgency and are eager to get things done, and show results; it is therefore necessary to find the ways and means of revitalising and animating the civil service with the same sense of urgency. This will call for drastic overhauling of the machinery of government and a simplification of the methods of work if we are to cope adequately with the urgent problems which need to be solved.

To all those civil servants who feel that they cannot, with a clear conscience, give loyal service to the Government, my advice is that they should resign from the service at once. If they are entitled to pension they will receive it. We will, at least, be sure that those who remain can be relied upon to carry out their duties loyally and efficiently. The Government will not continue to tolerate the kind of slovenly attitude towards work which has been so noticeable in many of the Ministries. It is our intention to tighten up the regulations and to wipe out the disloyal elements in the civil service, even if by so doing we suffer some temporary dislocation of the service. It is the Government's view that the defections in our Civil Service must be tackled vigorously and that now is the time to do so as we embark upon our Second Development Plan. For disloyal civil servants are no better than saboteurs and it is therefore better to make some sacrifice now, at the beginning of our herculean task, than to allow things to drift until a situation has been created which will be hard indeed to remedy.

I believe, however, that the disgruntled elements in our public service form an insignificant minority and that the service is fundamentally sound. I believe, therefore, that we can be assured of the maximum support from our public servants, both expatriate and Ghanaian. The size and breadth of the exercise which we are about to tackle should inspire and engender in our civil servants a deep enthusiasm, for it is the first time in the history of our country that they will have such an opportunity of giving of their best and of proving their worth. They should feel proud to be associated with a plan which aims at the fullest development of our country and the raising of the standard of life for all the people.

The battlefield is not the only place where men can demonstrate their patriotism and rise to great heights. The task which we are about to engage upon is no less heroic than war, for it is a struggle against poverty and want, backwardness and disease, illiteracy and ignorance. Our ultimate victory will bring greater satisfaction and well-being to all of us.

The Government, I said, was determined to root out corruption and other social evils. Regional Commissioners, District Commissioners and civil servants would be in the vanguard of the crusade against them. Everyone holding a responsible position should maintain the highest standards of integrity and probity both in private and in public life:

It is often said that God helps those who help themselves. I call upon each one of you, Chiefs and people, fellow men and women of Ghana, to make your maximum contribution to this concerted national assault on poverty, disease and ignorance. Tomorrow the battle will be joined. We move into the attack. If every soldier in this fight does his duty well and truly, victory is assured. Fellow countrymen and women, let us build not only for ourselves but for future generations, a brighter Ghana which will be an inspiration and shining example to all of Africa. I am confident that with your co-operation and with God's help we shall succeed. Let our battle cry be SERVE GHANA NOW. God bless you all and Good-night.

CHAPTER TWENTY-ONE

AFRICA MUST BE FREE

When I talk of freedom and independence for Africa, I mean that the vast African majority should be accepted as forming the basis of government in Africa. This does not imply that non-Africans should not live in Africa and play their full part in developing the continent, or that minority rights should be disregarded. As new African states emerge we look for a development of multi-racial understanding.

At the Accra Conference in April 1958, when representatives of eight independent African states met for the first time, a genuine African attitude to our basic problems became apparent. We agreed on three fundamental points; first, our desire to see all Africa free and independent; second, our determination to pursue a foreign policy based on non-alignment and positive neutralism, and third, our urgent need for economic development.

Since the Accra Conference there have been other meetings. In December 1958, the All-African Peoples' Conference opened in Accra. On that occasion, political and trade union leaders from all over Africa met. Once again, history was made, for never before had so many African leaders met together to discuss common problems. In the course of their discussions they made it clear that they wished to achieve not only the independence of their individual countries, but also some form of union which would bring the whole continent closer together. They decided to:

(i) work actively for a final assault on colonialism and imperialism in Africa;

(ii) use non-violent means to achieve political freedom, but be prepared to resist violence where the colonial powers resort to force;

(iii) set up a Permanent Secretariat to co-ordinate the efforts of all nationalist movements in Africa for the achievement of freedom;

(iv) condemn racialism and tribalism wherever they exist and work for their eradication, in particular, condemn the apartheid policy of South Africa;

(v) work for the ultimate achievement of a Union or Commonwealth of African States.

It cannot be denied that the process for the total liberation of Africa has begun in earnest, and that there is a strong case for very close association between the independent African states and those which will emerge as independent in future. I hope to see in Africa, not a large number of small and weak countries subject to all the dangers of Balkanisation, but rather the evolution of some sort of African union. Such a union need not prejudice the local autonomy of individual territories, but it would provide a mechanism which would allow Africa as a whole to co-ordinate its defence, its main lines of economic and foreign policies, and its economic development.

The first step along the road towards African union was taken on 23 November 1958, when Ghana and the Republic of Guinea united. We realised that our union might involve many difficult issues, but we were determined to unite in order to form a nucleus for a union of African states. In July 1959, I met the Presidents of Liberia and Guinea for a three-day conference at Sanniquellie. We discussed matters of common concern, and the whole question of African emancipation and unity. At the end of our talks we issued a Declaration of Principles which, I believe, may one day be regarded as of great historical significance. These principles are:

1 The name of the organisation shall be the Community of Independent African States.

2 Africans, like all other peoples have the inherent right to independence and self-determination and to decide the form of government under which they wish to live.

3 Each State or Federation, which is a member of the Community, shall maintain its own national identity and constitutional structure. The Community is being formed with a view to achieving unity among independent African States. It is not designed to prejudice the present or future international policies, relations and obligations of the States involved.

4 Each member of the Community accepts the principle that it shall not interfere in the internal affairs of any other member.

5 (a) The acts of States or Federations, which are members of

the Community, shall be determined in relation to the essential objectives which are Freedom, Independence, Unity, the African Personality, as well as the interest of the African peoples. (b) Each Member-State or Federation shall, in its acts or policies, do nothing contrary to the spirit and objectives of the Community.

6 (a) The general policy of the Community shall be to build up a free and prosperous African Community for the benefit of its peoples and the peoples of the world and in the interest of international peace and security. (b) This policy shall be based essentially on the maintenance of diplomatic, economic and cultural relations, on the basis of equality and reciprocity, with all the States of the world which adopt a position compatible with African interests and African dignity. (c) Its main objectives will be to help other African territories, subjected to domination, with a view to accelerating the end of their non-independent status.

7 The Community shall set up an Economic Council, a Cultural Council and a Scientific and Research Council.

8 Membership in the Community shall be open to all independent African States and Federations, and any non-independent country of Africa shall have the right to join the Community upon its attainment of independence.

9 The Community shall have a Flag and an Anthem to be agreed upon at a later date.

10 The motto of the Community shall be INDEPENDENCE AND UNITY.

Signed: W. V. S. TUBMAN, President of the Republic of Liberia.
Signed: SEKOU TOURÉ, President of the Republic of Guinea.
Signed: KWAME NKRUMAH, Prime Minister of Ghana.

The concept of a union of African states may seem visionary to some, but at least everyone would agree that great political forces have been released and are at work in Africa. With goodwill, sympathy and understanding, it should be possible to guide these forces into constructive and positive channels. We all have everything to lose from a failure to achieve a peaceful liberation of Africa.

CHAPTER TWENTY-TWO

LOYALTY AND THE SERVICES

In November 1959 Her Majesty the Queen was to have come to Ghana, but the royal visit had to be postponed. I was informed of the Queen's condition some weeks before the news that she was expecting a baby was made public. I believe I was the first person, outside the immediate royal circle, to be told. Shortly after the news was officially announced to the world, I was invited to see the Queen at Balmoral Castle to discuss revised arrangements for a later royal visit to Ghana. I did not know then that she intended to bestow a great honour on me by making me a member of the Privy Council.

On my arrival in London I had lunch with the Prime Minister, the Right Honourable Harold Macmillan. I also met the Lord Chancellor and the Secretary of State for Commonwealth Relations, Lord Home. These meetings afforded a useful opportunity for an exchange of views on the many complex problems facing emergent Africa. Afterwards, I went to Scotland, where I spent a most enjoyable few days. When I returned to Accra I broadcast to the people of Ghana to tell them about my visit:

I flew to Balmoral in an aircraft of the Queen's Flight which had been specially placed at my disposal to convey me to Scotland. This gesture was typical of the constant kindness and hospitality which was shown to me by the Queen during my entire visit. What impressed me most was not the grandeur of Balmoral, but the simplicity of the Royal Family and their deep sense of devoted family life. The spirit of a united, affectionate family circle – such as we treasure here in Ghana – made it very easy for me to convey to the Queen the sincere wishes of every man and woman in Ghana for her good health and happiness in her present delicate condition. I was able to assure Her Majesty that we in Ghana, men, women and children, shall rejoice with her when the new member of the Royal Family is born – a sentiment which the Queen greatly appreciated. At the time that I left Balmoral Her Majesty was looking wonderfully well and exceedingly happy.

I went on to say that although the Queen and the Duke of Edinburgh were very disappointed about the postponement of the royal visit, they hoped to come to Ghana in 1961. In the meantime, the Duke of Edinburgh had accepted an invitation to visit Ghana on his own in November (1959), to see for himself something of our progress since Independence. I continued:

It is with great humility that I must refer to myself at this stage. As you know, during my visit to Balmoral I had the honour of being made a member of the Queen's Privy Council. As the first African to be admitted into this great Council of State, I consider it an honour not only to myself, but also to the people of Ghana and to peoples of Africa and of African descent everywhere. I would like to take this opportunity to thank you all very sincerely for the hundreds of messages of congratulation that I have received by letter, telegram and telephone.

My homeward voyage by sea afforded me an invaluable opportunity to reflect on some of our urgent national problems. I would like to share with you some of my thoughts and to seek your co-operation in the implementation of the immense tasks that lie ahead of us all. As I lay in my bed in the peace and quiet of my cabin, I became convinced as never before of the high role that destiny has called upon the people of Ghana, not only in emblazoning the path in the new evolution and political awakening of our continent, but also in the struggle for African independence and unity.

That is why we must always keep steadily before us the vision of a Ghana socially stable and united, politically independent and economically free and prosperous. Now that we have achieved our first objective – political freedom – we must consolidate our independence by building up a solid economic foundation. This calls for a concerted effort on the part of all of us to give of our best to the national effort. I want to appeal to all of you to give me your fullest moral support to ensure that we establish in Ghana the highest standards of honesty and integrity both in our public and in our private lives.

It was my intention, I said, to visit those parts of the country which I had not been able to include in my previous itineraries. I hoped to meet people in their homes and at their work, to hear their views on the Five Year Development Plan and the future of Ghana. Constitutional development was a matter which had to be considered very soon:

As you know, the Government have been considering the establishment of a republican form of constitution in Ghana. We believe that this form of parliamentary democracy is better suited to our needs and will give new impetus to our rapid political and social development as well as enabling us to play a more effective role in the affairs of Africa, whose independent states are, many of them, republican in form. Such a republican form of Government in Ghana, like India and Pakistan, will in no way affect our relations with other members of the Commonwealth. This is a matter about which I shall keep the Prime Ministers of the other Commonwealth countries informed. When we have completed our final constitutional arrangements, I shall, of course, consult you, the people.

Regardless of the constitutional form which we evolve, the cardinal aim of Ghana's foreign policy will continue to be the cultivation of good neighbourliness and the promotion of world peace and security. That is why we are determined not to get ourselves entangled in the cold war between East and West. This, however, does not mean that my Government intend to be silent spectators in matters affecting our country's vital interests and the destiny of the African continent. It is for this reason that we have taken the initiative of expressing our strongest protest against the proposed test explosion of an atomic bomb in the Sahara by France, and we are encouraged by the impact which our protest and the protests of our sister States in Africa have had on world opinion. But just as we want peace and security for the world at large, so we ardently desire peace and tranquillity at home, for without law and order based on a solid economic foundation we shall not be able to carry out any effective foreign policy.

Consequently, the Government intend to devote their maximum energies towards achieving great progress in the next few years. It is thus that we will ensure the greatest happiness and well being for all people. But without your support our efforts will be in vain. I therefore once again appeal to you, my fellow countrymen and women, to rally behind the Government and to put aside all partisan feelings, and to re-dedicate yourselves to the patriotic service of your country, so that Ghana will continue to maintain the leadership which we have achieved in the vanguard of African liberation.

Three days later, on 4 September 1959, I once again emphasised the great opportunities for loyal service to the country. This time, I was speaking to Police officers who had just completed their course at the Police College in Tesano, and were newly-appointed Assistant Superintendents:

I am confident that the knowledge and experience which you have gained at the Police College will be put to good use in the service of the Force, and ultimately of the country. There is no need for me to tell you that you are entering the commissioned ranks of a proud and devoted Force, whose loyalty to the Government and the nation has been demonstrated repeatedly and on which my Government can confidently rely in the future.

It is of the greatest importance that you, and indeed all officers of Police, realise the duties of a Police Force in a free and independent State. The policeman is the servant of the public. There are colonial police forces which exist to enforce the authority of a foreign power on a colonial people. In such forces this will be demonstrated by the fact that the Police will be peremptory and even brutal in their dealings with the inhabitants of the colony, while they will be ingratiating and subservient to those in authority. In a free and independent country the conduct of the Police must be the exact reverse of this. They must demonstrate to the people at large that the country is free and independent by behaving towards the ordinary man in the street with exactly the same politeness as they would behave towards those in a superior position.

To a tremendous extent the reputation and the future of the country depends upon the conduct of the Police. For a new country there is perhaps no evil more deadly than corruption. Corruption can undermine industrial and social development and destroy the chance of raising the standard of living of the people. Above all, therefore, the Police must be absolutely and completely honest and incorruptible. You must remember always that to many citizens their everyday dealings with the Government are through the Police and the reputation of the State is very largely judged by citizens and those from outside on the way in which the Police behave.

A policeman must realise that his first duty is to be helpful to the public. The Police are, of course, helpful to the public in that they suppress crime and, in the interests of all, regulate the traffic and public gatherings, but they should always try and do these duties in such a way that they do not antagonise the ordinary man and woman, and that they do not give preference to any particular individual because of wealth or position, but are just, fair and courteous to all alike. In particular, it is necessary that you are not only efficient in your duties but that it is clear to the public that you are efficient. This is most important for the maintenance of public confidence. You should, therefore, always be smart in appearance and act in your duties in a well-drilled manner, appropriate to a disciplined Force. In all your dealings with the public, as I have said, you must not only be competent, you must let the public see that you are competent. If, for example, you are taking a statement from a citizen, you should do it with despatch and courtesy and not keep some member of the public, who has come to help the Police, hanging around at the Police Station or the Licensing Department, or wherever it is. You must remember that you are in a position of authority and you can use that authority very often to compel the public to come to you to fill in a form or make a statement to you. You must always exercise this authority with courtesy and with a realisation that you, too, are a citizen of Ghana and that the citizen whom you may be questioning, or marshalling in a crowd, has just the same rights as a citizen as you, yourself, possess.

I hope your future conduct in the discharge of your professional duties will demonstrate to the world that the training establishments of the Ghana Police, and those produced by these establishments, are second to none. I wish you luck in your future careers. I ask you all to devote the rest of your service to the good of the country, in the best interests of all its inhabitants, and in maintaining your highest traditions.

As I left Tesano, I reflected on the whole question of trained manpower to meet the rapidly growing needs of the country. In a developing nation like ours, the keynote to progress lies in the availability of qualified men to enter into the field in which development is designed to take place. The decision to raise a Ghana Air Force, for example, had to be quickly followed up by the establishment of a Flying Training School. I opened the School officially on 11 September 1959, although the pilots' course actually started on 20 July:

The Ghana Air Force is the latest addition to our defence forces and completes what is generally referred to as the conventional arms. Since the attainment of independence no effort has been spared to develop our Army and to establish the two sister arms – the Navy and the Air Force – both of which are being developed as rapidly as possible. The foundations of these forces are being carefully laid and we have the three service Chiefs – the Chief of General Staff, the Naval Chief of Staff and the Air Chief of Staff, working under the Chief of Defence Staff – for advising on the organisation and development of the forces as well as for their command and operational use. During the Second Development Plan period the Army will be expanded and the sister forces built up to fulfil their respective defence roles.

So far, the relatively unexplored field of aviation in this country, has in the main been confined to civil and commercial flying by a comparatively small nucleus of Ghanaian aircrew in Ghana Airways. The setting up of the Flying Training School will, I am convinced, result in the enterprising and right type of young Ghanaian coming forward in increasing numbers to take up an interesting, exacting, but nevertheless thrilling career in the parallel field of military aviation. I say *convinced*, because I have been told that the 15 young men you see before you on the parade ground were selected out of a batch of volunteers many times that number. It is this keenness that is so encouraging, and allays any doubts there may be on the healthy future for military aviation in Ghana. The aim of the Flying Training School is at present to impart basic training in service flying. The training schedule is spread over a fairly concentrated period of ten months, at the end of which the trainee will be in a position to assimilate more advanced forms of instruction prior to finally assuming responsibilities as an officer or a pilot in our Air Force.

The staff of the Flying Training School is made up of a team of flying instructors and maintenance personnel on loan from the Israeli Air Force, and a certain number of officers and other ranks from the Ghana Army. The object of the training schedule is in the first place, to impart basic military and academic instruction similar in pattern to the type given at the Regular Officers Special Training School at Teshie which is to form the main part of the proposed Ghana Military Academy. This schedule is suitably modified in its intermediate and final stages, laying emphasis on subjects peculiar to the Air Force and includes 100 hours of flying on an elementary trainer aircraft.

I said that the progress of the Flying Training School would be watched with keen interest by the Government and by myself. It was important to remember, however, that the Ghana Air Force needed ground staff as well as pilots:

It is pertinent to note that an Air Force is not made up of pilots only. It is also made up of men who labour behind the scenes, the ground staff and the various highly trained technicians without whom no operation either in peace or in war could be a success. In this field therefore there is also a great future, and I have no doubt that my Air Staff consisting of Indian Air Force officers are taking simultaneous steps to ensure that plans are being laid for the training of ground personnel who, in the not too distant future, will be responsible for keeping the aeroplanes flying. The concurrent growth of aircrew and groundcrew is a must, as only then can an Air Force be established on a sound footing, and so achieve expeditiously its rightful status as a completely independent and self-administering force within the defence forces organisation of Ghana.

I should now like to say a word to the staff and students. On those of you who pass out from this institution will eventually devolve the responsibility for the future of our Air Force. You must take every opportunity to absorb carefully every bit of instruction which is being imparted to you by experts in this special field of learning. It is on your ability to assimilate and later apply this instruction, that your mettle as pioneers of the Ghana Air Force will be determined. If your enthusiasm as reflected by the good turnout of your parade today, after only six weeks of training, can be taken as a pointer, then I am safe in predicting that you will be equal to the arduous task that lies ahead. Well done and keep it up!

As I said earlier, the Flying Training School is the first unit of a new service. We are agreed in our hopes that the seed has been cast in fertile soil and will bear much fruit in the form of an efficient fighting force, capable of shouldering its share of responsibility for the security of our nation. For this to be realised, it will need a spirit of enterprise, self-sacrifice and, co-operation, not only from those immediately and directly responsible for its establishment and growth, but also from the members of the public. I have every hope that the public will, at all times, ensure that in their own respective spheres they will use every available opportunity to encourage the cadets and co-operate to make an Air Force an efficient arm of our defence forces. Finally, as prospective officers you will have many responsibilities, and I could do no better than commend to you an inscription which is prominently displayed at a military college overseas which has inspired and will, I have no doubt, continue to inspire generations of cadets:

The safety, honour and welfare of your country comes first, always and every time. The safety and welfare of the men under your command comes next. Your own safety and welfare come last, always and every time.

These are challenging words and I trust they will ring constantly in your ears: Ghana expects from all its citizens, especially those belonging to the armed forces, a high sense of responsibility and selfless devotion to duty. Remember that the greatness of Ghana does not lie only in the physical achievements of our development plans but also in the quality of the life of its people. With these words, I have pleasure in formally declaring the Flying Training School open and, speaking in Air Force parlance, on behalf of the Government and myself, I wish you happy landings and the best of luck.

CHAPTER TWENTY-THREE

THE AFRICAN COMMUNITY

At the All-African Peoples' Conference in December 1958 we declared in no uncertain terms that only Africans can liberate Africa. Undoubtedly, the stirring message of the Accra Conference gave new momentum to the liberation movement. Riots broke out in the Congo. Many people were killed and hundreds imprisoned. Names hitherto unknown to the world, like Joseph Kasavubu, Lumumba, Tshombe and Ngalula have been spread across the front pages of the international press. The Congo riots were closely followed by risings in Nyasaland. The democratic one-man one-vote formula, which had been decided upon at the Accra Conference, and with which Banda caught the imagination of his people, proved too bitter a pill for the settlers to swallow.

I referred to the growing unrest in various parts of Africa, when I addressed the Steering Committee of the All-African Peoples' Conference in Accra on 6 October 1959. I said that the question of the apartheid policy of the South African Government had been raised in the United Nations, and that Ghana would continue to hold a vigilant brief until South Africa became free. South West Africa, the Cameroons, Algeria; all presented problems and Africa was in danger of becoming used as a battleground by foreign powers:

Africa is fast gravitating to the whirlwind of world politics. As new and developing nations, we must jealously guard against anything that threatens our independence and freedom of action; we must be careful of the activities of foreign powers in Africa and we must not do anything which will make us compromise our independence or lose our freedom of action. We must guard against any attempt by foreign powers to use African soil for their own political and economic advantage. In short, we must be vigilant in safeguarding our independence.

As regards our sister territories which are on the threshold of independence, we earnestly beseech them not to tie them-

selves up with agreements that may rob them of true independence. Independence must be free and unfettered, for
freedom of action on the part of a sovereign nation is essential.
The African Personality and the African Community must
have a free and fertile soil in which to flourish and blossom.

Freedom fighters all over the continent of Africa are mourning the loss of Comrade George Padmore. It was but yesterday
that Comrade Padmore was amongst us playing his humble
but no mean part in the great struggle for the total liberation
of Africa. Now he is no more. Let us pause and stand in silence
for one minute.

Friends and comrades: The Conference of the Independent
African States, the All-African Peoples' Conference, the Sanniquellie Conference and the Ghana-Guinea Union are all
pointers to the total liberation of Africa. Africa marches on
relentlessly to its cherished goal of independence and unity
and none can stem the tide any longer. It is therefore up to all
of us to contribute our share to facilitate this momentum so
that generations after us will be blessed. Fellow Freedom
Fighters of the All-African Peoples' Conference Steering Committee, I salute you and wish you every success in your
deliberations.

At another meeting of the Steering Committe, I stressed the
need for the regrouping of all trade union movements in Africa.
In the past, African trade unions had been grouped in either the
World Federation of Trade Unions, or in the International Confederation of Free Trade Unions. It seemed to me that the new
African outlook, evident in the conception of an African personality within an African community, merited the foundation
of an All-African Trade Union Federation. Such a federation
would be independent of any other organisation, and dedicated
to the movement for the total emancipation of Africa.

I spoke of this when I laid the foundation stone of the Hall of
Trade Unions in Accra on 17 October 1959, and to judge from
the applause which greeted the suggestion of an All-African
Trade Union Federation, my audience fully supported the idea.
I then went on to consider the labour movement within Ghana:

I would like to emphasise my determination to maintain the
unity of the country for our economic, political and social
reconstruction. The re-organisation of the Farmers' Council,
the Co-operative Movement, the Builders' Brigade, the
Trade Union Congress and the proposed establishment of

the Young Pioneers are all designed to achieve this objective. The Convention People's Party is the political vanguard of these movements within which we can find the expression of our ideals for the economic and social well being of our people. You will recall the resolution that was passed by the National Executive of the Party at Winneba last year exhorting members of the Party who are workers to belong to the Trade Union Congress, and Party members who are farmers to belong to the United Ghana Farmers' Council. I urge Party members to follow this decision.

It will continue to be the policy of my Government to give active support to the Trade Union Congress in their efforts to organise the workers and to win for them better living standards as well as respect for their rights as working people. Those who are against the labour movement, the co-operative movement or the farmers organisations are against me and the Convention People's Party. There can be no split loyalties. Nobody has the right to call himself a true labour fighter if he is not also an honest and loyal member of the Convention People's Party, because fundamentally the Convention People's Party is the political expression of the Ghana Trade Union movement.

The whole character of our labour movement was, I said, something new which we were giving to the world. Its success would demonstrate another method of achieving social harmony in the development of our new state.

Less than a month later, on 5 November, I welcomed representatives of African trade unions to Accra. Their task was to organise an All-African Trade Union Federation:

It is certainly not necessary for me, within this gathering of experienced and seasoned trade union leaders, to stress the strength, aims and responsibilities of the trade union movement in present-day Africa. The efforts that have been made by the various trade unions as the spearheads of the struggle for their countries' political independence are well-known. Your courageous efforts to raise the standard of living and to secure safe working conditions for African workers is also well-known.

The trade union movement in Africa is indissolubly linked up with the struggle for the political freedom, independence and unity of our continent. A trade union movement on a colonial territory cannot divorce itself from the national struggle for political independence. Indeed in a colonial

territory the struggle for freedom and independence is in-
extricably linked up with the success of the trade union
movement. Experiences in Ghana, Guinea, Morocco and
last, but not least, Algeria, are demonstration of this fact.
Political freedom and the rights of workers are indivisible. It
is only under genuine conditions of political freedom that the
workers can have the opportunity to assert themselves as
human beings and define their rights for better conditions
and for a better way of life.

The first duty of all organisations existing in a colonial
territory is for these forces in that territory to unite in the fight
for the nation's liberation. It is almost axiomatic that the
nationalist movements that have borne the brunt of the struggle
for independence have never ignored the trade unions. Everything possible has been done to draw the working classes and
the masses of the common people into the struggle as the only
effective challenge to the oppressive forces. In the past,
because of the partition and domination of Africa by colonial
powers, some African trade unions have been tied up to the
trade unions of the metropolitan countries of these colonial
powers. Another important factor is that African trade
unionism for the last quarter of a century has suffered splits
and divisions as a result of the cold war, about which we are
less concerned. The Conference of Independent African States
and the All African People's Conference gave a new ideology
to the African peoples to re-discover for themselves their
continent. To-day there is a new African in the world, a proud
African, free and independent, who is determined, despite all
obstacles, to assert his personality within the community of
the world. The African nations, having learnt their lessons
from the past, are no longer prepared to be pawns to foreign
nations and to allow their independence and freedom to be
sold on the altar of international politics. The desire of the
African people themselves to unite and to assert their personality in the context of the African community has made
itself felt everywhere.

The trade union organisations of the African countries who
have found themselves always in the vanguard of the national
movements, can no longer keep themselves aloof from this
upsurge which is permeating the whole of the African continent. That is why we in Ghana welcome with satisfaction
the unanimous declaration of the African trade unionists who
attended the All African People's Conference in Accra last
December calling for the formation of an All African Trade
Union Federation. You are here merely fulfilling an historical

mission as you reflect on the trade union movement which antedates your own. They, like you, started on a national scale before reaching international level.

We understand and support the desires of the African workers to be on their own. It is my hope that the world will understand your aspirations. We see in an All African Trade Union Federation an independent and united African organisation not affiliated to either the World Federation of Trade Unions, or to the International Federation of Free Trade Unions; a positively neutral federation, friendly to all international organisations but holding allegiance to none, except to Mother Africa. The Government of Ghana fully supports the desire of the African workers and, as in the past, we shall give every support and encouragement to the formation of such a federation. This federation should seek consultative status with the United Nations and its specialised agencies. In this way we shall have an African Trade Union International that will speak for the workers of Africa in the manner that the workers of Africa wish their voices heard. This new African Trade Union International has an important part to play in the struggle for African political freedom and in economic and social development. The national movements that are emerging in Africa to-day are decisive proof that our continent cannot be kept much longer in a state of political and economic dependence. From a purely trade union point of view, it should be one of the main objects of this new African federation to develop a strong trade union movement throughout Africa.

In coming here this afternoon to welcome you, I wish to express my faith, and that of my Government, in African labour. I wish you successful deliberations.

A further step forward in the direction of all-African co-operation was taken at about the same time, when the United Nations opened in Accra a Regional Office of their Food and Agricultural Organisation. The technical and human problems with which the international team intended to deal would cover the whole of Africa, and African governments would co-operate to solve their common food and agricultural problems.

At the opening ceremony, I recalled Ghana's entry into the United Nations Organisation two days after Independence:

Ghana, having joined the United Nations two days after her independence, now enjoys the company of other African countries who are strong and loyal members of the Organisation. As members, these African countries have obligations to the United Nations and, similarly, the United Nations and its specialised agencies have obligations to Africa. It is, therefore, heartening to see the United Nations extending its operations by establishing offices to deal with problems exclusive to Africa. In December, 1957, we were happy to see the United Nations Technical Assistance Board established here. This was followed by the United Nations Information Centre in March 1958. Earlier this year the Field Office of the International Labour Organisation was established in Nigeria and the Economic Commission for Africa began its operations in Ethiopia. The Office of United Nations Children's Fund for West Africa was established in Lagos and a Regional Office of the World Health Organisation has been operating from Brazzaville in recent years.

Realising the importance of agriculture to the nation and having regard to the fact that agriculture still provides the wealth of the country and employment for the majority of the people, the Government has laid a great deal of emphasis in the Second Development Plan on the development of agriculture and agricultural resources. It is our intention to diversify agriculture by the introduction of more cash crops and by the growing of all our food requirements in the country. Even though we can achieve much by our own efforts, there is much that we can gain from such organisations as the United Nations Technical Assistance Board. Ghana has therefore very special reason to be interested in having the headquarters of the Food and Agriculture Organisation in Accra and having in the same building officers for the other United Nations Agencies in Accra. As a mark of our interest in the United Nations and in the Food and Agriculture Organisation this building has been provided by the Government of Ghana for the Regional Office of the Food and Agriculture Organisation for Africa; it will also be occupied by the United Nations Technical Assistance Board.

What we see today as but an edifice in sand and cement will develop, we expect, into the centre of a vigorous African agency for disseminating improved agricultural practices so indispensable to the raising of the nutrition and general standard of living of the people of Africa.

CHAPTER TWENTY-FOUR

THE VISIT OF THE DUKE OF EDINBURGH

In November 1959 His Royal Highness the Duke of Edinburgh, piloting an aircraft of the Queen's Flight, arrived in Ghana for a short visit to see something of the progress made since Independence. He carried out a very full round of engagements, and helped to alleviate disappointment at the Queen's cancelled tour.

One particularly colourful occasion was the inauguration of the Ghana Academy of Learning, when the Duke agreed to become Honorary President for two years. In welcoming him to the first public meeting, I spoke of the reasons for the foundation of the Academy:

The objects of the Academy are, in the words of its Instrument of Incorporation, to promote the study and the extension and dissemination of all the sciences and learning; to establish and maintain proper standards of endeavour in all fields of science and learning; and lastly to recognise outstanding contributions to the advancement of science and learning in Ghana.

I have been convinced for some time that a stage had been reached in our educational development where additional thrusts and incentives were necessary to inspire our young scholars to aim for higher fields of endeavour. A few months ago, therefore, I proposed that we should examine the feasibility of establishing some sort of Association which would have for its main purpose the provision of a forum for the exposition of views in science and other fields of learning, and the stimulation of interest in the increase of knowledge in these fields. Most important of all, it was my belief that the existence of the right kind of institution would be of the greatest encouragement to many talented young men and women in Ghana, and lead them to aspire to academic distinction and recognition, to the ultimate glory of their country.

I then referred to the organisation and the standards of the Academy:

The government of the Academy has been vested in a Council, which is elected by the members. Membership of the Academy itself will be by election and a necessary requirement will be the production of some original work of significance in science or learning. The Council may elect as an Associate of the Academy any person who has completed an approved course of academic study, and who satisfies the Council of his intention to extend his studies and to carry out original work in a branch of science or learning. It is my firm hope that many Ghanaians will qualify for the Associateship of the Academy, as a first step to further academic work.

Finally any member of the Academy who is a citizen of Ghana may be elected to Fellowship of the Academy, provided that he shall have made an original contribution of outstanding merit in any branch of science or learning. Non-Ghanaians of eminence in science and learning who have rendered service to the extension of science and learning in Ghana will also be eligible for election by the Council to be Honorary Fellows of the Academy. In order, however, to ensure the full but gradual establishment of the Academy in an authoritative way, it is not proposed to elect any Fellows to it within the first five years of the Academy's existence.

The Ghana Academy of Learning will inevitably invite comparison with bodies like the Royal Society of London or the Royal Australian Academy of Science. We are fully aware of this, and are under no misconception as to the responsibility which devolves upon us to establish and maintain high and internationally acceptable standards. The Ghana Academy of Learning is therefore both an opportunity for, and a challenge to all scholars in Ghana. I am convinced that before very long, the Ghana Academy of Learning will be completely accepted internationally, and will exert the greatest influence in our national life by the raising and recognition of standards of achievement in research in various fields of knowledge relating not only to Ghana, but to the whole of Africa. You, Sir, have obviously appreciated our ambitions and have graciously agreed to accept the Honorary Presidency of this Academy for the first two years of its life. We are deeply sensible of the honour which you have conferred upon us, and we thank you for what you have done.

The Duke has great personal charm. Everywhere he went large crowds gathered to see him. He showed a keen interest in all aspects of our development plans, and inspected works completed and in progress. At the farewell dinner on 29 November, I thanked the Duke for all he had done:

We have come to the end of a visit which we shall long remember for the interest which Your Royal Highness has taken in everything that you have seen and for the pleasure which your visit has given to the Government and the people of this country. We were naturally disappointed that Her Majesty's visit had to be postponed but, on the other hand, the happy circumstance which led to the postponement has given us all a pleasurable anticipation. Although your visit, Sir, is not a substitute for the visit which Her Majesty and yourself were to have paid to Ghana at this same time, we have nevertheless been very happy to welcome you to Ghana and to show you some of our efforts. During the few days you have spent in Ghana you have seen a few of the developments upon which we have embarked in all fields, particularly in the fields of technology and construction. Some we have completed, others are still in the planning stage. All represent our hopes for a better life for our people and our aspirations for the future.

We are sorry that your visit has been so brief. But even in this time we hope that you have not failed to be struck by the great pride which the people of Ghana have in their independence, and their determination to build mostly by their own efforts a strong and peaceful nation in which equal opportunities will be provided for all; a nation that generations to come will be happy and proud to inherit. It is in this sense of freedom, independence and sovereignty that Ghana is proud to be a member of the Commonwealth family – all the members of which are sovereign and independent, none owing an allegiance to the other, but all of them working closely together within a special framework of understanding and friendship.

As we say goodbye to you formally, Sir, we should like you to carry to Her Majesty our loyal and sincere greetings, and to assure her how much we are looking forward to her visit in 1961. In fact, we are dying to see her! And I hope that the warmth of our welcome to you on this occasion has demonstrated the great pleasure with which we are looking forward to your return with her.

And now I have much pleasure, on behalf of the Government and people of Ghana in presenting you with this gift which we would ask you to accept as a small memento of your first visit to Ghana. It is in the form of a desk stand which is made in Ghana gold and Ghana ivory. We hope that it will remind you always of your visit and the great pleasure it has given to us. We wish you, Sir, a safe and enjoyable journey home.

I have just one more thing to say. As soon as you return to the Queen, please give to Her Majesty my personal good wishes, and those of all the people of Ghana. She is much in our thoughts, and we trust that she keeps in splendid health during the coming months.

CHAPTER TWENTY-FIVE

GHANA IN WORLD AFFAIRS

As the year 1959 drew to a close, we approached the end of the third year of our existence as a sovereign, independent state. Many important events had taken place in the field of international affairs which had directly affected not only Ghana, but other African peoples in various parts of our continent. It seemed an appropriate time to take stock of our performance and achievements in our relations with other nations, and to re-assess and re-state our policy in the light of changing circumstances.

In the National Assembly on 16 December, I introduced the motion: 'That this House approves the Policy of the Government in regard to Foreign Affairs.' In my speech I went over the whole field of our relations with foreign states and other peoples since we became independent:

Honourable Members are aware that a cardinal feature and objective of our foreign policy is to promote and maintain peace and security among the nations of the world. To achieve this objective, I have always stated that it is our desire to cultivate friendship with all nations and to be enemy to none. In pursuance of our policy of peace and friendship the Government and people of Ghana are determined not to get themselves entangled in the great ideological conflicts of the Great Powers as manifested in the cold war which divides the world into East and West power blocs suspicious of each other's motives and intentions.

This policy of non-alignment, of course, should not be interpreted to mean that my Government will choose to play the role of silent spectators in world affairs, or in matters which affect our country's vital interests and the destiny of the African peoples. Our policy of positive neutralism is not a passive or neutralist policy. It is a positive policy based upon our firm belief in positive action.

We believe that the United Nations is a useful instrument for harmonising the policies of states and for the promotion of peace and mutual understanding among the nations of the world. My Government will continue to co-operate with and support the United Nations in the effort to promote and maintain international peace and security. To this end, we reaffirm our faith in the Charter of the United Nations.

I said that the Government of Ghana welcomed the resolution on disarmament which had been presented to the General Assembly of the United Nations by the four great powers and sponsored by all the eighty-two member states:

The Government of Ghana welcome this healthy trend in international relations, and hope that no efforts will be spared on every side to bring about the general and complete disarmament upon which the continued existence of humanity so much depends, since failure to attain this desired objective could indeed result in the possible tragic extermination of mankind from the surface of this planet.

The United Nations Charter, however, recognises that disarmament matters are of world-wide interest and concern to all nations and peoples, and that they are not the exclusive preserve of the great powers.

Accordingly, ultimate responsibility for general disarmament measures or agreements should continue to rest with the United Nations. The setting up of the ten-power Disarmament Committee should thus in no way encroach upon United Nations responsibilities in this important field.

'Africa,' I continued, 'is the only continent where the majority of its indigenous populations are not yet free.' The independence of Ghana would be meaningless unless it were linked with the total liberation of Africa. I referred to conferences in which Ghana had taken a leading role, the Conference of Independent African States, the Sanniquellie Conference, and the All-African People's Conference:

My Government will continue to pursue this policy of independence and unity of Africa with all the vigour and resources at our command. We believe that until the whole of Africa is free, independent and united, there will be no lasting peace in the world. This is so because, in our view, the evils of colonialism and imperialist expansion have been the main cause of the wars which have afflicted Europe and the whole world in recent history. Therefore, in the interest of peace and security in Africa and in the world, we call upon the colonial powers to grant independence to all the African countries at present under their control.

We also appeal to all peace-loving nations and peoples of the world who believe in the ideals of democracy, freedom and justice, to support us in our efforts to secure unity among the African peoples.

The Union of Ghana and Guinea, agreed on in November 1958, may well serve as the basis for a larger Union of African States. I told members that Ghana and Guinea had established a system of exchange of Resident Ministers, who were deemed to be members of both the Government of Ghana and the Government of Guinea. There was no precedent in political practice for such an arrangement.

After condemning the proposed French atomic test in the Sahara, I went on to deal with the accusation that Ghana was fast becoming a centre for anti-colonial agitation:

There are many people in and outside Africa, who attribute the recent disturbances in Nyasaland, in the Congo and in other colonial territories of Africa, directly to the deliberations which took place at the All-African People's Conference held in Accra. Such people believe that Ghana has become the centre of anti-colonial forces and political agitation for independence in Africa. They view Ghana and the development of nationalism in modern Africa with alarm and increasing apprehension.

On our part, I wish to say that this accusation is perhaps the greatest tribute that the enemies of African freedom could pay to Ghana. If, indeed, the attainment of independence by Ghana, or the attendance at conferences in Ghana by youths from other parts of Africa has provided the spark of inspiration for nationalist action in the several African territories, then this is a situation of which we can justly be proud. In this regard, I wish to say in clear and unmistakable terms, that Ghana has no apologies to render to anybody; nor have we any excuses to make. Let me reiterate that our policies have been directed towards the total liberation of Africa from foreign rule. We accept this charge without demur, and we shall pursue it without rancour or violence, because of our unflinching faith in the inalienable right of all peoples to be free.

We call upon the world to witness and to take note that there is a new Africa dedicated to the task of complete

emancipation. Her sons and daughters will not rest until the
last vestiges of domination and discrimination and colonialism
in any form have been obliterated for ever from her soil.
Africa is on the march. There is no turning back.

A lively debate followed. Opposition members raised questions
about the Government's internal policy, and about relations
with French Togoland, the Ivory Coast, and other territories
bordering Ghana. One point, however, emerged clearly and unmistakably from the discussions, namely, that African freedom
and unity was the wish of all, irrespective of creed or party.

Early in the new year, on the tenth anniversary of Positive
Action, I addressed a large crowd in the West End Arena, and
again spoke of Ghana's role in world affairs:

> ... I must emphasise that our Party's foreign policy continues
> to be based upon positive neutralism and non-alignment. We
> are convinced that by our policy of non-alignment we are
> able to speak our minds frankly and without fear and favour
> on issues as they arise. Our policy is not a negative one.
> Positive neutralism and non-alignment does not mean keep-
> ing aloof from burning international issues. On the contrary,
> it means a positive stand based on our own convictions com-
> pletely uninfluenced by any of the power blocs. We believe
> that we could help to bridge the unfortunate and undesirable
> gap between the so-called East and West blocs by not aligning
> ourselves to either side. We hold the view that as to the issues
> between them, neither bloc can claim to be permanently
> right or permanently wrong. As such, it will not be in the
> interest of international understanding and unity for us and
> the other independent states of Africa to involve ourselves in
> the disputes of the Power blocs by taking sides. We should be
> free to take our stand without previously committing ourselves
> to any bloc on any matters which affect the peace, progress
> and, indeed, the destiny of Africa.
> We believe that it would be suicidal to involve ourselves in
> the disputes of the great powers by taking sides. We will con-
> tinue to cultivate and maintain friendly relations with all
> countries, and to be enemy to none.

Concerning Africa, I said that the Convention People's Party
was dedicated to the cause of African independence and unity.
The colonial powers had been compelled to recognise the grow-

ing tide of African nationalism, but there were still many dangers to be faced:

We must be vigilant, for colonialism and imperialism may come to Africa in different guises. We must therefore alert ourselves to be able to recognise this whenever and wherever it rears its head, and prepare ourselves to fight against it, for it is only with the complete internment of imperialism and colonialism that Africa will be free from menace and able to live and breathe in full liberty where not only men of colour everywhere but also men of all races shall walk with their heads high in human dignity.

As I have said, the colonial powers and their imperialist allies are beginning to advance a new, subtle theory – and a disguised one, at that – to safeguard their position in Africa and to beguile and bamboozle the Africans. They are prepared to grant political independence but, at the same time, they are also planning to continue to dominate the African territories in the economic field by establishing control over the economic life of the newly independent African countries. There is no difference between political imperialism and economic imperialism. By these methods, the enemies of African freedom hope to be able to use the new African states as puppets to continue to dominate Africa, while, at the same time, making the Africans believe that they are, in fact, free and independent.

This new type or concept of independence has been described as 'International Independence' and it is now the new slogan which is being preached in many colonial territories in Africa. Under certain conditions, the colonial powers are prepared even now to grant independence to many of their territories. As independent states, these territories are supposed to acquire international personality and establish diplomatic relations with other states and also have representation in the various international organisations, including the United Nations.

Once this stage has been reached, the devil of colonialism will put all its energies into establishing control over the foreign relations and policies of the new African states, and thus make it difficult or even impossible for the African people to work together to establish a Union of African States. The new policy or concept of 'conditional independence', which the colonial powers are now planning to adopt, is a policy which is intended to create several weak independent states in Africa. These states are designed to be so weak and unstable in the organisation of their national economies and administrations that they will be compelled by internal as well as external pressures to continue to depend upon the colonial powers who have ruled them for several years. The weaker and the less stable an African state is, the easier it is for the colonial power concerned to dominate the affairs and fortunes of the new state, even though it is supposed to have gained independence.

This policy of creating several unstable and weak, but none-theless independent states in Africa, was the same policy adopted by the great powers at the Congress of Vienna which balkanised Eastern Europe. It is now an indisputable historical fact that the creation of the small independent states in Europe, provided the fertile soil out of which developed the national jealousies, dissensions and disputes which culminated in the First and Second World Wars.

There is strength in the political unity of our continent and that is why the Convention People's Party, as the vanguard for African liberation, is always against any policy for the balkanisation of Africa into small weak and unstable states. We believe that considerations of mutual security and prosperity of our people demand that all the independent states in Africa should work together to create a Union of African States.

I explained that the Central Committee of the C.P.P. felt the time had come for all Africa to evolve a basic ideology based on our common Africanism. This would serve as a strong basis for the unity of Africa. Freedom fighters should meet together and formulate a common policy:

Accordingly, the Central Committee of our Party has decided to convene a conference of all political parties in Africa and consultation will begin at once. This conference, unlike its predecessors, will consist solely of African political parties dedicated to and engaged in the struggle for African emanci-pation. Its main task will be to forge a chain of ideology con-sistent with the present-day African political thinking, aspirations and way of life, and strong enough to bind our various parties together in the unity and oneness of purpose required for creating a formidable continental force which will ensure complete victory over colonialism and make possible the creation of a Union of African States.

Comrades, as we celebrate the tenth anniversary of the historic Positive Action, let us re-dedicate ourselves to the struggle for the economic emancipation and social progress of our country. Let us by hard work ensure that such legacies of colonialism as poverty in the midst of plenty, hunger, squalor, illiteracy and dishonesty disappear from the social fabric of our society.

The Government's Five Year Development Plan is aimed at achieving a stable economy and to ensure a high standard of living for our people. If we are to be able to play an increasingly important and effective role in African affairs, then we must ourselves put our house in perfect order; we must not only aim at making our country economically sound but also politically stable. In this regard the security of our state is of paramount importance to us. I am happy to state that in accordance with your wishes arrangements are now in progress to turn Ghana into a Republic.

We staged Positive Action to achieve independence so that with independence we could concentrate our efforts on economic and social development. Let us therefore on this memorable occasion of the tenth anniversary of Positive Action re-activate our sense of nationalism and patriotism which made it possible for us to achieve independence. Comrades, let us all remember that the greatness, indeed, the strength of our Party depends on discipline, loyalty, service and sacrifice. *Long live the Convention People's Party! Long live African Unity and Independence!*

CHAPTER TWENTY-SIX

THE WIND OF CHANGE

It was while he was in Ghana, in January 1950 that Mr Macmillan coined the now famous phrase 'the wind of change' which he said was blowing right through Africa.[1] The occasion was a state banquet given in his honour in Accra on 9 January, at the start of his long African tour.

At the banquet, I welcomed the Prime Minister of the United Kingdom and Lady Dorothy, and said that I hoped their visit would further strengthen the already firm bonds of friendship between Great Britain and Ghana:

Such visits as this are useful as a supplement to the long established methods of diplomacy. They provide, as it were, if I may use a school-room expression, visual aids to a better understanding of the problems of the host countries. We sincerely hope that Mr Macmillan's visit will enable him to have a better appreciation and understanding of our problems. We have had some useful and fruitful discussions over other problems and issues of mutual interests to our two countries. We have achieved by personal contact what no amount of intimate correspondence can provide. It is in this informal but frank manner in which relations in the Commonwealth are forged, that the real strength of the Commonwealth lies.

After speaking of Ghana's economic development and of the Volta River project, I next turned to the Commonwealth:

I believe, Sir, that this is the first occasion on which the Prime Minister of the United Kingdom has visited an African member state of the Commonwealth. Your visit thus dramatically reflects the growth and constant change of that remarkable institution, composed as it is of old countries and new countries, but all of them dedicated to the same principles of human dignity and political freedom. Naturally we in Ghana think of the Commonwealth in its present form. We know that some of the older nations were willing members of the British

[1] I have had occasion to refer to this as 'no ordinary wind, but a raging hurricane'.

Empire and we appreciate the historical significance of that institution, just as we look back with pride on our own African history to the Empire of Ghana. To us, however, the Commonwealth is a modern, flexible and adaptable institution, composed of sovereign, free and completely independent nations, none owing any special allegiance to the other, but all cooperating freely and as equals in the eternal pursuit of peace, and the abolition of poverty, ignorance, and disease from the entire world. It is in this sense that we welcome our membership of the Commonwealth, and I can assure you, sir, that the constitutional change which will be introduced this year will in no way affect Ghana's active participation in the affairs of the Commonwealth, nor affect the warmth of our affection for the Queen.

I wish to make one more comment, and it is this. Just as we, a young nation, are proud and jealous of our independence, so do we believe that the Commonwealth will gain its greatest strength and influence from an association of nations, each and everyone of which is fully sovereign and independent, and totally free from any external direction.

Mr Macmillan in his reply said that Africa had become a new world force. Ghana's experience in building a multi-racial nation could be an example to the world. 'Far reaching changes of tremendous importance,' he said, 'are taking place in Africa today. Your country, which achieved independence rather less than three years ago, is today one of the most important independent countries in Africa.' He went on to stress that the problems of race relations were harder in South Africa and the Central African Federation, where white men went to settle as well as to work; but in those countries too, the essential problem was one of nation building.

Many foreign press representatives accompanied Mr Macmillan on his tour, and I took the opportunity to speak to them. It was my first press conference for over a year. I said that Ghana was quite prepared to surrender her sovereignty if by doing so she could ensure a satisfactory union of African states. There was very great danger of African leaders in newly independent countries resting content with the idea of being 'little tin gods' in their own territories, when in reality Africa's future demanded that its countries should create the greatest unity. 'I hope the Ghana-Guinea Union will lead the way in countering this tendency,' I said. 'Otherwise, I am afraid that there will be balkanisation of this continent. We must be prepared to fight against it. African strength lies in our totality and union.'

Although Mr Macmillan and I had much to discuss, there was time for him to see something of the ordinary life of the country. He and Lady Dorothy visited the Accra market and received an enthusiastic welcome. Our market women spread out fine cloths for Mr Macmillan to walk on, and gave him many gifts selected from their stalls.

Earlier in the day, the British Prime Minister visited the harbour at Accra and saw the surf boats carrying cargoes ashore from the ships anchored in the bay. He himself was carried out to sea on the shoulders of four Ghanaian loaders and put on board one of the surf boats, which then took him out and carried him back on the crest of the waves.

One of the subjects I discussed with Mr Macmillan during our informal talks at Flagstaff House, was the Volta project and the need for financial support. I took Mr Macmillan to see the site where the dam was to be built, and explained that the Volta project included not only a dam but also an aluminium smelter and ancillary industries. On the way to the site, Mr Macmillan stopped for a few minutes to see the new Tema harbour which, like the Volta dam, was to play an important part in Ghana's economic expansion.

On leaving Ghana, the Macmillan party went on to visit other parts of Africa. The climax to the tour was the Prime Minister's speech in the South African Parliament, when he made it clear that Britain did not support the apartheid policy of the South African Government. I like to think that Mr Macmillan's stay in Ghana helped him to get the feel and sense of the new Africa.

CHAPTER TWENTY-SEVEN

A REPUBLICAN FORM OF GOVERNMENT

On the third anniversary of our Independence I broadcast the news that the Government had drawn up proposals for a new Republican constitution, and that a plebiscite would be held to allow the people to decide whether or not to accept them:

The Convention People's Party and the Government believe that the authority to govern a state should spring from the people and that the people's right to exercise these powers is based on the principle of one man, one vote. In the first Article of the draft Constitution it is stated that 'without distinction of sex, race, tribe, religion or political belief, every person who, being by law a citizen of Ghana, has attained the age of twenty-one years and is not disqualified by law on grounds of absence, infirmity of mind or criminality, shall be entitled to one vote'. We realise that only when this principle of one man, one vote is adopted throughout the length and breadth of the continent of Africa, can the misery and oppression, which prevail in many parts of this continent, come to an end. It is our aim to strive with all our might to bring this about.

The Convention People's Party and the Government believe also that the people of Africa will never be truly great, happy and prosperous while they remain divided into a number of small states. In the new Constitution we advocate strongly the principle of African unity. So deep is our faith in African unity that we have declared our preparedness to surrender the sovereignty of Ghana, in whole or in part, in the interest of a Union of African States and Territories as soon as ever such a union becomes practicable. The keynote of the Constitution which we are putting before you is: One man, one vote and unity of Africa, namely, the political union of African countries.

I explained that while the system of a ceremonial head of state might be suitable in some countries, it was quite contrary to the historical tradition and true character of Ghana. In the draft constitution, therefore, it was proposed that the head of state would also be the actual head of government, in accordance with the cherished traditions of our country. This would mean that, as in the case of India and Pakistan, which are Republics, and Malaya, which has a Paramount Ruler, the Queen would be recognised by Ghana as Head of the Commonwealth, but not as Head of State. The first President of Ghana would be elected by a direct vote of the people:

> The draft Constitution provides that the election of the President thereafter will be linked with the election of Members to the National Assembly in such a way that the President will be the leader of the party which commands a majority in Parliament.
> Under this draft Constitution, the President will be assisted in administering the country by a Cabinet drawn from Members of Parliament. In this way both the National Assembly and the political party which wins the general election will be closely associated in the running of the state.
> The sovereign law-making body will be Parliament which will consist of the President and the National Assembly. The President will not be a Member of the National Assembly, but he will have the same powers in relation to Parliament as the Head of State at present possesses.
> Parliament is not, however, given direct power to alter the basic principles of the Constitution. Only the people can do this, and only after they have been consulted in a referendum ordered by the President will Parliament be entitled to make any law which alters these basic principles of the Constitution.
> The essence of the Constitution which we are asking you to approve is that Ghana is a sovereign, unitary Republic, that there is a President responsible to the people and a Cabinet to assist him which is chosen from amongst Members of Parliament.
> Equally essential is the existence and the legislative power of Parliament. This cannot be taken away unless the people are consulted, nor can Parliament's exclusive rights over what taxes are imposed be abrogated.

I outlined other features of the proposed Constitution, which I urged everyone to study at leisure the following day when the constitutional proposals and a Government White Paper explaining them would be on sale:

> It is for you, people of Ghana, to decide on the form of constitution under which you wish to be governed. You cannot

arrive at this decision until you have carefully studied and clearly understood the proposals which have been submitted to you.

In many ways this Constitution is unique and contains a number of features which are not found in the constitution of any other country. This is so because it is fashioned to fit in with our historical experience and circumstances and designed to meet our own needs. It guarantees chieftaincy, preserves the Houses of Chiefs and in other ways is fitted to the general system of government which we have evolved in Ghana.

The Convention People's Party and the Government commend the proposed Constitution when the plebiscite is held next month. In that plebiscite I ask all of you to come forward uninfluenced and unawed to vote in an orderly and disciplined manner. The Government, for its part, will see to it that the plebiscite is conducted with absolute fairness and that every citizen of Ghana has a free and unfettered right to express his opinion. Furthermore, the Government is determined to suppress intimidation, coercion, malicious rumours and violence from whatever quarter it might come. It is essential for the well-being and good government of Ghana that the Constitution is enacted by the free will of the people. Countrymen, Ghana depends on each one of you to do your duty and I feel sure that you will rise to the occasion and do it well.

During the weeks which followed, plans went ahead for the holding of the plebiscite. Dr J. B. Danquah was named by the Opposition United Party as their candidate for the presidency.

My candidature was based on my leadership of the Convention People's Party. I made this point quite clear when I spoke at the opening of the Party Headquarters on 2 April. After reviewing the past work of the Party, I turned to the future:

Our Party is moving into what can become a most glorious chapter in the history of Africa. Our plans for the re-organisation of all sections of the community is to give everybody a chance to make his contribution to the development of our nation. The test of the future will be the amount of purchasing power we put into the hand of our workers and farmers, and the protection the Party and the Government can give to ensure a dignified existence and comfortable standard of living for all our people. There will be no place in that society for the exploitation of the labour of others for the enrichment of a minority. Our Party is great and strong because we aim for a socialist pattern of society. We are the Party of the workers, the farmers and all progressive elements in our community and we will remain faithful to the principles that guide us in evolving our own Ghanaian pattern of socialist society.

Everybody will be given equal opportunities for development whether it be in the fields of education or of cultural and economic advancement. Every worker and farmer will receive a fair share of the wealth of the country and their children will have the same opportunities as others for education, so that they can become doctors of medicine, engineers, barristers, professional workers and scientists. We want working-class intellectuals devoid of arrogance and an end to class distinctions based on privilege.

We want to give to the farmers, co-operators and workers equal status in our new society, and this explains our attachment to the Trade Union Congress, the United Ghana Farmers Council and the National Council of Co-operatives. These three Party organisations are the true and practical schools of our philosophy and those who go against them go against the Convention People's Party also.

The Convention People's Party is a powerful force; more powerful, indeed, than anything that has yet appeared in the history of Ghana. It is the uniting force that guides and pilots the nation and is the nerve centre of the positive operations in the struggle for African irredentism. Its supremacy cannot be challenged.

The Convention People's Party is Ghana, and Ghana is the Convention People's Party.

It was my firm belief that only the C.P.P. had the organisation necessary to build the new Ghana and safeguard its future:

It is on the basis of the Party's record that we contest the Presidential election and recommend our proposals for a Republican constitution. We have become convinced that it is only under a Republican form of government that the Ghanaian will realise his full sovereign stature and find the true expression of his aspirations. Our Party runs a stable government to guide us forward in planning an economy that will give us abundance of wealth for the improvement of our standards of living. The signs of what we can do for the country in the future can be seen around you everywhere. Hospitals are being built, highways modernised for communications, factories are springing up and modern townships are replacing the slums that we inherited. The Party's

Government has accelerated the construction of schools and colleges. We have built the University College at Legon, Kumasi College of Technology, the Nautical College and Flying Training School, the School of Law and the School of Business Administration. In the field of health, considerable improvement has been made. Health clinics, maternity homes, and dispensaries can now be found in your own vicinity.

Today you yourselves are the State, and those of us who bear the responsibility of government do so on your behalf. Thus the State exists in the image of the people and operates confidently in the service of the people. When the Party and the Government take your interests to heart and fulfil their responsibilities towards you, it is your duty in return to help the Party and the Government by your devotion to our cause and your steadfast loyalty to all our ideals.

Our record for the past ten years stands before the country as an example of what we can do in the future. I am simply asking you, on my own behalf and on behalf of the Convention People's Party, under all circumstances and at all costs, to stand united with us and vote solidly for the Republican constitution. This is the duty the Party expects of you and when to-day I open the National Headquarters Secretariat of the Convention People's Party, I also have the pleasure to launch the Party's Campaign for the plebiscite and offer myself to you as the first President under the new constitution.

CHAPTER TWENTY-EIGHT

POSITIVE ACTION AND SECURITY
IN AFRICA

A conference to discuss Positive Action and Security in Africa opened in Accra on 7 April 1960. It was called by the Government of Ghana in consultation with other independent African states. The reasons for the Conference, and the nature of its agenda can perhaps be best explained by quoting in full my speech of welcome to the many delegates and observers who gathered in Accra on that historic occasion:

Fellow Africans, Ladies and Gentlemen. It is a pleasant duty, on behalf of the Government and people of Ghana, to welcome here to-day our distinguished guests who have come from all over this vast but turbulent continent of ours to confer together in this conference on Positive Action for Peace and Security in Africa. We welcome also the many fraternal delegates and observers who have come to join us in our deliberations at this historic conference.

Once again it has fallen to me to play host to this gathering of dedicated sons of Africa, and, in welcoming you, fellow Africans, I would like to express my sincere appreciation of the promptness with which our invitations to this emergency conference were accepted.

As you are all no doubt aware, the beginning of the year 1960 has seen the climax of ruthless and concerted outrages on the peace-loving people of our continent. The explosion of an atomic device in the Sahara by the French Government and the wanton massacre just over a fortnight ago in the Union of South Africa of our brothers and sisters who were engaged in peaceful demonstrations against humiliating and repulsive laws of the South African Government, are two eloquent events in this climax, a climax which is a sign-post to the beginning of the end of foreign supremacy and domination in Africa.

In spite of several protests to General De Gaulle by the whole African Continent and the United Nations General Assembly against exploding an atomic bomb on our continent, the French Government arrogantly exploded this nuclear device on our soil. As a result of this callous and inhuman attitude, the Government of Ghana took immediate action by freezing the assets of French firms in Ghana. Other African leaders and Governments, indignant at this outrage, took other decisive measures against the French Government. I hope our reactions and protests will prevent the Government of France from exploding further atomic bombs on our continent.

Faced with this threat, the Government of Ghana, in consultation with other Independent African states, have invited you to this conference: first to discuss and plan future action to prevent the further use of African soil as a testing ground for nuclear weapons; secondly, to consider effective means to prevent further brutalities against our defenceless brothers and sisters in South Africa, brutalities which are the result of the South African Government's racial policy of apartheid. Thirdly, this conference must consider the ways and means whereby Algeria can be helped to bring an end to this dismal flow of human blood consequent upon this lingering physical conflict which does neither of the combatants any good. That Algeria, a country in Africa, is French, is a ridiculous concept. France is French and Algeria is Algerian. France belongs to the continent of Europe; Algeria belongs to the continent of Africa. The fact that there are a million Frenchmen in Algeria is a mere accident of history which does not, and can never make Algeria French. And the sooner this fact is realised, the better will the French Government be able to adjust itself to the idea of negotiating peace with our valiant fighting brothers in Algeria. This conference must discharge this pressing duty.

Lastly, but by no means the least important matter to be considered, is the great issue facing the whole of our people, namely, the total liberation of Africa and the necessity to alert the people of Africa against the new form of colonialism and its attempts to balkanise the continent and so prevent African unity. This conference is called, therefore, to plan concerted positive action for peace and security in Africa.

Fellow Africans, you all know that foreign domination in Africa effectively disintegrated the personality of the African people. For centuries during which colonialism held sway over our beloved continent, colonialism imposed on the mind of Africans the idea that their own kith and kin in other parts of Africa were aliens and had little, if anything, in common with Africans elsewhere. It was in the interests of the colonial

and settler rulers to perpetuate the subjection of us, the indigenous people, by pursuing a policy not only of 'divide and
rule', but also of artificial territorial division of Africa. It
played upon our tribalistic instincts. It sowed seeds of dissension in order to promote disunity among us.

It is therefore with great pride and happiness that we note
how resurgent Africa is witnessing to-day what is by no means
a humble beginning of the process of re-integration of the
African personality, and forging closer and stronger bonds of
unity which are bound to bring us to our ultimate goal: the
attainment of a union of African States and Republics which,
to my mind, is the only solution to the problems that face us
in Africa to-day.

Fellow Africans and friends: there are two threatening
swords of Damocles hanging over our continent, and we must
remove them. These are nuclear tests in the Sahara by the
French Government and the apartheid policy of the Government of the Union of South Africa.

It would be a great mistake to imagine that the achievement of political independence by certain areas in Africa
will automatically mean the end of the struggle. It is merely
the beginning of the end of the struggle. We must watch out
for and expose the various forms of the new imperialism with
which we are threatened. Among these, we must mention
nuclear imperialism that dawned upon Africa on a tragic day
last February when the French Government exploded an
atomic bomb on our soil. Winds carried the poisonous debris
from the explosion to various parts of Africa, including Ghana,
and thus confounded the confident forecasts by so-called
meteorological experts of France who claimed that there was
no wind that could carry radio-active debris more than 700
miles from the site of the explosion. From the point of view of
genetics, these atomic tests are extremely bad and can have
the most disastrous effects.

The French test last February resulted in a very substantial
increase in radio-activity. This was proved by British and
Canadian scientists who were manning our monitoring stations
here in Ghana. Their observations were confirmed by a
French scientist who was invited by us to Ghana to observe
things for himself.

Fellow Africans: on this matter of the evil effects of atomic
tests we refuse to allow anyone to throw dust in our eyes. I must
emphasise that five eminent physicists – three Japanese, one
American and one French, two of them Nobel Prizewinners –
have announced that more than one million people will die as

a result of such explosions. They stated also, among other things, that 'elementary calculation' showed that the fall-out from each 'superbomb' provoked the birth of fifteen thousand abnormal children. How can we, in the face of these facts, keep quiet? We must all with one voice vehemently protest against the holding of any more nuclear tests in the Sahara.

In spite of world protests and condemnation of its first test, the Government of France has actually carried out its intention by exploding the second bomb in the Sahara. This is an act of stubborn and inhuman defiance that not only challenges the very conscience of mankind, but also undermines the United Nations.

The action of the French Government in defying world considered opinion and exploding these atomic bombs becomes more heinous when it is considered that at the present moment the three leading world powers of atomic strength, themselves conscious of the grave dangers to human life of these tests, are leaving no stone unturned to arrive at an agreement to stop all tests and ultimately to abolish all nuclear weapons.

The Government of Ghana, as I have said, has already taken action by freezing all French assets until the extent of the damage to the life and health of her people becomes known. Since the explosion of the second bomb, she has also recalled her ambassador to France. But a critical situation such as this calls for concerted action and it will be for the committees of this conference to discuss what action can be taken to prevent further nuclear outrages in Africa. Another committee will discuss positive direct action to prevent further tests.

Last December and January an international team consisting of representatives from Ghana and other parts of Africa, as well as members from Britain, the United States and even from France itself, attempted to enter the testing site at Reggan in the Sahara. They left Ghana under the leadership of the Reverend Michael Scott, but were prevented from proceeding beyond the Upper Volta border by armed guards under the direction and control of French authorities. In order to make further attempts impossible, their vehicles and equipment were seized and have been kept by the French authorities up to now. Although they did not reach Reggan, they aroused many people to the dangers of nuclear imperialism. The team brought home to us the fact that the victims of these bombs are not less human just because they would probably never be known.

Positive action has already achieved remarkable success in

the liberation struggle of our continent and I feel sure that it can further save us from the perils of this atomic arrogance. If the direct action that was carried out by the international protest team were to be repeated on a mass scale, or simultaneously from various parts of Africa, the result could be as powerful and as successful as Gandhi's historic Salt March. We salute Mahatma Gandhi and we remember in tribute to him, that it was in South Africa that his method of non-violence and non-co-operation was first practised in the struggle against the vicious race discrimination that still plagues that unhappy country.

But now positive action with non-violence, as advocated by us, has found expression in South Africa in the defiance of the oppressive pass laws. This defiance continues in spite of the murder of unarmed men, women and children by the South African Government. We are sure that the will of the majority will ultimately prevail, for no government can continue to impose its rule in face of the conscious defiance of the overwhelming masses of its people. There is no force, however impregnable, that a united and determined people cannot overcome.

Future positive direct action against French nuclear tests might, for instance, take the form of a mass non-violent attempt to proceed towards the testing area. It would not matter if not a single person ever reached the site, for the effect of hundreds of people from every corner of Africa and from outside it crossing the artificial barriers that divide Africa to risk imprisonment and arrest, would be a protest that the people of France, with the exception of the De Gaulle Government, and the world could not ignore. Let us remember that the poisonous fall-out did not, and never will respect the arbitrary and artificial divisions forged by colonialism across our beloved continent.

In my view, therefore, this conference ought to consider the setting up of a training centre where volunteers would learn the essential disciplines of concerted positive action. Such an establishment might also become the centre for such needed research into the philosophy and technique of positive action which, in the age of nuclear madness and apartheid arrogance, offers the greatest single hope for peace, security and brotherhood among mankind.

General De Gaulle is reported to have said recently that while other countries have enough nuclear weapons to destroy the whole world, France must also have nuclear weapons with which to defend herself. I would say here, and no doubt you all join me, that Africa is not interested in such 'defence' which means no more than the ability to share in the honour of destroying mankind. We in Africa wish to live and develop. We are not freeing ourselves from centuries of imperialism and colonialism only to be maimed and destroyed by nuclear weapons. We do not threaten anyone and we renounce the foul weapons that threaten the very existence of life on this planet. Rather we put our trust in the awakening conscience of mankind which rejects this primitive barbarism, and believe firmly in positive non-violent action.

But while we consider the new forms of imperialism and colonialism, let us not forget its crude blatant forms that wreak havoc in parts of our continent such as Algeria, Angola, Kenya, Ruanda Urundi, Nyasaland and in South Africa. The passive sympathy of the African masses must be converted into active participation in the struggle for the total emancipation of Africa. Africa is too sacred a land to harbour hypocrites. Sooner or later, but sooner rather than later, our continent will be purged of all forms of colonialism, for the fire of intense nationalism is blazing all over Africa and burning to ashes the last remnants of colonialism. The civilised world stands aghast at the brutal massacre of unarmed Africans in South Africa. Yet this wanton outrage of the Government of South Africa is hardly more terrible than the explosion of French atomic bombs in the Sahara.

It is ironical to think that the rulers of South Africa call themselves Christians. If Christ were to appear in South Africa to-day he would be crucified by them if he dared to oppose the brutal laws of racial segregation. Apartheid and nuclear weapons must shake the conscience of the Christian world. But what are the churches of the world doing about these very contradictions of Christianity?

Fellow Africans: it is a misconceived view that Africans are incapable of shouldering responsibility for their own affairs and that it is in the African's own interest that European tute-lage should continue. In the light of such artificial doubts and antiquated ideas about Africa and her people, the need for a dispassionate presentation of Africa's case for complete freedom now cannot be over-emphasised.

The problem of peace and security on this our beloved con-tinent of Africa, is not an academic question. Even while we deliberate to-day, men, women and children die daily as a result of military action or police massacre. The Algerian refugees are an ever present reminder of this grim tragedy. At the southern end of the continent, the defenders of apartheid, the worst form of racial arrogance, have not only boasted openly of the new military equipment they are assembling to intimidate Africans who resort to non-violent positive action against that iniquitous system, but they have recently unleashed the murderous fire of Saracen tanks upon them, an action which has hit the conscience of the world. In eastern and central Africa, our heroic leaders and thousands of our freedom fighters suffer detention and banishment for daring to ask to be free.

Fellow Africans: the violence and threats of violence of the present day are but the continuation of a pattern which has been developing during the past ten years with an intensity both cumulative and alarming. The memories of the tragedy of Sakiet, and of the relentless harassing from ground and sky of the people of Kenya, are still vivid in our memory.

At this juncture, comrades, I would like to ask you to stand up and observe two minutes' silence for all those Africans who have been the victims of colonial and racial brutality.

We who are gathered here to-day wish to see all violent conflicts stopped; we wish to secure freedom and ensure security in Africa. In order to do so we must mobilise all of the forces of peace for non-violent positive action in protest against these outrages, and for making the social and political changes which are necessary to prevent future conflicts. This is the sacred task to which all of us are devoted, and the sublime objective to which every true lover of Africa must be dedicated.

I have often stressed the fact that Africa is not an extension of Europe or of any other continent, and that the attempts to balkanise her is inimical to African unity and progress.

We should not be so pre-occupied with the urgent problems of political independence as to overlook a scarcely less vital sphere – the economic sphere. Yet it is here, more than anywhere else, that we must look for the schemings of a politically frustrated colonialism. On the other hand, it is in the economic field also that we find the key to fruitful co-operation with other nations – at a functional level in the first instance – but leading to full political as well as economic unity that could be built up over wide regions, to extend finally throughout the length and breadth of our beloved continent.

A striking instance of the new Imperialism to which I referred earlier, is the inclusion of certain parts of Africa in common market and trade preference areas set up by industrial Europe, for example, the inclusion of Congo and the French Community states in the European Common Market. The main benefit of this is reaped not by the people of these parts of Africa, who cannot afford the expensive products of industrial Europe, but by European industry which is assured of cheap, tariff-free raw material. Furthermore, the arrangement prevents the building up of industry in Africa which, to survive, needs protection in the early years of its growth from the unequal competition of the industrialised nations.

But Africa must be developed industrially, for her own sake and ultimately for the sake of a healthy world economy. This can only happen if the artificial boundaries that divide her are broken down so as to provide for viable economic units, and ultimately a single African unit. This means an African common market, a common currency area and the development of communications of all kinds to allow the free flow of goods and services. International capital could be attracted to such viable economic areas, but it would not be attracted to a divided and balkanised Africa, with each small region engaged in senseless and suicidal economic competition with its neighbours. This international capital would more than offset any loss of capital from those who want to invest in Africa only when they can see quick and immediate profit in it for themselves, and who fear the industrial competition of a developed Africa.

I believe that independent African states should be able, even before actual political union takes place, to enter into an African treaty organisation whereby experts can work out details of the measures and the fields in which co-operation can take place immediately, and the elimination of waste through harmful competition can be realised first in the economic and social fields and later in others.

These measures cannot be put into force all at once. But a start could and should be made by the development, for instance, of better road and telegraphic communications between neighbouring African states and the setting up among the independent states of a common market in industrial products. This last may involve a little loss of revenue to any state but would certainly set the pattern for the whole future industrial development of Africa.

These questions may perhaps be raised among the matters to be discussed at the meeting of Heads of independent states at Addis Ababa next June. The technical details would be for expert commissions to work out. It seems desirable, however, that the occasion of this meeting of Government representatives, political parties and other organisations throughout Africa, should not be allowed to pass without preliminary discussions on issues that so vitally affect the future of our continent. It is hoped that the discussions at this conference, by underlying the economic needs and problems that we face, will pave the way to future co-operation.

The cardinal principle upon which the peace and security of this continent depends, is the firm insistence that Africa is not an extension of Europe or of any other continent. A corollary of this principle is the resolution that Africa is not going to become a cockpit of the cold war, or a marshalling ground for attack on either West or East, nor is it going to be an arena for fighting out to the East-West conflict. In this particular sense, we face neither East nor West: we face forward.

For the last ten years the tone of international politics has been set by the cold war. We understand the fears on both sides that have led to this tragic polarisation, but Africans have no intention of becoming a part of it. We have seen what happens when small nations become involved in it. We have also seen, on the other hand, what can happen when the spirit of Bandung prevails and the powers who stand outside this conflict use their good offices as conciliators and mediators through the United Nations, as in the stopping of the Korean War. That is the role which we Africans wish to play. I refuse to accept that dictum that if you are not for me you are against me. Our slogan is 'Positive Neutrality'. This is our contribution to international peace and world progress. It is in this context that military pacts and defence agreements between African states and former colonial powers and non-African nations are ultimately inimical to the interests of the continent as a whole. Since there is no suggestion that any African state has aggressive intentions, such pacts and agreements can only draw the states concerned into the cold war strategy of the bigger powers. Furthermore, they introduce one more obstacle in the way of harmonising our policies towards the achievement of African untiy.

There can be no peace or security in Africa without freedom and political unity. So long as one inch of African soil remains under colonial rule there will be strife and conflict. So long as any group on this continent denies the principle of one-man one-vote, and uses its power to maintain its privilege, there will be insecurity for the oppressors and constant resentment and revolt on the part of the oppressed. These are the elementary facts of life in Africa to-day. No man willed this situation and no man can stem the tide or divert the 'wind of change'. We decry violence and deplore it. We are devoted to non-violent positive action. Experience has shown that when change is too long delayed or stubbornly resisted, violence will erupt here and there – not because men planned it and willed it – but because the accumulated grievances of the past erupt with volcanic fury.

It is in this light that we must view those fortunately rare, but no less tragic episodes which have confronted us – the Mau Mau war in Kenya, the costly struggle in Algeria, events in the Cameroons and occasional riots here and there. The defenders of colonialism and settler domination should have eyes to see and ears to hear. Unless they respond to the pressures of non-violent petition and protest, they will ultimately reap a harvest of violence that no one wants. Where, as in Algeria, the bloody struggle still proceeds, it would be the essence of wisdom on the part of those who defend the privileges of colonial rule to negotiate a cease-fire now rather than to prolong a conflict which, should they even win, will in the long run raise its head again. Peace in Algeria must take first priority in the consolidation of peace and in laying the foundations of security.

Our emphasis upon Africa bespeaks neither chauvinism nor isolationism. We who pioneered the development of Pan Africanism have done so with a vision. History has described to us the tragedies which have beset every other continent upon this planet – the international wars, the rebellions and revolutions. We must be determined that this continent of ours shall not repeat that dismal history. The continent of Africa has been drenched with blood in the past, it has been raided for slaves, it has been partitioned, exploited and looted. Precisely because it has had this kind of past it is determined not to have that kind of future. If we succeed, and succeed we must, the whole of mankind – not Africa alone – will reap immense benefits. Men with great foresight and knowledge all agree that the future of the world will be decided in Africa.

We welcome men of goodwill everywhere to join us, irrespective of their race, religion or nationality. When I speak of Africa for Africans this should be interpreted in the light of my emphatic declaration, that I do not believe in racialism and colonialism. The concept 'Africa for Africans' does not mean that other races are excluded from it. No. It only means that Africans, who naturally are in the majority in Africa, shall and must govern themselves in their own countries. The fight is for the future of humanity, and it is a most important fight.

Fellow Africans: Africa is marching forward to freedom and no power on earth can halt her now.

Our salvation and strength and our only way out of these

ravages in Africa, lies in political union, and those who doubt the feasibility of such a union appear to have forgotten their history lesson too soon. The vastness of Russia and all the towering obstacles of her beginning did not prevent that country from building its greatness in unity by the union of eighteen different republics. The sprawling spread of America and her original colonial difficulties have not stopped that country from building a union of forty-nine states. If these countries can do this, why cannot Africa? I repeat that nothing but our own groundless fears and doubts can stop us from building a real practical political union. But remember – 'Our fears are traitors and make us lose what we might often achieve by fearing to attempt.'

If as African territories emerge into independence, they declare their intention to form a union among themselves, and countries like Congo, Nigeria, Ghana, Guinea, Liberia for instance, as well as others, come together in an effective political union in the West for a start, it is not difficult to imagine the impact that such an African union would create on the world. Then consider the weight of our influence if later our brothers of the East throw in their lot into the union, and greater still, the influence if our brothers of the North throw in their lot, too.

This is not a mere dream. This is an objective worthy and capable of achievement and I for one am prepared to serve under any African leader who is able to offer the proper guidance in this great issue of our time.

So dear is this African unity to our hearts, that in our proposed republican constitution a definite provision has been incorporated by a concrete proposal that Ghana's sovereignty should be surrendered in whole or in part as a contribution towards the attainment of the great objective. Fellow Africans: permit me the liberty of stating in categorical terms that the greatness of this objective so transcends all other purposes and its sublimity is so profound, that it behoves each and everyone in the leadership of this struggle to endeavour to subdue his own little interests, his individual pride and ego and other petty considerations which merely serve to create needless obstacles in our path. The overriding importance of African unity demands the sacrifice of all personal, tribal and regional objectives and considerations.

In my view, conferences, protests and petitions may have their usefulness, but such usefulness is undoubtedly limited. The only answer to the several difficulties facing our continent is actual union of our various states and territories. If we cannot make an effort in this direction, we might as well begin to throw up our hands in despair and forget about Africa. But dare we do so?

I firmly believe without the possibility of contradiction that the only and the best solution to our problems is union – real political union which will provide the necessary complement required to augment the efforts of other people for the consolidation of peace and security in the world.

Finally, by our concerted non-violent positive action, we can help to ensure that this march forward is a swift and peaceful one, and the formulation of the necessary plans to effect this must be the responsibility of this Conference. I thank all of you for your devotion, which your presence here indicates, to this great cause, and wish for God's guidance and success in our deliberations.

Again, I welcome you all to Ghana.

The full effects of the Conference will not be seen for several years. However, it achieved its main task of framing a policy consistent with modern African political thinking, strong enough to bind our various parties together in unity of purpose to create a continental force able to ensure complete victory over colonialism, and to make the creation of a Union of African States possible.

CHAPTER TWENTY-NINE

RACIALISM AND THE POLICY
OF APARTHEID

The Conference of Commonwealth Prime Ministers held in
London in May 1960 was one of the most significant of recent
years. Events in South Africa, the Sharpeville shootings, and the
whole question of apartheid, led many to believe that the
Commonwealth structure might break under the strain. There
was speculation in the Press about how the Indian and Malayan
Prime Ministers and I would regard the South African minister
Mr Loew.

On my arrival at London Airport I was asked by reporters
whether I would raise the question of apartheid at the Conference.
I replied that if no one else raised the matter I might very well
do so. My plane arrived almost at the same time as that bringing
Mr Nehru and his party from India. I was able to have a few
words with him before leaving for Grosvenor House, where I
stayed throughout the Conference.

It is greatly to the credit of Mr Macmillan and his superb
handling of a very delicate situation that the Commonwealth
survived intact, and emerged from the Conference probably
stronger than before. We discussed the policy of the South African
Government, but in private; not even our official advisers were
present.

Quite apart from what was said in the course of our private
discussions, Mr Loew must have been left in no doubt about the
view taken by most people on apartheid The British public, and
indeed world opinion, showed unmistakably that South Africa
stood alone in her racial policy.

While the Conference was in session I refrained from making
any public declaration of policy. But once it was over and our
joint statement published, I felt free to speak. The occasion was
a symposium held by the English Speaking Union in the Central
Hall, Westminster on 'What the Commonwealth Means in
Practice'. The Duke of Edinburgh was in the Chair, and there
were six speakers. I spoke last.

I said that Ghana, on gaining independence in 1957, chose to become a member of the Commonwealth, of her own free will:

Ghana regards the Commonwealth as an association of free and independent sovereign states, equal in all respects and bound together by a common desire to work together for the good and well-being of its members.

On the 1st July next, Ghana becomes a Republic. This change will not affect Ghana's membership of the Commonwealth nor her relations with other members, nor her deep interest in the successful functioning of the Commonwealth relationship. It is worth stressing what this relationship means to Ghana. The free and frank exchange of views on terms of complete equality between member-nations is of great value. So is the practice of non-interference in the internal affairs of its members, or with their independence of action and policy, domestic or foreign. These principles are a source of real strength to the Commonwealth. To those principles I would add the active co-operation which takes place among Commonwealth nations at international meetings such as the general agreement on trade and tariffs where the interests of member-states are concerned. Again, inter-Commonwealth Conferences and meetings, such as the Commonwealth Economic Conference which took place in Canada last year, the Commonwealth Education Conference held at Oxford recently, and the great number of other meetings between Ministers and others which go on all the time, are of great practical value.

It is natural that we in Africa should judge the effectiveness of the Commonwealth in terms of its significance to the African situation at present and in the future. I believe that the Commonwealth can win African goodwill if it genuinely addresses itself to the great problems which we face in our continent today. Africa is the land of the future. There is not only a ferment of ideas, but also a resurgence of keen national consciousness which seeks its natural outlet in political independence and African unity.

What are the aspirations of Africans? Above all, they desire to regain their independence and to live in peace. They desire to use their freedom to raise the standard of living of their peoples. They desire to use their freedom to create a union of African states on the continent and thus neutralise the evil effects of the artificial boundaries imposed by the imperial powers and promote unity of action in all fields. These are Africa's ideals.

The huge audience listened intently as I spoke of the next phase in Africa. The great wave of nationalism sweeping over the continent must be recognised, and the principle of 'one man one vote' must be accepted:

I am convinced that the Commonwealth has an important part to play in all this by demonstrating true and concrete friendship for the peoples of Africa in the critical times that lie ahead, and by co-operating in the task of creating those conditions which will make for dignity, self-respect and material prosperity for all those who live in Africa.

To be fully effective, the Commonwealth must be understood by other countries. Membership of it is of fundamental importance in securing this understanding, and I believe that we should therefore adhere rigidly to the principle that membership is limited to fully independent and sovereign nations. Today the Commonwealth has two anomalous aspects. The first is that over the years a special position has been accepted for Southern Rhodesia, and now for the Central African Federation. On that basis, a very strong case could have been made for the attendance at the recent conference of the Prime Ministers of the Federations of Nigeria and of the West Indies.

The second anomaly is the apparent linking of British colonies with the Commonwealth. This situation causes confusion with other nations, and must embarrass Prime Ministers such as myself and the governments of states such as Ghana, for the reason that we are unalterably opposed to colonialism in any form in any part of the world. In my opinion these colonies should be linked solely to the United Kingdom, and not to the Commonwealth.

After referring to defence and the economic development of Africa, I came to the issue of racialism, which strikes at the very heart of the Commonwealth. Ghana, as the only truly African member of the Commonwealth had a responsibility to make its views on the subject absolutely clear:

The Government of Ghana is concerned with racialism wherever it exists in the world, and particularly with apartheid as one aspect of the racial problem in South Africa. My

Government is concerned with racialism, not only as a practice repugnant to every decent principle and contrary to Christian faith and ethics, but also because of its effect on the basic principles which determine the existence of the Commonwealth. We believe that the Commonwealth cannot exist as an effective association of nations, all dedicated to the same basic principles of life, if exceptions are made. It is illogical and unreasonable to expect African states to be happy about joining and remaining within the Commonwealth if the Commonwealth tolerates governments which perpetuate policies of racialism and apartheid.

One of the principal aims of the Prime Ministers' Conference should be to preserve the Commonwealth as an effective organisation where racial policies of the member-governments are consistent with the multiracial character of the Commonwealth. This is a basic issue. It is a matter of principle, and the march to independence of many African territories makes it inevitable that it must be faced honestly by the individual members – and resolved – in order that we may not be faced with a crisis which could do irreparable harm to the Commonwealth as a whole.

Today the lives of thirteen million human beings in South Africa are at stake. If the Commonwealth has any meaning, it cannot – and it must not – let this situation drift until a revolution of desperation creates another Algeria on our continent. The warning has been written in blood for all to read. The Commonwealth cannot avoid this situation.

Another acid test for the Commonwealth will come later this year when the United Nations once more considers the problem of South West Africa. So far every attempt to negotiate with the Union of South Africa on this matter has failed, and the Union has refused to heed the views expressed by the Committee that their policy is a flagrant violation of the United Nations. The Commonwealth has a special responsibility for South West Africa because the mandate system of the League of Nations was established through Commonwealth initiative, and it was through the influence of the then Commonwealth members that the mandate for South West Africa was entrusted to the Union of South Africa.

I am certain that the heart of every person in the world today is troubled by this horrible issue of racialism. Today in Ghana, Africans and people of many other races are working together effectively in harmony and in understanding, and I hope that our achievements in this field, which reflect the fundamental tolerance of the African towards his fellow men, will give hope and encouragement to people in other parts of the world who are striving to find a solution to the problem of inter-race relations.

That the Commonwealth is a unique experiment in the history of the modern world no one can deny. That it has an important duty to mankind, most people will agree. I for one would wish to see it live and thrive and thus contribute to the peace, security and progress of the world.

Nearly a week later, on 18 May, I made a speech in Dublin and again emphasised the need for effective action against racialism. This time, I concentrated on the special responsibility of the United Nations:

In Algeria, in East Africa and in the Union of South Africa, the tensions, oppression and open warfare which mark the struggle arise from the determination of a minority to maintain their ascendency in a world where the social and economic basis of that ascendency has disappeared. The motives of the ruling minorities are, of course, complex and varied. But they have in them one common factor, a fear amounting to hysteria as to what might happen to them if they conceded to the principle – and, I believe, the only principle – which can bring peace and prosperity to Africa, the principle of one man, one vote.

The experience of Ireland, and also, I think, that of Ghana, shows how unreal such a fear is. Of course, the longer oppression continues, the more dangerous and explosive becomes the situation. Ultimately, if the majority are oppressed and degraded in the way they are today in Algeria, in the Union of South Africa, and in many other parts of the African continent, government becomes impossible. All organs of government break down and economic chaos supervenes, threatening not only the territory concerned, but possibly even the financial stability of the colonial power responsible for the oppression. What the ruling minorities should be afraid of is not that power will fall into the hands of the majority, but that by their own attempt to maintain a social order which can no longer exist, they will themselves be their own executioners.

The supreme task of the United Nations is to organise a peaceful transfer of power before it is too late to save the ruling minorities of Africa from the consequences of their own political blindness and folly. If the situation which exists in Africa today is allowed to develop, the inevitable defeat and destruction of the minorities will not only be accompanied by untold hardships and misery to all concerned, but will constitute a severe threat to world peace. What in my opinion is now required, is 'positive action' by the United Nations.

I spoke of the meaning of real independence. There must not be any patron-client relationship in the new Africa:

There are three alternatives open to the African territories now attaining nationhood. They can choose to stand alone, in which case they risk early and certain disintegration; they can be persuaded to agree to their being used to bolster up the imperialistic tendencies of their former colonial powers. When this happens, it is not difficult to see the grave harm which is done to the movement for the unity of the African states. The third alternative, and the wisest course for us in Africa, is to pursue resolutely our policy for the achievement of unity among ourselves, in order that in an African community, we can work for our political, economic and cultural development.

Within the framework of an Africa community, and as a first step to actual political union of African states, it should be possible to establish a council for economic co-operation and mutual development among the African states. Such a council can serve as an unfailing source of assistance in financial, technical and other services to new African states upon attaining their independence.

A council for economic co-operation and development among African states will also provide a pillar of strength and confidence for the new African states, and will thus make it impossible for the former colonial powers to continue to exploit the weak economic position of the new African states in the post-independence period.

To many people, the unity of African states which we regard as the primary basis of our African policy, appears visionary and unattainable. We do not hold this view. The unity of African states can be a reality, and it will be achieved earlier than many of us may suppose.

With regard to the Algerian question, I said that the basic issues were no different from those arising in other parts of Africa, where a minority of the population claimed the right to dictate the policy to be followed by the majority. The so-called 'Free World' should come down decisively on the side of the majority, both in Algeria and in South Africa.

The internal events in South Africa can, in my view, no longer be considered to be a domestic matter. You will recall that the resolution of the Security Council recognised that the situation 'arising out of the large scale killings of unarmed and peaceful demonstrators against racial discrimination and segregation in the Union of South Africa' was 'brought about by the racial policies of the Government of the Union of South Africa and the continued disregard by that Government of the resolutions of the General Assembly'. The resolution of the Security Council further called upon 'the Government of the Union of South Africa to initiate measures aimed at bringing about racial harmony based on equality in order to ensure that the present situation does not continue or recur. . . .'

The Security Council then called upon 'the Government of the Union to abandon its policy of apartheid and racial discrimination'. Finally, the Resolution requested the Secretary General of the United Nations 'in consultation with the Government of the Union of South Africa, to make such arrangements as would adequately help in upholding the purposes and principles of the Charter and to report to the Security Council whenever necessary and appropriate'.

The last thing which I would wish to do is to say anything which might make the task of the Secretary General more difficult. On the other hand, my own recent experience in attempting to persuade the South African Government to moderate its policies makes me not over-optimistic of the possibility of success of the Secretary General's mission. At this stage I would say only this: if the Secretary General is unable to agree with the Government of the Union of South Africa on such arrangements as would adequately help in upholding the purposes and principles of the Charter, then the Government of Ghana for one would find it embarrassing to remain in the Commonwealth with a Republic whose policy was not based upon the purpose and principles of the United Nations.

I then turned to the position in the mandated territory of South West Africa. The Union of South Africa, entrusted with the Mandate, was pursuing the policy of apartheid which, in the words of the United Nations Committee on South West Africa, was a 'flagrant violation of the sacred trust which permeates the Mandate and the Charter of the United Nations and the Universal Declaration of Human Rights'. The United Nations had called on the Union of South Africa every year for thirteen years, to place South West Africa under the international trusteeship system. The Union had repeatedly defied the authority of the United Nations by refusing to do this. It was, therefore, the duty of Ghana to propose a new policy in regard to South West Africa:

I have spoken freely and frankly about what I believe to be the inherent dangers of the African situation. I have done so because I believe any further delay in dealing with these problems may result in an outburst of violence caused on the one hand by panic and hysteria of the ruling minorities, and on the other hand by a sense of desperation by those who are oppressed and who can see no prospect of assistance from outside.

If the nations of the world can offer to the oppressed peoples of Africa some positive hope of action, then it is of course possible to counsel moderation and restraint. One can only counsel moderation and restraint or ask for that tolerance and forgiveness which will be necessary in an Africa of the future, if one is at the same time advocating a positive policy which will bring to an end the oppression and injustice which is at present occurring.

Nothing impresses me more than the discipline and restraint shown by the peoples of Africa in their protest against the oppression under which they are suffering. How can we ask them to continue to exercise this restraint and discipline if we ourselves, for reasons of diplomatic etiquette and politeness, are afraid even to indicate in public how we think it may be possible to bring to an end an intolerable situation! The lessons of history are quite clear. We have only to look at the history of Ireland itself for evidence of the fact that a minority which unjustly oppresses and dominates a majority, has no hope of survival in the modern world.

An important question to ask ourselves is: how is the change to be effected? Can it be done with tolerance and understanding and, above all, with forgiveness? Or must it be done through riot, civil war and economic and social collapse? The United Nations and the uncommitted countries of the world can, if they speak up and act at this moment, save the continent of Africa from that bloodshed and upheaval which must inevitably follow if the present situation is allowed to continue.

Now may I turn for a moment to the wider aspects of world politics. We in Africa have a vested interest in peace. There must be an enduring peace to enable us to consolidate our hard-won freedom and to reconstruct socially and economically the possessions of our heritage devastated by colonialism. It is indeed a regrettable and horrifying reflection on our age that the fate of the whole of mankind should be left in the hands of the leaders of four nations.

The situation in my view is alarming and frightful. This is the most crucial period in world history when the collective and concerted voice of the smaller nations must be heard. It is wrong that the rest of the world should sit idly by and allow the fate of mankind to be decided by political manœuvring between four powers, however important individually they may be. The other nations of the world, who together form the majority of the world's population, must now take steps to ensure that the four powers shall not toy with the fate of mankind just because they possess nuclear weapons.

Looking at the world political scene from the continent of Africa, the conduct of the four powers appears to be dictated by political expediency of the moment and is in no way related to the welfare of mankind as a whole. Let the other nations, indeed the majority of the world's people, take positive steps to bring to the notice of the four powers their grave responsibility to the rest of the world. History will never forgive any nation which, for its own ends, has gambled with the life of mankind.

CHAPTER THIRTY

THE REPUBLIC OF GHANA

Five hundred guests, including diplomatic representatives of more than fifty nations, arrived in Accra towards the end of June 1960 to witness the inauguration of the Republic of Ghana, freely voted for in the April plebiscite and authorised by a resounding majority. In the same plebiscite the people had elected me first President. The order of events was first, the departure of the Governor-General, the Earl of Listowel; second, the installation of the President and third the opening of a new Parliament under the republican constitution. In between these important ceremonies came the banquets, parades and other state occasions which justly accompanied so dramatic a change in the life of a people.

Chief among our guests was my brother President, Sekou Touré of Guinea and my old friend Dr W. E. B. Du Bois, an Afro-American scholar and one of the founders of the National Association for the Advancement of Coloured Peoples. Together we personified that identity of outlook which I hope will bring about a Union of African States. I firmly believe such a Union is the only complete solution to the problems facing all our peoples in Africa.

I could not but reflect on the contribution Ghana had made towards this end as I listened to the speech of Lord Listowel, departing Governor General, at a dinner we gave for him on 29 June. Ghana, he said, had given the world an object lesson in race relations, 'and this is something of inestimable value when one observes the tragic conditions resulting from bitter conflict in many other parts of the world.' In Ghana, he continued, things moved at breakneck speed. The advance from colonialism to unfettered self-government, from an agricultural to a growing mixed industrial economy had been achieved in a few years. Surely, I thought, there can be no other nation whose political development has been so swift, so bloodless and so certain. Lord Listowel's final words were a vote of confidence in the future:

I wish to extend to your new President and my old friend, Dr
Kwame Nkrumah, every good wish for success in the high
office to which you have so decisively elected him. Great
things have been achieved by Ghana under his leadership
and I am confident that, under his Presidency, the country
will continue to make steady progress in the service of Africa
and of mankind.

On the following morning, the Governor-General performed
his last duty, the prorogation of Parliament. In my speech on
this occasion, I paid tribute to Lord Listowel's devotion to duty
during his tenure of office and expressed my own regret at giving
up the office of Prime Minister and Member of Parliament:

Mr Speaker, in the same way as the Governor General must
feel sorrow at leaving Ghana, I feel a similar sorrow in that
this is the last occasion upon which I shall speak in this House
as Prime Minister and a Member of Parliament. This National
Assembly has been an historic body. I have known it from its
beginning. In fact, I have lived in it. I have seen it carry
through great constitutional changes. I myself have been a
fighter within its ramparts. Indeed, it has been the foundry
which has forged and moulded the new framework of our
nation.
    Though, however, from midnight tonight I shall cease to
be a Member of Parliament and cease to be an active partici-
pant in this august Assembly, I am certain that I shall not
lose that personal and intimate connection which I have
established with this House. I believe that no constitutional
change can affect the personal bonds which have been established in the ten years that we have worked together in this
House. I understand from the Clerk of the House that I shall
be provided with a seat in the new Assembly. I shall visit you
as often as is convenient.

That evening we saw the Governor General leave Ghana after
a moving farewell at the airport. The stage was now set for the
impressive ceremonies which would mark the entry of Ghana to
a new and more fully independent phase of government under
the republican constitution.
    The Government's proposals for a republican constitution had
been published in March as a White Paper. This document
explained the principles on which the Constitution was based
and indicated the way in which it would work. A plebiscite was

then held throughout the country in April, from which it was plain that the people of Ghana welcomed the new Constitution and by an overwhelming vote made me their first President.

In drafting the proposals for the new Constitution we had in mind the particular needs of the country and the principles which we had demonstrated again and again, namely that the ultimate power should reside in the people, that Ghana should be a unitary state, opposed to any form of federalism within its frontiers, but willing to surrender its sovereignty in whole or in part, if by so doing it could bring about African unity. An extract from the White Paper will show the essential originality of our Constitution:

The draft Constitution is not copied from the Constitution of any other country. It has been designed to meet the particular needs of Ghana and to express the realities of Ghana's constitutional position. It is therefore proposed that the actual Head of the Government should be the President of the Republic. In this respect the draft Constitution does not follow the traditional British model, where either a Monarch or a President (with only the same nominal powers as are exercised today by the Queen in the United Kingdom) is the technical Head of the State. Again, the Constitution of the Fifth Republic of France, which provides, in addition to a President, for a Prime Minister having little real authority, has not been followed. Nor is it proposed to copy the Presidential system as it exists in the United States and in other countries which have followed the United States type of government. Under the United States Constitution there is a division of authority between the executive part of the Government (the President and his Cabinet) and the legislative part of the Government (Congress, which consists of the Senate and the House of Representatives). Under the United States form of government Cabinet Ministers do not sit in Parliament and the Members of Parliament are elected quite separately from the President so that it is always possible that Parliament may be of one political complexion and the President of another. When there is a disagreement between the President and Parliament there is no machinery for an appeal to the people.

The proposed Republican Constitution for Ghana has been so devised as to provide as far as is possible that the person chosen as President will be the leader of the majority party in the Assembly. It is the Government's view that it is essential

in the interests of strong and efficient government that the
President and the Assembly should work as one and that this
can most effectively be secured by constitutional provisions
which link the election of the President to the election of
Members of the National Assembly and which provide that
if the National Assembly and the President disagree, the issue
can be decided by a General Election.

With this work behind us we came to the great moment when
as midnight struck on the First of July, Ghana was ushered into
a new era. Bells tolled; ships lying in Accra harbour blew their
sirens and men, women and children filled the streets to welcome
this new manifestation of Ghanaian advancement. They sang,
danced and shouted joyfully 'Long live Osagyefo[1] Kwame
Nkrumah'.

Later that morning at a solemn gathering in the State House
I was installed as first President of Ghana before the representatives of all those countries which have so closely attended the rise
and development of our nation. Holding in my right hand the
double bladed Sword of State,[2] I took this solemn oath:

*I, Kwame Nkrumah, do solemnly swear that I will well and truly
exercise the functions of the high office of President of Ghana, that I
will bear true faith and allegiance to Ghana, that I will preserve and
defend the constitution, and that I will do right to all manner of people
according to law without fear or favour, affection or ill-will. So help
me God.*

Thereafter I made my declaration, re-affirming that the independence of Ghana should not be surrendered or diminished
on any grounds other than the furtherance of African unity;
that no person would suffer discrimination on grounds of sex,
race, tribe, religion or political belief, and that chieftaincy in
Ghana would be guaranteed and preserved. Subject to restrictions
as might be necessary for preserving public order, morality and
health, no person would be deprived of freedom of religion or
speech, or of the right to move or assemble freely. No one would
be without the right of access to courts of law. 'The powers of
Government,' the Declaration continued, 'spring from the will

[1] 'Osagyefo': a title meaning Victorious Leader.
[2] Of solid gold, this sword is based in design upon the double-bladed Afesa-Nta,
the traditional symbol of inter-State peace. It is the symbol of Presidential authority.

of the people and should be exercised in accordance therewith. Freedom and Justice should be honoured and maintained.'

Leaving the Great Hall, I mounted a specially erected dais on the balcony and stood to receive a 21-gun salute. I was joined by President Sekou Touré of the Republic of Guinea and together we acknowledged the cheers of the crowd. Shortly after this ceremony, copies of the first issue of the Ghana Gazette was published, giving details of the Republican Cabinet and other Parliamentary posts. A new Order of Precedence was established and details were given of the newly created Orders, medals and awards.

Amid rising excitement I set off on a state drive of the city in an open car, with President Sekou Touré at my side. Behind us in a long motorcade followed the principal diplomatic representatives and distinguished guests, among them the Prime Minister of Nigeria, Alhaji Sir Abubakar Tafawa Balewa. The route was lined with gay, cheering crowds, many of them children who had waited for many hours to see the procession go by. From my car flew for the first time the President's personal standard, formed by the Black Star and the flying eagles of Ghana on a blue background.

Already it had been a long, historic day, but I had further engagements to fulfil. At six o'clock I broadcast to the nation to express the significance of our national achievements and to underline our hopes and outline our plans for the future. I called for continued support from the people to build Ghana into a prosperous nation and asked for their co-operation in the discharging of the heavy responsibility they had laid upon me as President. They would, I knew, seize the glorious opportunity now offered under our new constitution for service to Ghana 'in the final assault on the bastions of want, disease, poverty and indignity'. We would eliminate illiteracy completely from our midst.

On development, I promised to exert every endeavour to have Ghana's human resources trained to the full in science and technology. The women of the country would not be forgotten. 'I can even now see before my mind's eye,' I said, 'our women technicians in the factories, our women doctors in the hospitals, our women engineers building our bridges and even our women in overalls driving thousands of tractors in the fields.'

Turning to world affairs, I warned of the struggle still to come before all Africa could be free. I condemned 'those African leaders who are attempting to temporise by arranging behind the backs of their people' and said that the force of the mass movement towards freedom would not tolerate reactionary and double dealing politicians. I promised every support for African unity:

We shall not relax in our efforts to foster the concept of African unity and the creation of true political union among African states. I feel confident that in time our African compatriots will come to see our line and to know that Africa's salvation lies only in a political union of African states.

I reiterated that Ghana's policy of non-alignment remained unchanged. 'I believe that it is the best for us in our circumstances,' I said. 'We want to be friends to all and enemies to none.'

From the broadcast I drove to the race-course where preparations had been made for a fireworks display preceded by the ceremonial lighting of the flame of African freedom. This flame will be kept burning perpetually to symbolise the continuing struggle for African emancipation. As darkness began to fall over the city I rose to give a speech which moved me deeply as I spoke:

We have come here tonight to light the torch of African freedom. This flame which we are about to light will not only enshrine the spirit of the Republic of Ghana, but will also provide a symbol for the African freedom fighters of today and tomorrow. We shall draw inspiration from this perpetual flame for the struggle of African emancipation.

Day after day and year after year this flame will reflect the burning desire of the African people to be free – totally free and independent – fettered by no shackles of any nature whatsoever and will signify their ability to manage and direct their own affairs in the best interest of themselves.

I light this flame not only in the name of the people of Ghana but also in sacred duty to millions of Africans elsewhere now crying out for freedom. And I charge all of us here present to remember that this great struggle of African emancipation is a holy crusade to which we must constantly stand dedicated and which must be prosecuted to a successful end.

Your Excellencies, Ladies and Gentlemen: I now light this flame and may it burn perpetually and constitute a symbol of victory for our cause.

On Saturday, 2 July, by Presidential proclamation, the first sitting of the first Parliament of the Republic was held in the State House. At this brief session Speaker and Deputy Speaker were elected and all members took the oath of allegiance. This completed the constitutional preparations for the state opening of Parliament on the following Monday.

In the afternoon of Saturday a parade of the armed services including the police, and also the Builders' Brigade and many voluntary organisations was held in the Sports Stadium and witnessed by some fifty thousand people. After inspecting the parade I drove round the Stadium waving a white handkerchief in acknowledgement of the cheers of the crowds. The Prime Ministers of Nigeria, Sierra Leone and the Cameroons were on the dais as I addressed the gathering. Emphasising the need for the 'cardinal virtues of obedience, loyalty and courage', I went on to assure the armed forces of my regard for them:

As I assume the office of Commander-in-Chief of the armed forces of our country, I feel confident that every one of you, whatever your position, will also feel a keen sense of responsibility to your nation and be urged towards a resolve to offer of your best.

I will endeavour to keep in mind the necessity for making adequate provision for your needs, and as your Commander-in-Chief, I will jealously guard your interests.

Passing through this hectic period of transition, Ghana needs the patriotic services of all of us. Above all, she needs the requisite peace, internal and external, to pursue her life undisturbed. Your role as soldiers in this regard is of the highest importance. We are determined to build a stable society and you have a duty to guard with vigilance our hard won freedom.

I am highly impressed by your superb martial bearing and your smart turn-out and I wish to express to you my warmest thanks for the important role you have played in the inauguration activities.

The next occasion on which I spoke was perhaps the most colourful and impressive of all. This was the State opening of the nation's Parliament on 4 July. My arrival at Parliament House was heralded by the beating of traditional drums and the cheers of watching Ghanaians. A 21-gun salute was fired by a troop of the Ghana Reconnaissance Squadron, after which I inspected a guard of honour formed by the Third Battalion of the Ghana Regiment with the President's Colour and the Army Band. I was then escorted to the House in a procession led by the State Sword Bearer and including the Mace Bearer and eight Linguists drawn from many parts of the country. State horns – Mmenson – were sounded by the Juaben State Ntahera. I then took my seat in the Presidential throne, carved in the form of a stool and adorned with golden traditional stool symbols. In my speech I sought to give the clearest statement of our policy as a nation dedicated to freedom and justice, peace and goodwill. I spoke as follows:

Four days ago, the nation was ushered into a new life by the proclamation of the Republic of Ghana.

Today the first formal meeting of the Republican Parliament takes place in changed circumstances, both in regard to the physical arrangements of the House and to the spirit of excitement which possesses us all at this moment.

These are great times in the history of our country and you who are the chosen representatives of the people, have a glorious and unique opportunity to render service to the nation by endeavouring to change the state in which colonialism and imperialism have placed us and to create a society of men and women eager to give of their best in order to raise their country to a position of eminence and prosperity and enable her to give material help to other African countries.

By the voluntary act of our people we have chosen the path we wish to tread. We have done so in the utmost belief in our ability to shape our destiny by our own sustained efforts. We are creating the history of our nation as we translate into practical reality the dreams and visions of our forefathers. In twelve years from the fateful days of 1948, we have witnessed a remarkable transformation in our national life and have through tenacious effort worked steadily to our goal.

We have, moreover, started a movement that has set the whole of Africa ablaze and which aims to blast the last bastions of colonialism, imperialism and racialism from the face of the African continent. I am conscious of the gravity of the responsibility which the highest office in the nation has placed on me. But in the discharge of this responsibility I am comforted by the knowledge that I can rely on your support, co-operation and loyal service in the fulfilment of the great expectations and trust which our people cherish under this new regime.

We must remember, however, that our struggle is not yet over. We have merely moved into a new phase.

Our efforts must be constantly devoted to the aim of giving every individual the opportunity of living a fuller, richer and more useful life to prepare himself for greater devotion to the service of Ghana and of Africa. From each citizen will be expected loyalty, hard work, and the conscientious application of his talents to the nation.

The new era we have entered into, therefore, calls for a solemn pledge to ourselves to perform selflessly the duties entrusted to each one of us.

I am confident of the ability of this House, to bear the heavy responsibility which has been imposed upon it by our new constitution. I must emphasise, however, that today Ghana has been reborn. I trust that this new spirit may guide and influence you in all your deliberations and infuse you with a determination to reach yet greater heights in your supreme efforts to transform this country into a place worthy of the part it is destined to play in the future of the human race.

Since this is the first formal meeting of the Republican Parliament it is my duty to outline to you the policies which the Convention People's Party Government will follow during this session.

I will start by making it quite clear that the operation of the republican constitution will not in any way involve a change of policy as far as our foreign relations are concerned. Ghanaian foreign policy will continue to be one of positive neutralism and non-alignment. As I have explained many times before this does not imply that the Government of Ghana will be a mere silent spectator of world events.

On the contrary, the Government will continue to take positive steps through the United Nations Organisation to promote and maintain peace and security among all nations.

We shall always adopt whatever positive policies will do most to safeguard our independence and world peace.

To that end the Government solemnly re-affirm their faith in the Charter of the United Nations and undertake to be friends with all nations and enemy to none.

The Government will continue to denounce the arms race, and the manufacture and testing of nuclear weapons anywhere in the world. In particular, it will, in concert with other Governments of Africa, find ways of persuading the French or any other Government to desist from such tests on African soil. Secondly, the stand we have taken on foreign policy will steadily add impetus to the role that Ghana has to play in the projection of the African personality in the international community.

At an early stage we intend to urge that the independent African states should agree to the formation of a free African non-nuclear bloc, independent of East or West, on the basis of refusal to allow their territories to be used as military bases and particularly the rejection of alliances dependent upon nuclear weapons. I will even be bold to offer the proposal that all uncommitted non-nuclear countries of the world, particularly of Africa and Asia, should summon themselves into a conference with a view to forming a non-nuclear third force – a war preventing force – between the two blocs of the so-called East and West.

We in Africa have a vested interest in peace. There must be an enduring peace in the world to enable us the new emergent countries, to consolidate our hard won freedom and to reconstruct economically and socially the possessions of our heritage devastated by colonialism and imperialism. As far as Africa is concerned, I have long ago stated a postulate that Ghana's independence is meaningless unless it is linked up with the total liberation of Africa and with the projection of the African personality in the international community. Our resolution on this issue is unshakeable and the Government will continue to give every support to freedom fighters in all parts of Africa.

I would like to pay tribute here to the gallant men and women who had laid down their lives for the liberation of Algeria, to the victims of apartheid in South Africa, and to all those struggling against the degradation brought about by colonialism and racialism. The Government will, therefore, continue to work for African unity and independence and will endeavour in accordance with that objective to make the political union of African states a living reality.

It is against this background that we must view the significance of the presence at the celebrations ushering in the republican constitution of my brother, President Sekou Touré of the Republic of Guinea. Together, Guinea and Ghana will continue to wage war on the old and new colonialism until both the independence and unity of Africa are achieved.

Before African unity can be achieved however, it is necessary for there to be real and genuine independence. The current of African nationalism and freedom is flowing so strongly that no colonial power can hope to swim against it and survive in Africa.

Turning to South Africa, the Government is unalterably opposed to the inhuman policy of apartheid practised by the South African Government and will relentlessly continue to fight against this policy. The Government will give every support to the Political Bureau which the leaders of the banned African nationalist organisations of South Africa have decided to set up here as the mouthpiece of their people. As I stated recently in London, it will be extremely embarrassing to Ghana to remain indefinitely in the Commonwealth with a Government that recognises and practices apartheid and racial discrimination.

I will now turn my attention to our domestic policy. The Government will embark upon an intensified programme of industrialisation which, with the diversification and mechanisation of agriculture will provide the main basis for the transformation of the economic and social life of this country. The momentum of this development will increase so that in a relatively short period Ghana will become a modern industrial nation, providing opportunities for all and a standard of living comparable with any in the world.

For industrial development and the establishment of factories ranging from steel mills and aluminium smelters to sugar refineries, we shall need abundant and cheap power. That is why the Volta River project is foremost among the many schemes which we have for increasing our industrial productivity. Negotiations are now reaching the critical stage for the construction of the dam at Akosombo and the establishment of the complex industries associated with the project.

The Government will continue to safeguard and expand the cocoa industry. Furthermore, the Government intends to put new life into agricultural development not only by the diversification of agriculture through the growth of other cash crops, or by tackling the problems of food deficiency through the production of foodstuffs and protein foods sufficient for our needs, but also by seriously embarking upon active mechanisation of our agriculture.

The industrial and commercial infra-structure of the country will continue to be given attention as one of the conditions for ensuring increased agricultural and industrial production. Roads, river communications, harbour facilities and other communications will be developed in accordance with the present plan.

The Government attaches great importance to educational advancement as one of the means of transforming the society of Ghana to a higher standard. Our goal is to achieve a free universal primary and middle school education within the shortest possible time. A commission is being appointed to investigate and report upon university education and the Government intends that a University of Ghana will be created which will not only reflect African traditions and culture but will also play a constructive part in the programme of national awakening and reconstruction.

The Government has embarked on a complete reorganisation of the health and medical services of the country and greater impetus will be given to research and health problems, the attack on endemic diseases, health education, nutrition and development of hospitals and health centres.

The Government intends to give new orientation to our financial policy, to expand trade between Ghana and other countries, to pursue plans for increased economic co-operation in Africa and to give encouragement to the establishment of co-operative enterprises as one of the means of modernising the economic and social life of Ghana.

Last year has been a remarkable record of freedom from industrial and other disputes. This vindicates the policy which the Government has pursued for reorganising the trade unions. It will be an important element of the Government's policy to help establish and develop the All-African Trade Union Federation as an expression of the African personality and the solidarity of all the workers of emergent Africa.

It will be the policy of the Government not only to maintain and consolidate the existing organisation of the Armed Forces and the Police Force but also to embark on a steady programme of expansion to match the growing need to safeguard the external and internal security of Ghana.

The Government is determined to ensure that a sound base is provided for the modern and stable society which we are endeavouring to build for our people in Ghana. For that reason we will adopt a most ruthless attitude to stamp out all corrupt and mercenary practices. Greater vigilance also will be exercised in maintaining and ensuring internal security and in rooting out all subversive elements.

On the same day I gave a luncheon to some five hundred guests in the Ambassador Hotel. The guest of honour was President Sekou Touré who made a courteous speech in which he outlined the policy of his government and expressed 'the genuine solidarity that binds the people of Ghana and the people of Guinea together in one and the same struggle, whose aim is to shape the

historic destiny of all the people of Africa within the framework
of peace, based upon social freedom and democratic progress'.
He was replying to a short speech in which I welcomed our guests
and expressed once again my own convictions of the importance
of African freedom through political unity. I told of our feelings
of gratitude to those nations and individuals who had sympa-
thised with us in our task:

> I have said much in the past few days to give a clear indication
> of the policy which the Government of Ghana, with the sup-
> port of the people, intends to pursue. I do not propose to repeat
> myself here on that subject. What I wish to do at this point is
> to express to our guests, who have come from all corners of the
> earth to join in these celebrations with us, my own personal
> gratitude and the gratitude of the people of Ghana for this
> concrete expression of their goodwill and encouragement to
> us. We are deeply appreciative also of the many messages of
> congratulation and goodwill which we have received from
> leaders and statesmen from all over the world. I am sure that
> our guests have seen something of the new life which we are
> trying to create in this part of Africa. They will also have had
> an indication of our aspirations and our hopes. We trust that
> they have enjoyed their short stay and that they will one day
> visit us again. We ask our visitors to carry back to their
> Governments and people and to our many friends abroad,
> our good wishes and our hope that the immense goodwill that
> has been shown to Ghana in the last few days will contribute
> to our ability to play a useful role in the community of nations.

Lord Hailsham, the U.K. delegate, then proposed the health
of Ghana in a speech of sincere goodwill. Following upon con-
gratulatory messages from the Queen as Head of the Commonwealth and from the President of the United States and India as
well as from the Governments of Russia and China, Lord Hailsham's words made me feel that our policy of steady non-alignment with political blocs, of friendship to all and hostility to none
might well be entirely successful.

CHAPTER THIRTY-ONE

THE CONGO STRUGGLE

The day before our Republic came into being, the Congo declared its independence. This was to start a succession of crises in which Ghana and other independent African states were to become more and more deeply involved. It was only to be expected that Congolese independence would be accompanied by all sorts of political difficulties. Not only was the country divided against itself, but there had been no policy of Africanisation to prepare the way for independence. There were few experienced Congolese politicians or civil servants. The Force Publique, the Congolese army, had no African officers. The Belgians had quite clearly never intended to prepare the country for self-government.

Far from being a unified state, the Congo was torn by political dissension. At the elections before independence, only one man, Patrice Lumumba, won seats in all the provinces. His party, the Congo National Movement, gained 33 of the 137 seats in the National Chamber. The next nearest was the People's National Party, with 19 seats. Mr Kasavubu, leader of the Abako and Lumumba's rival for power, won only 12 seats.

Somehow, Lumumba patched up a working majority in the Chamber and at independence he became Prime Minister, and Kasavubu, President. Moise Tshombe was elected chairman of the Provincial Council of Katanga. Surprisingly enough, Tshombe began negotiations to join Lumumba's government. Unhappily, the negotiations broke down on the question of the number of seats demanded by Tshombe. He withdrew to Katanga. This was an ominous indication of the serious trouble to come.

The breakdown of law and order began on 7 July with a meeting of the Force Publique at Thysville. Disappointed because independence did not immediately bring more pay and the removal of Belgian officers, the soldiers seized arms, arrested white officers and N.C.Os and finally broke up into rioting bands. The Belgians fled, abandoning their homes and their work,

and tales began to pour into Leopoldville of violence and disorder all over the country. It was at this crucial point that
Tshombe, with the assistance of Belgian advisers, maintained
that Katanga Province should secede even though he held only
one-third of the seats of the Provincial Council of Katanga while
the Balubaket, the supporters of Lumbumba's Congo National
Movement, held a convincing majority in the Provincial
Council. Without the rich resources of Katanga Province the
new Republic of the Congo could not hope to survive. On 12
July, Lumumba appealed to the United Nations for aid. Two
days later, the vice-premier, Antoine Gizenga, asked the United
States for military help. Next day, Kasavubu sent a telegram,
threatening to call in the Bandung Powers if the U.N. did not
act. In the meantime, Katanga appealed to the Federation of
Rhodesia and Nyasaland for military help.

I watched this rapidly worsening situation with growing concern. In a press release on 13 July, I made it clear that the
Government of Ghana took the most serious view of attempts to
destroy the territorial integrity of the Congo. Intervention by
any power in Congolese internal affairs would be regarded as an
unfriendly act amounting to aggression. I announced that a
mission had been sent by the Ghana Government to the Republic of the Congo 'to offer all possible aid, including, if it is
desired by the Government of the Congo, military assistance'.
The press statement continued:

Ghana is prepared, if requested, either alone or in concert
with the United Nations to provide any other form of technical
aid which the Republic of the Congo may require.

Ghana considers, however, that the present difficulties in
the Congo should be solved primarily through the efforts of
the independent African states within the framework of the
United Nations machinery. Intervention by Powers from outside the African continent, in the view of the Government of
Ghana, is likely to increase rather than lessen tension.

The Government of Ghana has made this statement in the
belief that the present situation in the Congo is one capable
of peaceful and quick solution, provided that rival outside
Powers do not interfere as a means of serving their own particular interests.

The Government of the Congo Republic asked the Ghana

Government for military aid, and at once, on 13 July, I sent this message to the Belgian Government:

The Government of Ghana have been invited by the Government of the Republic of the Congo to provide military aid. The President will be in touch with the Secretary General of the United Nations during the night so as to see how far it will be possible to use United Nations transport to convey the Ghanaian forces to the Congo.

In responding to the request for aid, the Government of Ghana are not, of course, acting in any spirit of hostility to the Government of Belgium. If the Belgian Government so desire, Ghanaian troops might by arrangement with the Belgian commander on the spot replace Belgian troops in an agreed manner. In order to assist the planning of Ghanaian military aid, the Chief of the Ghana Defence Staff, Major-General Alexander, will be arriving in Leopoldville tomorrow morning, and he will naturally call on the Belgian Commander.

The Government of Ghana hopes that the present close cooperation between Belgium and Ghana will continue, and that it will be possible for Belgium to give all assistance to the Ghana force in their mission.

At 11 p.m., Ghana time, on Wednesday, 13 July I spoke by telephone to Mr Hammarskjöld, Secretary-General of the United Nations. I told him that the Congolese Parliament had requested the Ghana Government for military aid, and said that Ghana, *as an African state*, was ready and willing to send troops. Air transport, however, was needed urgently. I asked Mr Hammarskjöld to urge the United States Government to place the four American Globemasters at Wheeler Field, Libya at the disposal of the U.N. These aircraft, together with the two R.A.F. Comets alredy at Accra could carry Ghanaian troops to the Congo, and fly out of the Congo all foreigners – Europeans, Asiatics and Americans, who wished to leave the country. In the same way, at my request, the Soviet Union sent five ILI8 aircraft to Accra on 20 July 1960, to assist the Ghana Government in the airlift of troops and equipment to the Congo.

The same evening, the Security Council of the U.N. met to discuss the resolution that was to establish U.N. forces in the Congo. Mr Hammarskjöld decided to make it a predominantly African operation, although Sweden and Ireland, both unquestionably neutral, were asked to send troops. The Great powers, excluded from the U.N. military force, provided air transport, and on 15 July the first Tunisian soldiers, closely followed by Ghanaian troops, landed in the Congo.

My Government wholeheartedly supported U.N. intervention in the Congo. We hoped that law and order would be quickly and effectively restored, and Katanga compelled to renounce her secession. Only then, would the Congo be able to work out its own destiny, unhindered by any outside interference.

While events in the Congo continued to occupy the headlines of the world press, a significant conference took place in Accra. Ghanaian women, and African women from all parts of the continent, assembled to discuss common problems. At the opening ceremony on 18 July, I spoke of the part women could play in the great struggle for African liberation and unity:

Your role is of great importance. Not only can you carry back this message to the men of your respective countries, but, if you are convinced that unity is the right answer, you can also bring your feminine influence to bear in persuading your brothers, husbands and friends of the importance of African unity as the only salvation for Africa. For my part, I stand resolutely and inexorably by this conviction and will work with unrelenting determination for its attainment.

There is a great responsibility resting on the shoulders of all women of Africa and African descent. They must realise that the men alone cannot complete the gigantic task we have set ourselves. The time has come when the women of Africa must rise up in their millions to join the African crusade for freedom. All over Africa the cry goes out for action – political, social, economic, cultural and educational.

A vivid picture of the danger besetting us is provided by the present example of colonialist and imperialist intrigue in the Congo. The fact that the Congo has achieved independence has not prevented her detractors from causing trouble and dissension by subversion or overt treachery in denying the province of Katanga as an integral part of the Congo Republic. This example of what has happened in the Congo is a positive warning to all Africa to unite in action to defend and preserve the independence of Africa.

Women of Africa, the history that you make today records not only the iron determination of our people to be free, but also our proclamation to the world to take note of the fact that colonialism and imperialism are a decadent force with their backs to the wall, and that they can only help to liquidate themselves. Our rich heritage must be restored to us.

Women of Africa, yours is the duty and privilege of hoisting high the nationalist banner of redemption; yours is the glory of answering the call of our beloved Africa; yours is the enviable opportunity to call a decisive halt to the ruinous penetration of colonialism and imperialism in Africa; yours is the honour to fight relentlessly for the total emancipation of this great continent; yours is the task of projecting the African personality to the world of today.

Sisters of the African Liberation Front, the last century was one of European occupation of Africa. This century, is one of African liberation. The year 1960 is the most challenging and significant year in this historic development. It is the year of the climax of the revolution in which Africa has rebelled against the shame and injustice which for so long has been meted out to her. The clarion command echoes across the mountains and the valleys across the rivers and the lakes, across the oceans and the deserts: Hands off Africa! Hands off Africa!

I told them that we in Africa had a vested interest in peace. Under no circumstances should nuclear bases be established on our continent. Central and South America, the Middle East, China, India and S.E. Asia, together with the Far Eastern countries and other non-nuclear powers, should form a non-nuclear association. Such an association could do much to promote peace in the world. I said that free Africa was determined to make its own contribution to the world, and that this could only be done in an atmosphere of political and economic freedom:

My sisters, I have said much to give you some idea of the danger facing our continent and of the obvious remedy. We believe in the destiny of the African continent, and will continue to labour with purpose and faith until Africa is united in freedom. May God's blessing rest upon your conference and guide your deliberations.

As the days went by, and the U.N. forces in the Congo did not drive the Belgian troops out, or hand Katanga back to the central Congolese Government, it became clear that the real struggle was only just beginning. Dr Ralph Bunche, who repre-

sented the United Nations at the independence celebrations and
had stayed on in Leopoldville, visited Katanga in an attempt to
persuade Tshombe to allow U.N. forces to enter the province.
He failed. Tshombe, backed by Belgian soldiers and officials,
insisted that Katanga could manage her own affairs.

On 8 August I received a telegram from Tshombe in which he
contended that the Government of the Congo was illegal and
Communist-dominated. I at once replied:

> In answer to your last telegram to me I should like to make
> one final appeal to you to act with a sense of responsibility
> and in accordance with the interest of Africa which I know
> you also have at heart. The whole world knows that your pre-
> tended state has been set up with the support of foreign
> interests. Your actions are applauded in South Africa and the
> Rhodesias, and are condemned by every other independent
> African state. This at least should give you food for thought.
> Your whole administration depends on Belgian officials who
> are fundamentally opposed to African independence, and
> who are merely using you as their tool. They will discard you
> as soon as you have served their purpose. No true African
> nationalist can have confidence in you while you continue to
> allow yourself to be used as such. Your name is now linked
> openly with foreign exploiters and oppressors of your own
> country. In fact you have assembled in your support the fore-
> most advocates of imperialism and colonialism in Africa and
> the most determined opponents of African freedom. How can
> you, as an African, do this? I appeal to you with all sincerity
> to denounce those who are merely using you as a puppet, and
> who have no more respect for you than they have for African
> freedom and independence.
>
> Your allegations of Communism against the Republic of
> the Congo show how far you are under the influence of South
> Africa, who regards any movement for African freedom as
> Communist. You have allowed the Belgians to control the
> news coming out of Katanga. Nevertheless, it is clear that
> serious disorder is occurring in the northern part of the pro-
> vince of Katanga, and that your policy is endangering the
> lives of Africans and Europeans alike. Let me once again
> appeal to you and Ngalula to consider the position into which
> you have placed yourselves, and to work for the unity of the
> Congo and of Africa.

The same day I addressed the National Assembly on African
affairs. I spoke of the danger of a power vacuum in Africa:

The new African nations must, from the very nature of the conditions under which they became independent, be in their early days weak and powerless when contrasted with the great and older established nations of the world. Potentially, however, an African union could be one of the greatest forces in the world as we know it. One of the most encouraging things which have taken place within the last six months or so is the growing realisation among African statesmen that we must unite politically and that, indeed, in the words of the Prime Minister of Northern Nigeria, that a United States of Africa is inevitable. As I have stated elsewhere, there are three alternatives open to African states; firstly, to unite and save our continent; secondly, to disunite and disintegrate; or thirdly, to sell out. In other words: either to unite, or to stand separately and disintegrate, or to sell ourselves to foreign powers.

I then turned to the Congo struggle, and reminded Assembly members of the speech I made in Dublin nearly three months before, when I urged the United Nations to organise, before it was too late, a peaceful transference of power in Africa:

Though this speech was made long before the event, it does, I consider, describe exactly the situation which has subsequently arisen in the Congo. Fundamentally, Belgian influence in the Congo has been destroyed, not because the Belgian Government agreed to hand over power to the Congolese Republic – this was inevitable – but because for far too long the white minority in the Congo had excluded Africans from all positions of authority. . . . No one can, of course, condone or excuse assault, violence and murder, however great the provocation. It is necessary, however, to understand that it is possible for a colonial power to create a situation in which such violence is bound to occur, and that, in fact, is what the Belgian Government did by a consistent policy of colonialism over a period of 80 years.

I said that it would be a mistake to look upon the Congo as a case apart, or suppose that the same conditions which had produced the Congo crisis did not exist in one form or another throughout the whole of the African continent. The problem of Africa was essentially bound up everywhere with a struggle between a ruling minority and an under-privileged and economically exploited majority. It was, therefore, no solution for a colonial power to hand over authority to a small clique of African politicians who were not generally representative of the people from whom they had sprung. I went on:

The Government of Ghana support wholeheartedly the United Nations intervention in the Congo. The only thing that is wrong with United Nations intervention is that it came too late and is acting too slowly.

Recent events in the Congo have shown that independent African states are capable and better equipped to deal with the great problems of Africa than are the powers outside the African continent. This does not mean that Africa will not need the disinterested and impartial aid of the United Nations and other powers working through the United Nations, or through the African states themselves. A situation, however, has been reached when African states are technically competent to tackle any problem arising on the African continent. I would not be so presumptuous as to put forward a Monroe doctrine for Africa. I must say, however, that the great powers of the world should realise that very often African questions can be settled by African states if there is no non-African intervention or interference.

Action at an early stage by the United Nations need not involve the costly and difficult task of assembling a United Nations force. Early and prompt action by the African states can avoid the disorganisation and disorder which always accompany the final disintegration of a colonial power.

I am greatly heartened that there is a growing realisation that outside intervention, backed and supported only by the United Nations, is essential if chaos is not to envelop large parts of the African continent.

After referring to the troubled situation in Algeria, the Union of South Africa, the Rhodesias and Nyasaland, I went on to examine the history and effect of balkanisation in Europe, and warned my listeners that unless we were extremely vigilant, the same sort of thing might happen in Africa:

In the same way as defensive alliances by the Balkan powers, with rival powers outside the Balkans, resulted in a world war, so a world war could easily originate on the African continent if African states make political, economic and military alliances with rival powers from outside Africa. The new colonialism creates client states, independent in name, but in

point of fact pawns of the colonial power that is supposed to
have given them independence. When an African balkanised
state concludes a pact with its colonial power, then that state
has lost control over its foreign policy, and is therefore not free.

On the other hand, if Africa is converted into a series of
tiny states, such alliances are inevitable. Some of these states
have neither the resources nor the personnel to provide for
their own defence, or to conduct an independent foreign
policy. Nor can they become economically independent. They
have not the resources to establish their own independent
banking systems and they are compelled to continue with the
old colonial framework of trade. The only way out is to stand
together politically.

The African struggle for independence and unity must
begin with political union. A loose confederation of economic
co-operation is deceptively time-delaying. It is only a political
union that will ensure a uniformity in our foreign policy, projecting the African personality and presenting Africa as a
force important enough to be reckoned with. A political union
envisages a common foreign and defence policy, and rapid
social, economic and industrial developments. The economic
resources of Africa are immense and staggering. It is only by
unity that these resources can be utilised for the progress of
the continent, and for the happiness of mankind.

Territories in Africa which have become independent, or are
likely to become independent in the near future, and which have
populations of less than 3 million, include the Central African
Republic, Chad, the former French Congo, Dahomey, Gabon,
the Ivory Coast, Niger, Sierra Leone and Togoland. I said that
I thought it impossible that the colonial powers seriously believe
that independence could be of much value to these African states
in such a terrible state of fragmentation:

It has often been said that Africa is poor. What nonsense! It
is not Africa that is poor. It is the Africans, who are im-
poverished by centuries of exploitation and domination.

To give one example: in Northern Rhodesia, the Government considers that the country is so poor that to quote the
Colonial Office Report for 1958, 'no rapid progress can be
expected in secondary education'. In fact, with an African
population of nearly 2 million there are only 1,900 African
children in secondary schools. Northern Rhodesia, however,
is not poor. Its copper mines are among the most successful

and profitable in the world. They pay a far higher rate of interest on the capital invested than would be found in other parts of the world.

Let me give you another example. The mandated territory of South West Africa is always described by the Union of South Africa as one of the poorest territories in the world. But it is not poor from the point of view of the foreign shareholders in the Tsumeb copper-lead-zinc mine.

I have frequently emphasised that imperialism in the present stage of African nationalism will employ many feints. With one hand it may concede independence, while with the other, it will stir up the muddy waters of tribalism, feudalism, separatism and chicanery in order to find its way back in another guise. What is now going on in the Congo is a typical example of this latest kind of imperialist and colonialist manœuvre. And there are very good reasons why we should have expected something of the kind to happen. The interests that are engaged in the Congo are empires in themselves, and those in Katanga especially, have fabulous advantages which they are loath to abandon.

Foremost among these is the immensely ramified Société Générale de Belgique, whose pyramidal structure covers the Comité Spécial du Katanga. This Comité holds property of a size which is breath-taking. That a single concern would hold property of the size of 111,111,111 acres is a staggering thought. But this is the size of the empire of the Comité Spécial du Katanga, and it contains some of the world's most valuable mineral rights.

A subsidiary of this giant structure and the Compagnie du Haut Katanga, which is linked to the Union Miniere, has procured for itself in the Katanga area a concession of 7,700 square miles; that is, a territory more than half the size of Belgium itself. This concession was not due to expire until 11th March 1990. These interests feared that the independence which passed to the people of the Congo on the 30th June this year, would cut across the privileges enjoyed by the Union Minière to exploit the riches of this vast region for its shareholders and the Belgian Government, which has a two-thirds interest in the Comité Spécial du Katanga, the organisation owning 25 per cent of the Union Minière.

Here are interlocking connections which are of considerable importance, and it is easy enough to understand what there is at stake when we realise that the Union Minière produces out of its Katanga concessions 7 per cent of the total world production of copper, 80 per cent cobalt, 5 per cent of zinc, as well as substantial quantities of cadium, silver, platinum, columbium, tungsten and many other important minerals. It also operates the uranium mine at Shinkolobwe, which provides the raw material for some nuclear weapon nations. The amount of this production is a closely guarded secret, as is also the price paid for it.

The Union Minière produces at least 45 per cent of all Congo exports, and these are so profitable that its net profits, that is, its profits after all reserves and allocations have been made, are well over £20,000,000 per annum.

When we consider these facts in relation to the present serious situation in the Congo, it is not at all difficult to appreciate the efforts that have been made to separate Katanga from the Republic of the Congo.

I pointed out that when the Congo was declared independent, the financial arrangements of the Union Minière were rearranged, and a substantial portion of the shareholding went to the Congo Government. The rest of the capital was held by the Société Générale de Belgique and Tanganyika Concessions Limited. The latter company was originally registered in London, but in November 1950, control was transferred to Southern Rhodesia:

Capital investment from outside is, of course, required in Africa. But if there is real political independence the profits from the investment of this capital can be shared in a way which is fair both to the outside investor and to the people of the country where the investment is made.

The evil of balkanisation, disunity and secessions, is that the new balkan states of Africa will not have the independence to shake off the economic shackles which result in Africa being a source of riches to the outside world, while grinding poverty continues at home.

There is a real danger that the colonial powers will grant a nominal type of political independence to individual small units so as to ensure that the same old colonial type of economic organisation continues long after independence has been achieved. This in itself is a source of the gravest potential danger for the whole world. The peoples of Africa do not seek political freedom for abstract purposes. They seek it because they believe that through political freedom they can obtain economic advancement, education and a real control over their own destiny. If there is a grant of independence to a state which is so small that it cannot mobilise its own resources, and which is tied by a series of economic and military agreements to the former colonial power, then a potentially revolutionary situation is at once created. These are the situations facing the new Africa today.

I spoke of the Ghana Government's offer of armed assistance to the Congo, if no U.N. solution was forthcoming. I said that I had been in constant touch both with the Secretary-General and with the leaders of the African states. I asked members of the National Assembly for a mandate for the complete mobilisation of all Ghana armed forces for such military action as might be required.

The call of the hour is: 'Hands off Congo', and we must press the Security Council of the United Nations to effect the speedy and unconditional withdrawal of all Belgian troops from Katanga and all other parts of the Congo. There are some people who are at present talking of a loose form of federation between Katanga and the rest of the Congo. In my view, any person who talks of a federal type of constitution for the Congo is a supporter of the imperialist cause. This proposal to establish a loose federation in the Congo is merely an attempt by those who failed to detach Katanga from the Congo Republic, to get balkanisation of the Congo by the back door.

The question of a constitution for the Congo is entirely a matter for the Congolese people themselves to decide; and the Congolese people can have the opportunity to decide the issue in perfect freedom and security only when the Belgian troops have withdrawn completely and unconditionally from Congolese territory, including Katanga.

It was essential, I said, that the Congo question should be solved primarily with our own African resources:

Therefore, however heavy the burden, I believe that military action should be taken primarily by the independent states of Africa, and at the conclusion of my address to you, you will be invited to support a Government motion authorising the Government to take such military action against Belgium as may be necessary. The Government wishes to have this authority from Parliament in order to be able to inform the United Nations that Ghana will fight under U.N. leadership against Belgium in support of the Security Council resolution.

However, if the United Nations are unable to implement the Security Council's resolution, Ghana would co-operate with the military forces of other independent African states to drive the Belgian aggressors from African soil.

This is a turning point in the history of Africa. If we allow the independence of the Congo to be compromised in any way by the imperialist and capitalist forces, we shall expose the sovereignty and independence of all Africa to grave risk. The struggle of the Congo is therefore our struggle. It is in-incumbent on us to take our stand by our brothers in the Congo in the full knowledge that only Africa can fight for its destiny. In this struggle we shall not reject the assistance and support of our friends, but we will yield to no enemy, however strong.

I left the Chamber to loud applause, and members went on to discuss the various questions I had raised. Later, by a large majority, they voted my Government the necessary powers to mobilise Ghana's armed forces, and so approved our Congo policy.

CHAPTER THIRTY-TWO

GHANA AND THE UNITED NATIONS

On 10 August 1960 I sent a note to our delegate at the United Nations, Mr Quaison Sackey, informing him of the Government's views on the Congo situation. I suggested that a copy of the note should be sent to all members of the Security Council, and to the delegates of independent African states. I hoped, in this way, to clear up any misunderstanding about Ghana's policy which might have arisen as a result of certain inaccurate press reports. The note was as follows:

The view of the Government of Ghana is that United Nations forces are in the Republic of the Congo at the request of the lawfully constituted Government of that Republic, and Ghanaian forces were contributed to the United Nations contingent on that understanding. In these circumstances it would be in the view of the Government of Ghana entirely inappropriate for the United Nations to have any dealings with any group of persons who have their authority to negotiate on a repudiation of the authority of the Congolese Government.

The Government of Ghana takes the view that in relation to internal matters in the Congolese Republic, the only authority from whom the United Nations can obtain an authoritative view of the obligations existing under the Constitution of the Republic is the Government of the Republic which requested United Nations intervention.

It is the responsibility of the United Nations to restore order in the Congo. It would be a gross breach of faith, in the view of the Government of Ghana, if, after this has been done with the consent of the Government of the Republic, the United Nations were to agree to any conditions under which any other rival and illegal groups were allowed to retain their arms.

The United Nations force has, in the view of the Government of Ghana, a duty to see that no arbitrary or unjust act is committed by any authority or person under the shadow of the military force provided by the United Nations. So long, however, as the provisions of the constitution of the Republic are preserved, the United Nations should not take any step

to prevent the Government of the Republic enforcing the constitutional provisions, or of prosecuting persons who have
offended against the municipal laws of the Republic of the
Congo.

The Government of Ghana considers that the future constitution of the Republic of the Congo is one entirely for the
people of the Congo, and the Government therefore hopes that
it will be possible for the United Nations to create a situation
in which free and uninhibited constitutional discussions are
possible. It would, however, be entirely wrong if the military
force of the United Nations were used to protect an illegal
Government. The so-called shadow of Belgian military
occupation, which in itself was contrary to the resolution of
the Security Council. The puppet nature of this regime has
been a subject of almost universal acknowledgement in the
press of the world.

The Katanga impasse was finally broken by Mr Hammarskjöld, who went into the province with a token force of U.N.
troops. But Mr Tshombe still refused to recognise the central
government. Premier Lumumba, I think with some justice at
that stage, bitterly accused the U.N. of betrayal, because they
had failed to 'provide the Government with such military assistance as may be necessary'.

My Government and the Government of Guinea promised
Mr Lumumba military aid. We hoped that he might succeed in
uniting the Congo into a single state, and so prevent the country
from becoming involved in the East-West conflict.

Lumumba declared martial law, and threatened to attack
Katanga unless the U.N. enforced his rule there. During this
time I was in close touch with him. Colonialist intrigue was such
that he demanded that all white troops should leave the Congo.
This, and other aspects of the Congo situation made me very
uneasy.

As one political crisis followed another, Mr Hammarskjöld
flew back to New York to ask the Security Council to endorse his
actions, and to clarify his position. In the past I had a strong
personal regard for the Secretary-General. During the 1960
Commonwealth Prime Ministers' Conference we had lunch together in London, and discussed Africa and world affairs
generally. He has also visited me in Accra. He has a keen grasp
of African problems, and impressed me as a man sincerely dedi-

cated to the cause of peace. He, I thought, if anyone, could successfully guide U.N. intervention in the Congo.

The Russian representative on the Security Council, Deputy Foreign Minister Mr Kuznetsov, however, complained about the way in which the Secretary-General had interpreted the powers given to him. He reminded him that the Security Council had, on 9 August, laid down that the U.N. force in the Congo 'will not be a party to, or in any way intervene in or be used to influence the outcome of any internal conflict'.

Yet with each day that passed, it became clearer that the Congo Government could neither command full political support, nor maintain order in the country without external help. I repeatedly made it known that the forces of Ghana would be at the disposal of the United Nations so long as the U.N. acted in support of the Security Council resolutions. Nevertheless, my Government decided to consult with other independent African states to prepare a joint plan for military assistance to the Congo should it be needed. The world had to be shown that this was an African issue, and that African states, with U.N. assistance, could be trusted to find a solution.

A conference of independent African states was held, at Mr Lumumba's invitation, in Leopoldville from 25–30 August. At the suggestion of the Sudan Government, it was held at foreign ministers' level. Mr Lumumba addressed the conference more than once, and the delegates had a chance to air their views on the problems put before them. More important still, they were able to see for themselves what was going on in the Congo, and to report back personally to their governments.

Early in September, the crisis atmosphere in the Congo sharpened as the rift between President Kasavubu and Premier Lumumba widened. First one, and then the other, seemed to be on top. To add to the general confusion, fighting broke out on the borders of Katanga between soldiers acting on orders from Mr Lumumba, and Katanga tribesmen. Later Colonel Mobutu, the Army leader, seized control, and the dingdong struggle for power in the Congo took a new turn.

It was expected that the Congo crisis would loom large in the discussions at the United Nations headquarters later in September. Mr Khruschev announced his intention of attending, and it was expected that both President Eisenhower and Mr Macmillan would also address the Assembly. Many other heads of state said they would attend, among them President Tito of Jugoslavia, Fidel Castro of Cuba, President Nasser of the United Arab Republic, and Prime Minister Nehru of India.

I also decided to go. It was clearly going to be an historic session, with a record number of heads of state attending, and some 42 foreign ministers taking part in the debates. Just under 4,000 delegates, advisers and assistants were to be on hand, and the agenda was the longest ever proposed for an Assembly.

During the opening days of the session, fourteen new members were admitted: Cameroun, the Central African Republic, Chad, Togo, the Congo, Dahomey, Gabon, Ivory Coast, Malagasy Republic, Niger, Somalia, the Voltaic Republic and Cyprus. Their admission increased the membership of the United Nations to 96. The membership later rose to 98 when the constitutional situation in the Mali Federation was clarified.

This entry of the newly independent African states into the United Nations Organisation has made the Afro-Asian group very strong. Out of some 98 countries represented, 46 belong to the Afro-Asian group, and of these, 24 are African. Clearly it is our duty to use our strength in the cause of peace by remaining steadfastly neutral in the cold war.

When I arrived in New York, Mr Khruschev was already there, practically a prisoner in his hotel, so stringent were the security precautions taken by the American police. President Eisenhower had delivered a long speech in the U.N. General Assembly in which he put forward five proposals for assisting the emerging states of Africa. They were:

1 Non-interference in the internal affairs of the African states.
2 Help in assuring their security without wasteful and dangerous competition in armaments.
3 Emergency aid to the Congo, with the United States contributing substantially to the £35,700,000 U.N. Emergency Fund.
4 International assistance in shaping long-term development programmes; and
5 United Nations aid to education.

He went on to urge all countries to refrain from exploiting the Congo crisis, and called for full support for the U.N. and the Secretary-General.

Mr Khruschev made the following main points:
1 That the policy of the preparation of war and the violation

of the sovereign rights of nations must be condemned and ended.

2 That colonialism and all colonial regimes must fully and finally end.

3 That there should be general and total disarmament.

4 That peaceful co-existence is the only of reasonable way developing international relations in our time.

5 That the United Nations must demand the restoration of law and order in the Congo so that the parliament lawfully elected by the Congolese people should function, and that it should refrain from any action likely to prejudice the territorial integrity and independence of the Congo Republic.

6 That the United Nations secretariat should be revised.

7 That the People's Republic of China must be admitted into the United Nations.

I addressed the General Assembly on Friday, 23 September. I quote my speech in full:

Mr President, Distinguished Delegates:

The great tide of history flows and as it flows it carries to the shores of reality the stubborn facts of life and man's relations, one with another. One cardinal fact of our time is the momentous impact of Africa's awakening upon the modern world. The flowing tide of African nationalism sweeps everything before it and constitutes a challenge to the colonial powers to make a just restitution for the years of injustice and crime committed against our continent.

But Africa does not seek vengeance. It is against her very nature to harbour malice. Over two hundred millions of our people cry out with one voice of tremendous power – and what do we say? We do not ask for death for our oppressors, we do not pronounce wishes of ill-fate for our slave-masters, we make an assertion of a just and positive demand. Our voice booms across the oceans and mountains, over the hills and valleys, in the desert places and through the vast expanse of mankind's habitation, and it calls out for the freedom of Africa. Africa wants her freedom, Africa must be free. It is a simple call, but it is also a signal lighting a red warning to those who would tend to ignore it.

For years and years Africa has been the footstool of colonialism and imperialism, exploitation and degradation. From the north to the south, from the east to the west, her sons languished in the chains of slavery and humiliation, and Africa's exploiters and self-appointed controllers of her destiny strode across our land with incredible inhumanity, without mercy, without shame, and without honour. Those days are gone and gone for ever, and now I, an African, stand before this august assembly of the United Nations and speak with a voice of peace and freedom, proclaiming to the world the dawn of a new era.

Mr President, distinguished delegates, I wish to thank the General Assembly sincerely for this opportunity of addressing you. Let me say here and now that our tribulations and suffering harden and steel us, making us a bastion of indomitable courage, and fortifying our iron determination to smash our chains.

I look upon the United Nations as the only organisation that holds out any hope for the future of mankind. Mr President, distinguished delegates, cast your eyes across Africa's. The colonialists and imperialists are still there. In this twentieth century of enlightenment, some nations still extol the vain glories of colonialism and imperialism. As long as a single foot of African soil remains under foreign domination, the world shall know no peace. The United Nations must therefore face up to its responsibilities, and ask those who would bury their heads like the proverbial ostrich in their imperialist sands, to pull their heads out and look at the blazing African sun now travelling across the sky of Africa's redemption. The United Nations must call upon all nations that have colonies in Africa to grant complete independence to the territories still under their control.

In my view, possession of colonies is now quite incompatible with membership of the United Nations. This is a new day in Africa, and as I speak now, thirteen new African nations have taken their seats this year in this august assembly as independent sovereign states. The readiness of any people to assume responsibility for governing themselves can be determined only by themselves. I and the Government of Ghana, and I am sure the Governments and peoples of independent African states, share the joy of welcoming our sister states into the family of the United Nations. There are now twenty-two of us in this Assembly and there are yet more to come. I would suggest that when the Charter of the United Nations comes to be revised, a permanent seat should be created for Africa on the Security Council in view not only of the growing number of African members of the United Nations, but also of the increasing importance of the African continent in world affairs. This suggestion applies equally to Asia and to the Middle East.

Many questions come to my mind at the moment all seeking to be dealt with at once: questions concerning the Congo, disarmament, peace, South Africa, South West Africa, China and Algeria. However, I would like to start with the question of the Congo and to take the others in their turn.

The Congo, as we all know, has been a Belgian colony for nearly a century. In all those years Belgium applied a system of calculated political castration in the hope that it would be completely impossible for African nationalists to fight for emancipation. But to the dismay of Belgium, and to the surprise of everyone outside the African continent, this dreaded nationalism appeared and within a lightning space of time, secured the independence of the Congo. The policy of political frustration pursued by the Belgian colonial regime created a situation in which the Belgian administration was unable to continue to take over and run the state. The struggle for independence in the Congo is the shortest so far recorded. The Belgians were so overtaken by events that they pulled out but fully expected to return in one way or another.

The high positions in the army, the police and the public services had been the exclusive preserves of the Belgians. No African could hope to rise to the lowest commissioned rank in the army. The whole of the Force Publique was subject to extremely harsh discipline and had very low rates of pay. This situation made it impossible to build up a cadre of indigenous personnel to man the services. As soon as an African became Minister of Defence, the incongruous position of the African in the Force Publique became evident.

Great discontent resulted. Even so, the situation might not have erupted had the Belgian commander of the Force Publique adopted a realistic attitude towards the men, and made an attempt to redress the legitimate grievances of the Congolese soldiers. Even a promise of future reform might have done some good. On the contrary, emphatic statements were indiscreetly made by Belgian officers that nothing had changed and that life would go on much the same way as before independence; in short, the soldiers were told that independence was a sham and that Belgium still wielded the big stick. This produced the mutiny.

When the mutiny occurred, large numbers of Belgians began to leave the country. The President of the Republic, Mr Kasavubu, and the Prime Minister, Mr Lumumba, went to Matadi in order to appeal to the Belgians to remain. But instead, they were all taken on board a ship on the advice of the Belgian consul. The next day the town was machine-gunned from the air by Belgian military aircraft and shelled from the sea. Despite the fact that there were no Belgian civilians whatever to protect, Belgian troops entered the town and shot in cold blood a number of unarmed police and civilians. It was following upon this incident that acts of organised violence by members of the Force Publique began to occur. These incidents in their turn, provided an occasion for Belgian military intervention.

Meanwhile, ostensibly on the grounds of safeguarding the lives of Belgians in the province, Belgian troops entered Katanga in considerable numbers and enabled the chairman of the Provincial Council, Moise Tshombe, to set himself up as the head of a so-called independent state. The whole of the administration of this so-called state was in Belgian hands and it was supported and maintained openly by Belgian troops. The situation was thus one of extreme danger. The Belgian army was virtually occupying the Congo, pleading as their excuse circumstances which were fundamentally all of Belgium's own making.

The Congo Government called for aid. Congo asked Ghana for help and also wisely called in the United Nations. From this point, distinguished delegates, you are more than conversant with the story and there is no need for me to dwell in detail on the facts. It is only necessary to say that something has happened in the Congo which has justified my constant warning to the African countries to be on their guard against what I call clientele-sovereignty, or fake independence, namely, the practice of granting a sort of independence by the metropolitan power, with the concealed intention of making the liberated country a client-state and controlling it effectively by means other than political ones. What has happened in the Congo has more than justified my continuous outcry against the threat of balkanisation in Africa and more than justified my daily condemnation of neo-colonialism, the process of handing independence over to the African people with one hand only to take it away with the other hand.

The Congo question is a test case for Africa. What is happening in the Congo today may happen in any other part of Africa tomorrow, and what the United Nations does today must set a precedent for what it may have to do tomorrow. The United Nations will be judged by the success or failure of its handling of this Congo situation.

Certain propositions seem to me to be self-evident. The first of these is that the United Nations need not go to the assistance of any country which invites its intervention. But once it has done so, it owes an obligation to the Government and people of that country not to interfere in such a way as to prevent the legitimate Government which invited it to enter the country from fulfilling its mandate. In other words, it is impossible for the United Nations at one and the same time to preserve law and order and to be neutral between the legal authorities and the law breakers. It is, unfortunately, exactly this which the United Nations has attempted to do in the case of the Congo, and which is the cause of all the present difficulties and dis-agreeements.

My second proposition is, that in any sovereign state there can only be one national army. If a soldier disobeys the superior officer and uses his arms to murder and to loot, he is a mutineer. There is, however, no difference between his position and that of a colonel who disregards the authority which appointed him and uses the troops under his own com-mand for his own purposes. The United Nations in enforcing law and order, must deal equally sternly with either of these two types of mutineer.

This failure by the United Nations to distinguish between legal and illegal authorities had led to the most ludicrous results, embarrassing both to the Ghanaian forces who were called upon to carry them out, and to the United Nations itself, which was exhibited in a ridiculous light. For instance, the very troops which Ghana sent to help the legitimate Lumumba Government at the request of Lumumba were employed by the United Nations in preventing Lumumba, the legitimate Prime Minister of the legal Government of the Congo Republic, from performing the most obvious functions of his office – for instance, using his own radio station.

Distinguished delegates, these difficulties are in essence growing pains of the United Nations, and it would be entirely wrong to blame either the Security Council or any senior officials of the United Nations for what has taken place. How-ever, a new approach is clearly required. I believe that it is not difficult to devise methods by which the issue can be appropriately dealt with.

Let us get down to realities. The United Nations were invited to enter the Congo in a message from the Head of State, Mr Kasavubu, and from the Prime Minister, Mr Lumumba. Both these gentlemen were appointed to their respective offices in accordance with the will of the Congolese people expressed through election. Here, then, is the legal Government which should be supported and behind which the United Nations should throw its authority.

I am sure that the independent African states will agree with me that the problem in the Congo is an acute African problem which can be solved by Africans only. I have on more than one occasion suggested that the United Nations should delegate its functions in the Congo to the independent African states, especially those African states, whose contributions in men and materials make the United Nations' effort in the Congo possible. The forces of these African states should be under a unified African command with responsibility to the Security Council in accordance with the first resolution of the Security Council under which the United Nations troops entered the Congo Republic.

I suggest that the General Assembly should make it absolutely clear that the United Nations contingents in the Congo Republic have an overriding responsibility to preserve law and order which can only be done by supporting, safeguarding and maintaining the legal and existing Parliamentary framework of the state. In order to prevent illegal actions of all sorts, it is necessary that in co-operation with the legitimate Government of the Republic, the National Army should be re-trained, regrouped and reorganised so that there is finally established one army responsible only to the central Government. These proposals, if accepted, would result in the withdrawal of all non-African troops from the Congo and make easy to identify and eliminate the Belgian troops who have been infiltrating into the territory in defiance of the security council resolution.

In this connection one must mention Katanga, which brings to mind the regrettable and most vicious attempts being made by vested interests to bolster up a puppet regime there, using poor Moise Tshombe against his own Government to break up the Congo Republic by secessionist activities. I am sure, Mr President and distinguished delegates, that no African state would lend support to any secessionist move in the Congo. The Congo is the heart of Africa and we shall do our utmost to prevent any injuries being inflicted upon it by imperialist and colonialist intrigue. The Congo, including Katanga and Kasai, is one and indivisible. Any other approach is mere wishful thinking, for not all the mineral wealth in that integral part of the Congo can create Katanga into a separate State. The crisis in the Congo must be arrested now before it sparks off another world conflagration. But some powers do not appear to realise the gravity of the situation and are playing with fire by attempting to use the United Nations as a cloak for their own aims.

I personally and my Government have done everything possible to assist and advice the leaders of the Congo to resolve their differences and place their countries and Africa's interests first. Both of them, President Kasavubu and Prime Minister Lumumba, speak the same language of peace and unity. Both of them are anxious to see stability achieved in their country. Both of them agree to reconciliation. What, then, prevents them from coming together? What has led to the fake Mobutu episode?

I can assure distinguished delegates that, but for the intrigues of the colonialists, a document of reconciliation which had been drafted in the presence of my Ambassador in Leopoldville and approved by both Mr Kasavubu and Mr Lumumba would have been signed by them. Imperialist intrigue, stark and naked, was desperately at work to prevent this being signed. The policy of divide and rule is still being practised energetically by the opponents of African independence and unity.

It is quite clear that a desperate attempt is being made to create confusion in the Congo, extend the cold war to Africa, and involve Africa in the suicidal quarrels of foreign powers. The United Nations must not allow this to happen. We for our part will not allow this to happen. That is why we are anxious that the United Nations, having reached a point where intervention on the side of the legitimate Government of the Congo appears to be the obvious and only answer to this crisis, should act boldly through the medium of the independent African states.

Let these African states act under the canopy of the United Nations and produce the effective result. In these particular circumstances the Congo crisis should be handed over to the independent African states for solution. I am sure that, left to them, an effective solution can be found. It is negative to believe and hesitate until the situation becomes irredeemable and develops into another Korea.

I would go further and suggest that all financial aid or technical assistance to the Congo Republic should be arranged only with the legitimate Government of the Congo Republic, channelled through the United Nations and guaranteed and supervised by a committee of the independent African states appointed by the Security Council who should be accountable to the United Nations.

Having dwelt at length on the Congo situation, which is

only natural in view of its gravity, I now wish, Mr President and distinguished delegates, to turn to other matters. But before I do so, it is pertinent here to sound a strong note of warning; namely, that if some people are now thinking in terms of trusteeship over the Congo to carry out the exploitation of her resources and wealth, let those people for ever discard that idea, for any such suggestion would be resisted. There can be no question of trusteeship in the Congo. The Congo is independent and sovereign. The colonialists and imperialists must remember this fact and remember it for all the time.

I would now like, if I may, to turn to the question of South West Africa. Although opinions delivered by the International Court show that South West Africa is strictly not a trust territory, there can be no doubt whatever that the United Nations, as the successor of the League of Nations, has a particular responsibility towards South West Africa.

I consider also that Ghana has a particular responsibility in regard to what is taking place in South West Africa. The justification for depriving Germany of this colony and of vesting its Government in South Africa was based upon a United Kingdom document entitled 'The Native Tribes of South West Africa and Their Treatment by Germany'. Explaining the attitude of Imperial Germany towards Africans, this United Kingdom publication exposed the acts of brutal suppression perpetrated against the Africans of this territory by the Germans.

In fact, however, the policy laid down by the old German Imperial Colonial Office exactly reproduces the policy now being pursued in South West Africa by the Union of South Africa. In his 1957 Report to the Committee on South West Africa, the Secretary-General has quoted a speech by a Senator nominated by the Union Government to represent South West Africa in the Union Senate. This Senator, Dr Vedder, actually delivered a long and detailed speech to the Senate pointing out that in every respect the Union Government was merely carrying on the traditional methods for ruling Africans devised by Imperial Germany and enforced in South-West Africa by Dr Goering, the father of the notorious Fascist, Herman Goering.

The United Kingdom document which made the case against Germany in regard to South West Africa was, in reality, a Commonwealth document. At the Peace Treaty of Versailles the Commonwealth was collectively represented by the United Kingdom which acted in the name of and on behalf of the then British Empire. What, therefore, was done at Versailles was done in the name not only of the United Kingdom, but of Canada, Australia, New Zealand, South Africa and, though they were not yet independent, of India and Ghana.

In a Report made to the General Assembly last year by the Committee on South West Africa, and approved by the General Assembly, the Committee stated that the policy of apartheid as practised in South West Africa 'is a flagrant violation of the sacred trust which permeates the Mandate and the Charter of the United Nations and the Universal Declaration of Human Rights'. For thirteen years now the Union of South Africa has consistently disregarded the requests of the United Nations in regard to South West Africa. The Union imposes the most harsh and degrading regime upon the inhabitants which is not in any way in accord with the provisions of the Mandate. There is a duty on the United Nations to enforce the Mandate and the United Nations must not fail in this duty.

Mr President, in this connection, I wish to make the following proposal. The Union of South Africa should be asked to surrender the Mandate to the United Nations and a committee of all the independent African states should be set up to administer the territory on behalf of the United Nations. If the Union of South Africa is unable to accept this, then the next General Assembly of the United Nations should take steps to terminate the Mandate, make the territory a trusteeship area, and appoint the independent African states to undertake the Trusteeship.

I now turn to the Union of South Africa itself. The Union Government, against all moral considerations and against every concept of human dignity, self-respect and decency, has established a policy of racial discrimination and persecution which in its essential inhumanity surpasses even the brutality of the Nazis against the Jews. The interest of humanity compels every nation to take steps against such inhuman policy and barbarity and to act in concert to eliminate it from the world. To this end, Ghana has taken the following action. We have as from 1 August this year, caused a total boycott of South African goods, closed all Ghanaian ports – sea as well as air – to South African shipping and aircraft, except in cases of distress, and have required South African citizens entering Ghana to have in their possession travel documents issued by the Ghana Government or passports with valid Ghanaian transit visas.

This action is in implementation of the unanimous resolution adopted by the independent African states in Addis Ababa last June. Indeed, the hollow social basis of apartheid and the grievous practical harm it causes can be judged by the gruesome massacre of defenceless men, women and children at Sharpeville in March this year by the Union police. The untenable claim of a minority in South Africa is steadily building a wall of intense hate which will result in the most violent and regrettable consequences in the future unless this minority abandons the iniquitous racial policy which it pursues.

Mr President, distinguished delegates, I now turn to the question of the Portuguese colonies in Africa. Portugal, a member of the North Atlantic Treaty Organisation, has by her metropolitan law claimed the territories she has colonised in Africa as an integral part of Portugal. I have always emphasised that Africa is not, and can never be, an extension of Europe, and this Portuguese arrangement is repugnant to any concept of African freedom.

The NATO Treaty states in the Preamble that member States 'are determined to safeguard the freedom, common heritage and civilisations of their peoples founded on the principles of democracy, individual liberty and the rule of law'. May I ask all members of NATO who are members of the United Nations to point out, when they come to speak in this debate, any single instance where Portugal has observed the NATO principles in regard to her colonies in Africa. In Portuguese Africa there exists forced labour which is akin to slavery, all political freedom is denied and though this is difficult to believe, the condition of the ordinary African is worse even than it is in the Union of South Africa. If the situation in the Portuguese Territories has not yet become, as has the situation in South Africa, a threat to world peace, this is merely because the inevitable explosion has not as yet taken place. In regard to Portugal, my view is that a particular responsibility rests on the North Atlantic Treaty members who are also members of the United Nations. They can bring pressure to bear on Portugal to accord the same independence to her colonies in Africa as other North Atlantic Treaty powers have granted to their former colonial possessions.

As I have said elsewhere, the wind blowing in Africa is not an ordinary wind. It is a raging hurricane and it is impossible for Portugal or, for that matter, any other colonial power, to prevent the raging hurricane of African nationalism from blowing through oppressed and down-trodden colonies.

May I turn now, with your permission, Mr President, to the

most regrettable question of the war in Algeria. For the past six years or more this war has remained a big problem for us all. For more than six years the sands of Algeria have been stained red with blood, and French and Algerian youth in their thousands have marched to their death. The flower of French youth is being wasted in an attempt to maintain an impossible fiction that Algeria is part of France, while at the same time the youth of Algeria are forced to give their lives in a conflict which could be settled tomorrow by the application of the principles of the United Nations. This utter waste of the flower of youth of France and Algeria as a result of a senseless war must now stop, and the responsibility for stopping it should rest squarely on the United Nations. No argument about it being an internal problem of France can solve the issue. The subject of a shooting war can never be the internal problem of any power, since a spark in the wrong direction by some madman could spread the fire and cause a world conflagration.

France cannot win a military victory in Algeria. If she hopes to do so, then her hopes are false and unrelated to the realities of the situation. Indeed, any person who thinks that France can win a military victory in Algeria, lives in a world of utter illusion, and time will prove me to be right. The only way out of this tragic impasse is the way of negotiation. There was indeed a bright ray of hope a year ago when the President of France made his declaration accepting the principle of the right of self-determination for the Algerian people. It is sad that the purpose of this declaration was later treated with contempt by France herself, thereby defeating this fine gesture of goodwill for the solution of the Algerian problem.

I feel strongly that whatever has happened in Algeria, France and the Algerian Nationalist Government can still sit face to face on equal terms at the negotiating table and produce workable results, which could bring peace to both sides and put an end to this catastrophe. But from whatever angle you view this problem, you cannot escape from the fact that Algeria is African and will always remain so, in the same manner that France is French. No accident of history, such as has occurred in Algeria, can ever succeed in turning an inch of African soil into an extension of any other continent. Colonialism and imperialism cannot change this basic geographical fact. If colonialism and imperialism attempt to do this, we shall have nothing but the strife and confusion that we are witnessing in the world today. Let France and the other colonial powers face this fact and be guided accordingly.

The problem of Africa, looked at as a whole, is a wide and diversified one. But its true solution lies in the application of one principle, namely, the right of a people to rule themselves. No compromise can affect this cardinal and fundamental principle, and the idea that when a handful of settlers acquire a living space on our continent the indigenes must lose this right, is not only a serious travesty of justice, but also a woeful contradiction of the very dictates of history.

Out of a total African population of over 230 million people, some three per cent are of non-African origin. To suppose that such a small minority could in any other continent produce acute political difficulties would be unthinkable. Yet such is the subconscious feeling of certain European settlers in Africa that to them the paramount issue is Africa is not the welfare of the 97 per cent but rather the entrenchment of the rights of the three per cent of these European settler minorities in Africa.

To these minority settlers a solution seems impossible unless what they describe as 'justice' is done to the foreign three per cent. Justice, they say, must be done to this group irrespective of whether it means that injustice continues to be done to the remaining inhabitants. I believe that a reasonable solution can be found to the African problem which would not prejudice the minorities on the continent. No effective solution, however, can be found, if political thinking in regard to a solution begins with the rights of the three per cent and only considers the rights of the 97 per cent within the framework which is acceptable to the rest. The world must begin at last to look at African problems in the light of the needs of the African people and not only of the needs of minority settlers. Colonialism, imperialism and racialism are doomed in Africa, and the sooner the colonial powers recognise this fact the better it will be for them and the world.

I have spoken at length on African questions and I must now turn my attention to other matters. I will accordingly make a few observations on disarmament. In my view, we are passing through another scientific and industrial revolution which should make unnecessary the division of the world into developed and less-developed areas. We must therefore avoid economic thinking based upon the conditions of the past. Above all, we must avoid an attitude of mind which applies in an era of abundance the economic theories worked out to serve an age of scarcity.

Fundamentally, the argument in favour of disarmament must be looked at in two ways. First, it is ridiculous to pile up

K

arms which must destroy the contestants in a future war impartially and equally. Secondly, it is tragic that preoccupation with armaments prevents the big powers from perceiving what are the real forces in the world today. If world population continues to grow, and if inequality between the so-called developed and under-developed countries is allowed to remain in conditions where it is no longer technically or scientifically justified, then however great the armaments piled up, an international explosion cannot in my view be averted. While there exists the means for providing world prosperity, the great numerical majority of mankind will not agree for ever to remain in a position of inferiority. Armaments, therefore, not only threaten the future of mankind, but provide no answer to the major problems of our age.

Possibly, the cause of disarmament has suffered because it is looked upon in a negative way. In some countries, at any rate, industrial prosperity is associated with rearmament and military preparation and a recession with a slowing down of military effort. This is because disarmament is looked at in a vacuum. It should be looked upon as a means for the redeployment of the capital resources and the technical skills now being used for military purposes.

What is required at the United Nations is some fundamental thinking and planning about the re-deployment of the armament capacity of the countries which disarm. Side by side with technical discussions as to how nuclear weapons can be controlled, there should be proceeding discussions as to how resources released by the control of these weapons could be used in the service of mankind. No such planning is at present being undertaken by the United Nations. I propose, for your consideration, that some such study should be undertaken immediately and that an international team of scientists, technicians and administrators should be formed under United Nations auspices to produce a plan to show what could in fact be done with the resources which are at present being wasted in armaments.

In the meanwhile, of course, it is essential that we on the African continent take positive steps to isolate ourselves as far as is possible from the effects of nuclear warfare. One of the first and most practical steps which could be taken in this regard is to prevent any state having nuclear weapons from possessing military bases on the African continent. This is one of the main reasons why the Government of Ghana believes that no African state should enter into an alliance of a military nature with any outside power. Any such alliance not only involves the state concerned in the risk of being drawn into nuclear warfare, it also endagers the security of the neighbouring African states.

'Fall-out' is no respecter of frontiers and a declaration of neutrality cannot save the people of any African state from nuclear poisoning, once atomic war is introduced into the African continent. A military alliance with any atomic power is, therefore, in the view of the Government of Ghana, a threat to the security of Africa and world peace. The Government of Ghana feels that it is its duty to support all measures taken within the framework of the United Nations charter and in collaboration of like-minded African states to prevent the establishment or maintenance of military bases on the African continent. In order to ensure that such bases are not established in Africa, I suggest that an arrangement should be made by the United Nations whereby new states admitted to this organisation should register with it any treaties they may have entered into with their former colonial powers.

I hope that the great powers who possess atomic weapons will appreciate our feelings in this regard and will voluntarily relinquish any bases that they may at present possess in Africa. I believe that it is the duty of the United Nations to encourage the growth of zones free from nuclear warfare. A start in this policy must be made somewhere, and I therefore make the positive proposal that whatever other steps may be taken to effect nuclear disarmament, a start should be made by all nuclear powers agreeing to keep Africa out of their nuclear warfare plans.

Looking at the problem of nuclear disarmament generally, the small nations of the world can make a useful contribution. Since the great powers suspect each other so much, and since inspection on the spot appears to me to be one of the most effective means of obtaining concrete results, these great powers should agree to a system of inspection where the inspection teams are only composed of certain members of the small uncommitted nations. This would eliminate all suspicion, create confidence in the inspection method and help to solve this crucial and vital issue. And here I must refer in particular to the question of French atomic tests in the Sahara. The element of French intimidation contained in the tests was a positive provocation against Africa and a threat to world peace. We have no doubt that France chose the Sahara to demonstrate to African states their political weakness. This nuclear blackmail brings home forcibly to the independent African states the importance of creating and maintaining their solidarity against any attacks upon the peace and security of the African continent.

We cannot overlook the fact that France is militarily allied to certain other powers and that in fact France is only able to carry on these nuclear tests through the support which she receives militarily from other nations. We believe that the allies of France could do much more than they have done hitherto to dissuade the French Government from resuming atomic tests. The very least they could do would be to offer France the use of their own testing grounds. I hope that when the representatives of the military allies of France come to deal with this particular matter, they will make it perfectly clear that they are opposed to the French atomic tests in the Sahara and do everything possible to stop France from carrying out any further tests.

In Africa we judge the great powers not by their words but by their deeds. We have a right to know which of the great powers support atomic tests and perhaps, more important than everything else, in assessing the situation which of the great powers hold African opinion in so little regard that though in their hearts they oppose the French action, they are prepared to sacrifice African friendship for the interests of appeasing French pride and ambition.

Mr President, distinguished delegates, one of the most interesting facts of political evolution in Asia is that the old relationship between East and West is gone. Whatever this relationship was, whether it was exploitation or paternalism, it is no longer consistent with the new sense of dominant nationalism in Asia. This is an important background from which to consider the problem of pacification, unification and containment which have emerged in Korea and Vietnam.

In the case of Korea, it is now of great interest to recall the Indian Prime Minister's plea against advancing the United Nations forces beyond the dividing line of the 38th parallel after the North Koreans had been driven back to their own domain. The Indian Prime Minister was extremely critical of the unfortunate disposition of the Western Powers towards making decisions affecting Asia without a full understanding of the mind and sentiment of its peoples. How right he was, has been demonstrated by recent events. It is possible even now to resolve this intractable problem by having general elections in Korea.

The situation in Vietnam is too well known to need recapitulation here. I wish, however, to invite attention to a crucial obligation that remains unfulfilled in regard to the question of reunifying the two Vietnams. As a result of the armistice signed at the 1954 Geneva Conference, it was agreed that elections were to be held within two years with the object of re-creating a unified Government for Vietnam. When, however, the two co-chairman of the Geneva Conference, namely, the United Kingdom and the Union of Soviet Socialist Republics met in 1956, the elections were postponed. They have not yet been held. These countries will no longer submit to political subjection in any form, and in the interests of world-peace, we ask that elections should be held as soon as possible.

Mr President, distinguished delegates, while on Asian problems I feel constrained to pass a few remarks on the continued existence of the People's Republic of China outside the framework of the United Nations. The Government of Ghana has always supported the view that the People's Republic of China should be admitted to the United Nations so that the representation of China in this Assembly will be more realistic and more effective and useful.

We believe that the People's Republic of China, representing some six hundred and thirty million people, and with the vast economic, scientific, and technological resources that she is rapidly developing, can have a useful and constructive contribution to make towards the maintenance of peace and the advancement of civilisation in our time. The issue of whether China should be admitted to the United Nations or not should, I submit, be determined on the basis of principle rather than expediency. It would be unfortunate to underestimate the force of the socialist revolution that has taken place in China, and Ghana is convinced anyhow that any attempt to impose a form of tactical isolation on the People's Republic of China is bound to prove abortive in the long run.

Mr President and distinguished delegates, let me now turn to the Middle East. I do so because we in Africa have a vested interest in international peace and security and we view with considerable concern problems in any part of the world likely to affect such peace and security.

The Middle East covers an area of a little over three and a half million square miles and possesses vast oil resources which make the region both economically important and politically vulnerable. From the foundation of the Roman Empire the Middle East has been of great commercial significance and persistent efforts have been made by various countries to control and profit from the petroleum deposits in the area. However, the real danger to international peace is the attempt made by vested interests to prevent the inhabitants and others from profiting by the natural wealth of the region.

It is the view of the Government of Ghana, therefore, that the Western Powers which are the principal consumers of oil from the Middle East have a vital obligation to safeguard the peace and political equilibrium of the area. As long as these powers continue to exploit the oil resources of the Middle East on a competitive basis, the friction resulting from a clash of their economic and commercial interests is bound to endanger the peace of mankind.

It is my view that the time has come for a supreme effort to be made at the international level to reduce the fever and heat of tension in this part of the world, and I would propose that the United Nations should consider as a matter of urgency inviting the various states in the Middle East to provide a just and permanent solution to these problems. It seems to me that the most vital question would be to find out how best the petroleum deposits of the regions could be exploited on a non-competitive basis for the development of the Middle East and for feeding the productive capacity of industrialised countries for the benefit of mankind. If this were done the existing tensions between East and West would be significantly reduced. For there is no doubt that with the invention of long-range ballistic missiles and other forms of nuclear weapons, the importance of the Middle East as a base for any struggle for the mastery of the world has been greatly minimised.

Nevertheless, even when this clash of economic interests has been resolved, there will still remain the burning issue of Arab-Israel relations in the Middle East. This is one of the thorniest problems facing this world organisation today, and unless a permanent and realistic solution is found, the danger of its developing into an armed conflict still remains. The solution of the Middle East question lies in the recognition of the political realities there.

In the light of this, I submit that the United Nations should set up a committee to study and evolve a machinery in which it would be impossible either for Israel to attack the Arab states or for the Arab states to attack Israel, and for some sort of arrangement to be made to keep the cold war out of the Middle East.

Mr President, distinguished delegates, I must crave your indulgence to make a few concluding observations by way of emphasis on the African situation. For a long time Africa has been subjected to a harsh form of colonialism. In consequence there is now a most strong, powerful and positive rebellion in Africa against this system. I think that the upheaval in the Congo is a manifestation of that rebellion.

The responsibility for keeping the cold war out of the Congo and, for that matter, out of Africa, rests squarely on the United Nations. This responsibility, as far as the Congo is concerned, can only be discharged if the United Nations acts promptly and realistically in the present situation there. It is impossible to ignore the realities of continued Belgian intervention in the Congo in defiance of the Security Council resolution. Unless such intervention is promptly and effectively checked, and the private armies of all sorts now operating in the Congo eliminated by the United Nations, there will be no end to the chaos and confusion which now reigns in the new state. It is as impossible for a saint to be neutral on the issue of good and evil as it is for the United Nations to be neutral on the issue of legality and illegality. The United Nations must determine what is lawful and what is right and then see that this is enforced; otherwise the United Nations will betray the principles which were proclaimed in the first resolution of the Security Council on the basis of which the legitimate Government invited them to enter the Congo Republic.

Mr President, distinguished delegates, knowing the situation in the Congo as I do, and in order to save the Congo from chaos and confusion, from strife and political and economic instability to, drive the cold war out of Africa, save the reputation of the United Nations itself, and safeguard the legitimate Government which invited the United Nations to the Congo, I strongly recommend to the United Nations the adoption of certain measures which I am sure will definitely provide the only solution to the present impasse in the Congo. In proposing these recommendations, I wish to take this opportunity of expressing my personal appreciation of the way the Secretary-General has handled a most difficult task, and my own personal belief in the ideals of the United Nations Charter which constitutes in our time the strongest bulwark for international peace and security.

The following are the recommendations of the Government of Ghana:

1 That the United Nations command in the Congo should be changed forthwith and a firm strong command established with clear positive directions to support the legitimate Government with Kasavubu as President and Lumumba as Prime Minister, whose jurisdiction should be recognised throughout the whole Congo Republic. In other words, the

present composition of the United Nations command should
be changed and the composition of the United Nations
force, its military command and administration altered so
that it is drawn entirely from continents of the forces of the
independent African states now serving in the Congo.

2 That every support should be given to the central
Government, as the legitimate Government of the Congo,
with the full support of the United Nations.

3 That all private armies, including the Belgian-officered
forces in Katanga, should be disarmed forthwith and the
Congolese National Army be regrouped and reorganised
for the purpose of training so that ultimately it can play its
proper role as a National Army of the Congo Republic
until such time that the central Government considers it
possible to dispense with the services of the United Nations
forces.

4 That this new command of the United Nations forces
should support the central Government to restore law and
order in the Congo in accordance with the first resolution
of the security council, in reliance of which Ghana and
other independent African states placed their contingents
under United Nations command.

5 That the United Nations should guarantee the territorial
integrity of the Republic of the Congo in accordance with
the provisional constitution agreed at the time of independence.

6 That all financial aid and technical assistance to the Congo
Republic should be arranged only with the legitimate
Government of the Congo Republic and channelled
through the United Nations and guaranteed and supervised
by a committee of independent African states appointed by
the Security Council and who should be accountable to the
United Nations.

Mr President, distinguished delegates, I must now thank
you for the patience with which you have listened to me and
also for the honour of this opportunity of addressing you.

On Sunday, 25 September, I issued a statement appealing to
all countries in Africa and Asia to stay neutral in the conflict
between East and West. It might well be that East-West tension
has reached a point where the leaders of the Great Powers are
unable to find solutions to major problems. The Afro-Asian

nations, if they act together, might prove strong enough to be a decisive force for peace in the world.

But the whole of Africa must be free and united. Only then will we be able to exercise our full strength in the cause of peace and the welfare of mankind.

INDEX